The Broken Spoke

John and Robin Dickson Series in Texas Music
Sponsored by the Center for Texas Music History
Texas State University–San Marcos
Gary Hartman, General Editor

The Broken Spoke

Donna Marie Miller

Austin's Legendary Honky-Tonk

Donna Marie Miller

Foreword by Charles Townsend

TEXAS A&M UNIVERSITY PRESS • COLLEGE STATION

Copyright © 2017 by Donna Marie Miller
All rights reserved
First edition

This paper meets the requirements
of ANSI/NISO Z39.48–1992 (Permanence of Paper)
Binding materials have been chosen for durability.
Manufactured in the United States of America

LIBRARY OF CONGRESS CATALOGING-IN-PUBLICATION DATA

Names: Miller, Donna Marie, 1956– author.
Title: The Broken Spoke : Austin's legendary honky-tonk / Donna Marie Miller.
Other titles: John and Robin Dickson series in Texas music.
Description: First edition. | College Station : Texas A&M University Press,
  [2017] | Series: John and Robin Dickson series in Texas music | Includes
  bibliographical references and index.
Identifiers: LCCN 2016047168| ISBN 9781623495190 (cloth : alk. paper) |
  ISBN 9781623495206 (ebook)
Subjects: LCSH: Broken Spoke (Dance hall)—History. | Country
  music—Texas—Austin—History and criticism. | Country
  musicians—Texas—Austin. | Dance halls—Texas—Austin—History. | Bars
  (Drinking establishments)—Texas—Austin—History. | Popular
  culture—Texas—Austin—History. | White, James M., 1939- |
  Businessmen—Texas—Austin.
Classification: LCC ML3477.8.A97 M55 2017 | DDC 792.709765/31—dc23 LC record
available at https://lccn.loc.gov/2016047168

Cover photograph by Kirk Weddle.
All photographs by Donna Marie Miller unless otherwise credited.

Contents

Foreword, by Charles Townsend   vii
Acknowledgments   ix
Introduction   1

Part I. The 1930s, 1940s, and 1950s   13
    Chapter 1: Dance Hall Tradition   15
    Chapter 2: James White Receives His Honky-Tonk Education   18
    Chapter 3: Dance Hall Influences on James White   22

Part II. The 1960s   27
    Chapter 4: Origins of Country Music   29
    Chapter 5: The Broken Spoke Opens   31
    Chapter 6: First Performers Booked for Dancing at the Spoke   43

Part III. The 1970s   63
    Chapter 7: The Progressive Country Movement   65
    Chapter 8: The White Family Expands   67
    Chapter 9: George Strait, Alvin Crow, Jerry Jeff Walker, and the Wheel   72

Part IV. The 1980s   103
    Chapter 10: *Urban Cowboy, Dallas,* and South by Southwest   105
    Chapter 11: "The Broken Spoke Legend" Song   107
    Chapter 12: Mixed Drinks and Loyal Customers   111

Part V. The 1990s   129
    Chapter 13: Austin Becomes the "Live Music Capital of the World"   131
    Chapter 14: "If There's a Willie, There's a Way" Fund-Raiser and the "Broken Spoke Series"   132
    Chapter 15: Making Movies and Introducing New Talent   142

Part VI. The 2000s   157
    Chapter 16: Movie and Music Mecca   159

James and Annette White. Courtesy of Will van Overbeek.

Chapter 17: Sale of the Land and a Rash of Health Issues 160
Chapter 18: The Dixie Chicks, Kinky Friedman, Ray Price,
    and a Bus Crash 166

Part VII. The 2010s 179
Chapter 19: The Whites' Small Family Business Thrives 181
Chapter 20: New Neighbors, Dance Lessons, and Celebrations 182
Chapter 21: Documenting the Broken Spoke 198

Notes 207
Bibliography 213
Index 229

Foreword

When one of Frederick Jackson Turner's students at Wisconsin or Harvard pioneered a new area of research and writing, the famous historian of the American West would often say, "You have broken new ground." This is exactly what Donna Marie Miller has done in this book. She "broke new ground." Like Turner, she has courageously opened a new frontier for historical studies, telling the story of a famous dance hall in Austin, the Broken Spoke. At the same time, she has told the story of James and Annetta White. Miller writes in minute detail how the Whites built the Broken Spoke and remodeled it again and again.

For over half a century, the Broken Spoke has been part of the landscape of Austin. Miller's book is a necessary page in the overall urban history of the capital of the Lone Star State. In the mid-1940s during "The Golden Age" of American music, "The Age of the Big Bands," I was a student at Austin High School. Glenn Miller, Tommy and Jimmy Dorsey, Harry James, Benny Goodman, and even Bob Wills led popular dance orchestras. Their music was about all one heard in Austin and most other places.

The Whites and their Broken Spoke played a major role in introducing many other musical genres to Austin, which ultimately created musical diversity that made Austin a sort of "Nashville West." The Broken Spoke introduced country music, western swing, rockabilly, outlaw music . . . the list is almost endless.

The artists who performed at the Broken Spoke include Ernest Tubb, Bob Wills, Jerry Jeff Walker, Kinky Friedman, Willie Nelson, Asleep at the Wheel, Dolly Parton, Ray Price, Kitty Wells, Don Walser, Gary P. Nunn, Jason Roberts, George Strait, Billy Mata, Jody Nix, and Alvin Crow, the nearest thing to a house band the Broken Spoke has ever had.

As the fame and appeal of the Broken Spoke spread, so did the appearance of celebrities such as Robert Duvall, Coach Darrell Royal of the University of Texas, Mario Andretti, and that most gracious of women—the First Lady of Austin and Texas' Lady Bird Johnson.

Miller seems to have the same spirit and love for the Broken Spoke that its founders have. She writes about the old place with the passion one has in a true love affair. I hope other writers who read this book will be infected with Miller's spirit, her love for dance halls and their music. In that spirit, hopefully they too will break even more new ground by telling the story of more dance establishments.

With this book, Donna Marie Miller has made certain that, even with one broken spoke, the Broken Spoke will keep on rolling along as a popular dance hall and into the annals of history.

—Charles R. Townsend

Acknowledgments

This book would not have been possible without the unconditional love and support I receive daily from my husband, Myles R. Miller III. Thank you for taking that leap of faith with me when I retired from teaching in 2013. I am so grateful that I did not have to find another "job." Thank you for the times that you escorted me to the Broken Spoke and sat alone while I took photographs or schmoozed with people, for your expert editing advice, and for reading every draft of this book and never once complaining.

Thank you to my son, Myles R. Miller IV, for telling me to "go write, Mom," starting in 2009 as I blogged for the Texas State Teachers Association and before I returned to writing full time in 2013. You are a wonderful writer yourself; please always find time to write.

I thank my father, Elmer Musshorn, for reading everything I have ever written. I also thank God for all the priceless insights I learned from my beloved mother, Connie, who taught me routine, organization, and a respect for deadlines before she passed away in 2005.

Thank you to my extended family, including my brother-in-law and sister, Doug and Karen Bickel; to my brothers Ed and Eric and my sister-in-law Tina; nieces Jennifer and Tracie; nephews Mike, Stephen, and Eric Jr. and Eric's wife, Nicole, for reading excerpts of this book. Thank you also to my brother-in-law and sister-in-law Marcus and Debbie Miller and their daughters, Alyssa and Amanda Joy, for their constant support of all of my writing endeavors.

To my cousin Gene Melchionne, thank you for your limitless generosity and for giving me my very first Macintosh computer and a Hewlett Packard printer to begin writing again in 2000.

I also thank Charles Townsend, former college history professor emeritus at West Texas A&M University, for writing the foreword. In 1975 he won a Grammy Award for his brochure notes inside the United Artists' release of *For the Last Time*, the final recording of Bob Wills and his Texas Playboys. Townsend also wrote *San Antonio Rose: The Life and Music of Bob Wills* in 1976 and inspired my love for classic country music and Bob Wills.

Thank you also to my former journalism professor Sara Stone, now at Baylor University, for her friendship and support during my college years. I also feel grateful to the late Bill Lee, former editor of the now defunct *El Paso Herald-Post*, who hired me in 1978 fresh out of college. Thank you to the former executive editor of the *Amarillo Globe-News*, Jerry Huff, and its former city editor and design editor Ben and Nan Keck, who helped land me a job reporting there from 1979 until 1984 and at the *El Paso Times* five years later. Together they and my dear mentor, the late *Times* columnist Mary Margaret Davis, taught me how to be an active listener and take good notes. Thank you also to the thousands of students I taught for twenty-four years in Texas public schools within the Amarillo, Austin, El Paso, Eanes, and Manor districts, who inspired me daily.

Thank you to James and Annetta White for providing me with the facts about your lives that span more than fifty years. Since our initial meeting in May 2013, you were all in on my book project. Thank you also to your daughters, Terri White and Ginny White-Peacock; Ginny's husband, Mike Peacock; his brother, Gary, and Gary's wife, Marcia, for all of your support. Thank you to Terri's daughters, Ashley Carey and Mollee Jo Montague. I feel especially grateful to Mollee, who first introduced me to her grandpa, James "Poppy" M. White, that wonderful afternoon on May 20, 2013.

Thank you to all of the musicians, singers, and songwriters who contributed their time for interviews with me. Thank you to the friends, fans, and dancers at the Broken Spoke who allowed me interviews; to the celebrities who contributed prepared statements for this book; to the agents, publicists, personal secretaries, and family members of celebrities who behind the scenes helped me to arrange interviews or prepared statements.

Thank you to the entire staff at Austin History Center for spending hours with me searching for archival information about the Broken Spoke; and to Judith Dale, chief of staff to Representative Elliott Naishtat, and to the entire staff of the Texas Historical Commission for bestowing the Whites with the Texas Treasure Business Award in 2014. A special thanks to Greg Smith, coordinator for national programs at the THC, for considering the Broken Spoke as a nominee to the National Register of Historic Places.

Thank you to the entire staff at Travis County Historical Commission for

ACKNOWLEDGMENTS

help with my application for a Texas Historical Marker for the Broken Spoke in both 2014 and 2015. The Broken Spoke deserves the designation.

I thank all the staff at Riverside Resources and Transwestern developers for their support of this book project.

Thank you to the staffs at Travis County tax office staff and the Southeast Texas field office for the Bureau of Alcohol, Tobacco, Firearms and Explosives, for searching the archival records about the Broken Spoke's opening in 1964.

Thank you to the entire staff of Wild Blue Yonder Films for collaborating with me and for allowing me to conduct some of the interviews for your 2016 documentary, *Honky-Tonk Heaven: Legend of the Broken Spoke*. I felt honored to do it.

Thank you photographer Kirk Weddle for my book's cover photo. Thank you to photographers Rick Henson, Donald "Winker" Emmons, and Will van Overbeek for the use of your Broken Spoke photos. Thanks also goes to the entire staff at Texas A&M University Press, especially acquisitions editor, Thom Lemmons, and copyeditor, Cynthia Lindlof, and associate editor Pat Clabaugh. Also, thank you Sue Gaines for creating the index for this book.

I also want to thank my closest girl friends, Deborah Abbott, Susan Abbott, Carole Barasch, Chris Brown, Mary Brown, Bettye Cross, Terrie Cross, Erin Eid, Melissa Frasquieri, Robin Reed, Daphne Rye, Janet Sokell-O'Gara, and Sylvia White, for reading the many excerpts of this book and for your constant love and support.

Y'all have made my exciting transition from teaching to writing full time so much fun!

Introduction

In November 1964 when James and Annetta White opened the Broken Spoke in South Austin, I was just eight years old, living more than eighteen hundred miles away in Waterbury, Connecticut. We may have shared the same planet, but we could have lived worlds apart for all our differences.

I was born a Yankee, but I have long considered myself a Southerner. Whenever I tell people that I moved eleven times as a child before my parents settled in El Paso, I am always asked if my father was a military man or wanted by the FBI. The answer is neither. I like to think of Dad as a bit of an explorer. He always searched for a better job, a bigger house, and a new adventure. He worked as a manager for a number of companies before starting his own company in El Paso.

I can trace my early music education to a single piece of furniture that became the focal point of my adolescent family life in El Paso during the 1970s, a rectangular solid wood mahogany cabinet fitted with a television and built-in speakers. The RCA twenty-five-inch "entertainment center" also housed a turntable stereo on one side, a radio and an eight-track tape deck combination on the other. On weekends the turntable provided the music from my parents' favorite vinyl recordings of the Count Basie, Tommy Dorsey, Duke Ellington, Benny Goodman, and Glenn Miller orchestras. That tape deck often provided me with a variety of music genres culled from my father's "Tape of the Month Club" selections after they arrived by mail. However, unequivocally for me at fourteen years old, the radio provided my daily doses of country music.

My mother often turned on the radio weekday mornings before school. One morning Mom tuned the radio dial to the country KHEY-FM station, so I awoke to hear Marty Robbins's 1959 Grammy Award–winning song, "El Paso," for the first time.[1] Immediately the lyrics captivated me: "Out in the West Texas town of El Paso / I fell in love with a Mexican girl / Nighttime would find me in Rosa's cantina / Music would play and Felina would whirl." I imagined Rosa's cantina as a colorful place with live music and dancing. It mattered little to me that such a place might also draw a few undesirables. By comparison, my own sheltered world seemed boring and confining. I longed to grow up and to learn to dance like Felina.

In the meantime, our television provided my family and me with evening distractions from the unrelenting political and social conflict of the times. The weekly hosts of *Hee Haw*, a countrified variety show, featured singer-songwriters Buck Owens and Roy Clark.[2] Their irregular antics and some of the show's popular performers made us laugh in spite of ourselves. Louis Marshall Jones, "Grandpa Jones," played banjo; Alvin "Junior" Samples told bad jokes in a slow monotone; and Sarah Colley, known as "Minnie Pearl," provided self-deprecating monologues about her hillbilly family.

By June 1972 when the *Washington Post* began its investigation into the break-in at the Democratic National Committee headquarters at the Watergate offices in Washington, DC,[3] I began reading all of Bob Woodward's and Carl Bernstein's investigative articles and felt inspired to pursue a career as a newspaper reporter. Though I aimed to attend Columbia University in New York, my father, who had just started his own business, convinced me to consider attending a Texas college with cheaper tuition. About the same time that President Richard Nixon ordered the withdrawal of US Armed Forces from Vietnam, I began my junior year of high school. Coincidentally another TV show joined my family's weekly lineup: *Dean Martin Presents Music Country*. The sound of country music had become the new staple in our household.

My world expanded in 1974, the year I graduated from high school, when a constitutional amendment allowed Texas to lower the drinking age from twenty-one to eighteen. This opened up a new world for me inside establishments that served up both alcohol and live music and further expanded my cultural and entertainment universe. That fall I enrolled at West Texas State University (WTSU), now known as West Texas A&M University, in Canyon, just a thirty-minute drive from Amarillo. I headed off to the Texas Panhandle, listening to what would soon be termed "progressive country" music on the radio of my metallic-green 1965 Ford Galaxie 500 sedan. While a disgruntled band of Nashville musicians who called themselves country "outlaws" began to experiment with country music, I grew into my rebellious dancing boots. Soon I discovered Johnny Cash's "Cocaine Blues," Waylon Jennings's "Lonesome, On'ry and Mean," and Willie Nelson's "Whiskey River." Their words rang like pure poetry to me and put a bounce in my independent steps for the next four years.

I found my own true love of classic country music as a freshman at WTSU. My history professor, Charles Townsend, introduced all of his students to the music of Bob Wills and the Texas Playboys and in 1975 won an Emmy Award for writing the liner notes to their final album, For the Last Time.[4] In 1976 Townsend wrote San Antonio Rose: The Life and the Music of Bob Wills. That summer I began listening to Wills's vintage vinyl recordings and those of the singing cowboys: Gene Autry, the Sons of the Pioneers, and Jimmie Rodgers. I soon learned to dance the two-step, Cotton-Eyed Joe, polka, and schottische on weekend nights in two of Amarillo's most famous dance halls, the Aviatrix and the Joker.

In 1978 I went to work as a feature reporter at the El Paso Herald-Post right after graduation, but a year later I took a job as an entertainment and feature reporter at the Amarillo Globe-News and soon discovered the Texas Moon Palace. There I reviewed live concerts, including the performances of Ray Benson and Asleep at the Wheel, Alvin Crow, and Rusty Wier. On other weekends I sought out local country bands at a variety of dance halls within the Panhandle area, stretching from Amarillo to Guymon, Oklahoma. In 1980 I was assigned to police beat.

During the fall of 1982 I took a six-month sabbatical from the Globe-News to string stories for several Austin entertainment publications as I followed the waves of progressive country music to their root establishments, especially at the Broken Spoke and Threadgill's. However, my brief freelancing adventure had taught me the merits of earning a steady paycheck, so I returned to the Globe-News in the spring of 1983. I was soon reassigned to the police beat, which nearly ruined my love for newspaper journalism. By the fall of 1984 I had had enough of bad news, so I took a job teaching advertising, newspaper, and creative writing at Amarillo High School for the next four years.

In 1988 two former Globe-News editors who had relocated to El Paso helped me land a job writing for the El Paso Times. While working for the Times, in 1990 I enrolled in graduate-level creative writing classes at the University of Texas at El Paso. On the weekends I danced in bars that offered live country music, especially those off Interstate 10 in places like Union Station in Anthony, New Mexico, or Cowboy's in Las Cruces. Along the way, I reconnected with an old family friend whom I had known for more than twenty years and who would eventually become my husband.

While I was reporting about a bond election for the construction of Franklin High School in El Paso, its new principal offered me a job teaching journalism. In 1994 I married and gave birth to my son. My new family and I moved to Austin during the summer of 1996. I taught English and journalism classes for one year in Manor, followed by four years in Eanes, and then twelve years in the Austin Independent School District. Together teaching and parenthood had changed my life and my priorities. I spent less time dancing inside any of Texas' dance halls, but my love for country music and the Broken Spoke never faded. Over the years my husband and I have visited the Broken Spoke whenever possible.

The Broken Spoke in 2016 seems as ageless as its proprietor and founder, James M. White. Most Friday and Saturday nights, seventy-seven-year-old James still makes rounds at the Broken Spoke dressed in his standard "uniform": his best Wranglers, a Swarovski crystal–studded vintage western shirt with five snap-button cuffs, a Gene Autry–era neckerchief, his Lucchese ostrich-skin boots, and his Stetson Silverbelly cowboy hat. His black leather belt features twenty-one Texas Ranger star insignias the size of cinco pesos. He often greets people at the door as they enter. James walks through the crowd and shakes everyone's hands. He allows people to take pictures with him and never says no to an interview. Interviewing and having his picture taken remain two of his most favorite roles at the Broken Spoke. His genuineness has become his greatest selling point. Visitors often share compliments like "Mr. White was right there at the door and he shook my hand." His wife, Annetta White, often works behind the bar serving cocktails and beer, running the cash register, or helping to fill orders in the kitchen. She also manages parties for up to five hundred people; she cooks the entire day before the event and often serves as well. Since 1964, James White's name and the Broken Spoke have been synonymous. The building and the man who helped create it remain indelible icons in Austin. It is a real country joint, it has a great dance floor and incredible bands, and famous performers have and continue to grace its stage, but without James White, there would have been no Broken Spoke.

In the dance hall on weekends, beginning about 10:00 p.m., visitors stand as close to the bandstand as possible to see and to photograph James delivering his "Broken Spoke Speech." Meanwhile, behind him the night's band plays on his cue. James preselects a female member of the audience to roll

Broken Spoke proprietor James White parks his 1954 Cadillac Coupe de Ville in the parking lot in front of the Broken Spoke. Photo by Kirk Weddle.

an authentic wagon wheel across the dance floor in front of the stage while he readies himself at the microphone. Most regular patrons have heard James's speech so often that they can recite it verbatim. It goes something like this: "Fifty years ago, I came out under that big ol' oak tree out there, and I visualized a place like no other, and when I got it built, I named it the Broken Spoke. So we want to welcome you to the Broken Spoke—the last of the true Texas dance halls and damn sure proud of it. We ain't fancy, but we dang sure are country. We ain't changin' nothing; we ain't gettin' none of those hangin' fern baskets on our ceilin' out here, none of that Perrier water neither. When you order your hamburger, don't ask for the Grey Poupon, because you're getting the real mustard out here, the real deal. Well let me tell you what we do got. We've got cold beer, good whiskey, and we're the home of the best chicken-fried steak in town. We've got good country music—and last but not least, we've got all these good-lookin' girls to dance with out here tonight."

James always stops for a moment to announce the name of the girl rolling the night's wagon wheel. "We're glad you're here, because we have rolled through the '60s, the '70s, the '80s, the '90s, the 2000s, and the 2010s. We've rolled past our fiftieth year; thanks to you for making it all possible. Y'all stick with us right here at the Broken Spoke because we ain't goin' nowhere. We're gonna keep on rollin' because we've had people like Bob Wills, right here, Willie Nelson, George Strait, Dolly Parton, Ernest Tubb, Tex Ritter, and the list just goes on and on, but I couldn't be more happy than to be right here in Austin, Texas." James tailors his introduction for the night's band by changing little more than the names of the performers. At least once a month for over forty years one regular performer has held a familiar presence on the Broken Spoke stage: fiddler and singer-songwriter Alvin Crow. He usually wears sunglasses as an accessory to his cowboy hat, flashy vest, western shirt, jeans, western belt, and boots.

James's introduction for Crow goes like this: "What seems like just a short time ago, a young man from the Panhandle put his fiddle under his arm and told his mama and his daddy, 'I'm gonna go to Austin, Texas, and I'm gonna play country music at the Broken Spoke.' So he came right here up under that big old oak tree out front, he walked across that old dirt parking lot, threw the doors open on this red rustic old building, and knew damn good and well he wasn't at Carn—eg—ie Ha—all." The audience echoes back the last two words of James's speech in unison from the dance floor by extending syllables. "Let's make him welcome. We've got Alvin Crow and the Pleasant Valley Boys with us here tonight," James says, always with an arm raised to the ceiling. Audience's cheers and whistles follow. Immediately afterward, Crow breaks into singing the first verse from the original song that James White wrote and the two recorded first on the Pure Country CD in 1988, "The Broken Spoke Legend," while the band behind them plays. Crow's part goes like this: "*If you like waltzes and polkas / two-steps, and Cotton-Eyed Joes / deep in the heart of Texas / there's a place that you should go.*" James joins in on the second verse: "*It ain't fancy / but it's country / wear your jeans and your cowboy hat / just across that ol' river / 'cause that's where it's at. / It was born on the south side of Austin / the Broken Spoke was its name, / it'll always be a winner, it's destined for fame.*"

The decor at the Broken Spoke has not changed much at all in the past five decades. It has an old Americana feel to it and houses more than fifty years of country music history and memorabilia. Hundreds of framed pictures line the walls, each telling a story about its star celebrity performances, dancers, and visitors. In the dining room, café-style curtains cover the windows, depicting western themes of cowboys and cowgirls participating in campfire sing-alongs. Patrons sit on vintage peg-leg chairs at handmade round tables complete with built-in lazy Susans that hold condiments or at booths upholstered in imitation calfskin vinyl. Before 6:00 p.m. each Tuesday through Saturday, classic songs from the canons of country music emanate from the dining room's jukebox. In the evenings a local country band entertains the dinner crowd for tips in a corner of the dining room nearest to the pool table; the dance hall opens at 8:00 p.m. for dance lessons, and a band performs beginning about 9:00 p.m. Glass cases along the walls house vintage embroidered and embellished western suits, star-autographed acoustic guitars, and an authentic handcrafted black leather and silver saddle.

The Broken Spoke's very own mascot, Rowdy, a cowboy mannequin with a black handlebar mustache and long hair, dressed in leather chaps, vest, western shirt, boots, and black felt cowboy hat, sits at one of the round tables. James bought Rowdy from a street vendor along Ranch to Market Road 620 years ago. Women like to sit on Rowdy's lap to take selfie photographs. However, the mannequin has suffered some abuse in recent years;

no one knows who broke off one of the fingers on Rowdy's right hand or who gave him a hairline facial fracture. Meanwhile, someone keeps stealing his hat and sunglasses. The dance hall at the Broken Spoke stands empty by day, with all of its vintage beer signs lit up in neon red, yellow, and blue. A sign hanging from the ceiling reads: "No standing on the dance floor." The stage stretches the entire sixty-four-foot width of the dance floor. Powder-blue-painted paneling depicts a country scene of giant yellow Texas stars, a crescent moon, and a guitar player that bears a likeness to Bob Wills. The Texas Lone Star flag waves above some blooming prickly pear cactus beside an old corral where a sleepy-looking gray horse peers out. Anyone can see the hole made above the stage years ago to accommodate a six-foot seven-inch Asleep at the Wheel frontman, Ray Benson, standing onstage.

Folks still head to the Spoke for good music, good food, and plenty of dancing. Benson and Asleep at the Wheel, Dale Watson, Gary P. Nunn, Bruce Robison, Marcia Ball, Alvin Crow, and others still perform regularly at the honky-tonk. The Spoke's iconic standing in the city has grown even more in the past few years as the two four-story, multiuse commercial and residential properties known as The 704 have been built around it. Now, when driving down South Lamar Boulevard, residents can literally see the juxtaposition of "new Austin" and "old Austin" in the shadow that neighboring buildings cast over the Spoke. For more than five decades the Whites have rolled with the inevitable wheels of change that have come their way.

On May 20, 2013, about two weeks before my official retirement from teaching, one of my journalism students, Mollee Jo Montague, asked me to help her make a video documentary about her grandfather, James White. I spent hours that day interviewing her grandfather and his daughter, Terri White, who is also Mollee Jo's mom. James told me about the people who had performed at the Broken Spoke over the last five decades. Terri told me how much she loved growing up at the Broken Spoke and how much she enjoys teaching dance lessons. When our video recording ended, Mollee Jo had created a wonderful documentary about her grandfather, and I had given James my promise that I would write a book about the Broken Spoke.

In June 2013 I began spending at least one day each week interviewing James for two to three hours at the Broken Spoke or at his private residence in South Austin. I recorded his recollections and stories about the old days. Following our recorded interviews, I transcribed them into Microsoft Word documents. Afterward, I printed them out and allowed him to read my chapters. I kept a calendar with all of the dates of those meetings, and we e-mailed, texted, or called one another often. I quickly began to know James and his wife, Annetta, as two of the most endearing people I have ever met. They are nothing short of loving, honest, and hardworking folks. James White and his extended family members have all become part of my own inner circle. The Whites invited me to their ranch twelve miles south of town for James's seventy-fifth birthday party on April 12, 2014. I also photographed the weeklong fiftieth-anniversary party at the Broken Spoke November 4–8, 2014. I interviewed guests while the enigmatic country singer Dale Watson performed. I photographed Austin's first Ameripolitan Awards when James accepted the award for the "Best Venue" in the United States on behalf of the Broken Spoke on February 18, 2014.[5] Four hundred guests showed up at the 100 percent fan-funded premiere event at Austin's Wyndham Garden Hotel. Watson had coined the name "Ameripolitan" as a new genre of music that includes country, honky-tonk, western swing, rockabilly, outlaw, and roots categories. Honorees included Johnny Bush, who received the "Founder of the Sound" award and accepted a posthumous "master award" on behalf of the late great country crooner Ray Price. Other local performers honored included James Hand, Ray Benson, Rosie Flores, Dawn Sears, Wayne "The Train" Hancock, Whitey Morgan, the Derailers, and the Heybale band.

The second annual Ameripolitan Awards, in 2015, moved into Austin's hundred-year-old Paramount Theater, a bigger and better musical venue for guests with all the fanfare of a star-studded country awards show. I photographed James White as he bestowed Steve Wertheimer, friend and owner of the Continental Club, with the 2015 "Best Venue" award. Joe Ely also accepted the "Founder of the Sound" award on behalf of Billy Joe Shaver, who was absent due to illness that night. Other performers who received awards included Amber Digby, James Hand, the Derailers, Sarah Gale Meech, Jesse Dayton, the Freightshakers, Kenny Sears, Mojo Nixon, Elana James, Bobby Flores, Hot Club of Cowtown, Kim Lenz, James Intveld, and Big Sandy and His Fly-Rite Boys.[6]

My love for the Whites has often compelled me to act as their advocate on a number of occasions. I successfully applied on their behalf for a 2014 Texas Treasure Business Award for the Broken Spoke from the Texas

Historical Commission. District 49 representative Elliott Naishtat delivered the award to the Whites during the Broken Spoke's fiftieth-anniversary celebrations on November 6, 2014.[7] I have attempted to help the Broken Spoke obtain historical markers from both the Texas Historical Commission and the National Registry of Historic Places; both these efforts are ongoing. I also wrote an article about the fiftieth anniversary of the Broken Spoke for *Austin Monthly* magazine for its November 2014 issue.[8]

In October 2015 I created a photo composite for the wall of a video-conference room inside Austin's Facebook offices that features Dale Watson, several regular Broken Spoke dancers, and three members of a bachelorette party offstage wearing "Dale" T-shirts, as well as James and Annetta. Miller Imaging and Digital Solutions printed and installed the image inside "the Broken Spoke conference room" at Facebook. A special guest performance by Watson and James White in the company lunchroom followed the installation.

Frequently I act as the Whites' unpaid personal assistant; I have worked on their home computer or printer, framed their awards and documents, and brought them soup and homemade goodies whenever they have fallen ill or have been hospitalized. I continue to do these things because I have always felt that I could not and still cannot thank the Whites enough for their friendship and support while writing this book.

The Whites have introduced me to a wide circle of their friends, regular patrons, and celebrity performers. I have tracked down agents or managers for the famous bands and musicians who have performed at the Broken Spoke. I personally interviewed nearly all of the entertainers either before or after their performances or by phone. I recorded the interviews, transcribed them, and e-mailed the finished documents to the performers themselves, seeking their approval before adding any of the material to this book.

I also helped to interview the White family members, friends, and country stars in collaboration with the directors and production crew of Wild Blue Yonder Films while they recorded the feature-length documentary *Honky Tonk Heaven: Legend of the Broken Spoke*, directed by Brenda Greene Mitchell and Sam Wainwright Douglas. Producers were Michelle Randolph Faires and Jenny Holm; executive producers, Maria J. McDonald and Scott Mitchell; and directors of photography, Lee Daniel and David Layton. Brian McNulty served as a story consultant. The documentary screened at film festivals around the country, including the 2016 South by Southwest (SXSW) Interactive, Film, and Music Festival in Austin where it won the "Audience Choice Award."

Over the course of twenty-seven months from June 2013 until March 2016, I interviewed more than one hundred people about the Broken Spoke. The best of those dialogues appear in this book together with my observations and research. I have divided the book into seven sections by decades with the exception of part 1, which includes three—the 1930s, 1940s, and 1950s. Parts 2–7 cover the 1960s through the 2010s. Within each part are three chapters or story threads using a "braided" narrative structure that provides perspectives from (1) the local, state, and national history and music scene of the time; (2) the Whites' family lives; and (3) the Broken Spoke's cast of characters, performers, dancers, and fans. Like any good braid, its center thread—in this case the White family—weaves in and out and around its subparts over time to build a strong interlocking new construction. I hope that this story, like the Whites' own tale, withstands the test of time.

Navigating along the periphery of the Broken Spoke for more than two and a half years has been a joy. I have gained a deep appreciation for James and Annetta White and the entire extended White family for their roles in fostering live country music at the world-renowned venue known as the Broken Spoke in Austin. I would not have traded this experience for anything.

PART I

The 1930s, 1940s, & 1950s

CHAPTER 1

Dance Hall Tradition

Like so many Texas dance halls throughout the late nineteenth and early twentieth centuries, the Broken Spoke has served as a gathering place that allows its patrons to catch up on regional news while providing a community social nerve center. Immigrants built the first dance halls as community centers throughout Texas beginning as early as the 1800s to provide space for meetings, refreshment, relaxation, live music, and dances. Gail Folkins wrote in 2013 that "Texas dance halls offer a history as complex and varied as the musical notes drifting through their open doors."[1] Texas' German, Czech, Polish, Tejano, and African American settlers built the structures to help perpetuate their dance styles and cultures far from their homelands. In 2014 Larry Bleiburg identified the top-ten surviving Texas dance halls: the Broken Spoke, Gruene Hall in Gruene, Neon Boots Dancehall and Saloon in Houston, Billy Bob's Texas in Fort Worth, Music City Texas Theater in Linden, Stagecoach Ballroom in Fort Worth, Luckenbach Dance Hall in Luckenbach, Crider's Rodeo & Dancehall in Hunt, Schroeder Hall in Scroeder, and John T. Floore's Country Store in Helotes.[2] Bleiburg calls these dance halls "cultural landmarks," where music lovers gather regularly for entertainment. The Texas Dance Hall Preservation organization keeps an inventory of all the state's historic dance halls, creates public awareness, and provides financial or technical assistance for their restoration and rehabilitation by having them listed on the National Register of Historic Places.[3]

The term "honkatonk" may have originated with a type of ragtime piano music popular during the turn of the twentieth century and performed in Tin Pan Alley, a neighborhood once located along West Twenty-Eighth Street between Fifth Avenue and Broadway in Manhattan.[4] After Prohibition ended in 1939, "honky-tonk" came to define any one of a variety of roadside venues stretching from Texas to Oklahoma and along the West Coast that sold beer and provided live music. Singer, guitarist, piano player, and bandleader Clarence Albert Poindexter, alias Al Dexter, first used the term within the title of his song "Honky Tonk Blues" in 1939.[5] During the 1950s, musicians Ernest Tubb, Hank Locklin, Lefty Frizzell, George Jones, and Hank Williams began referring to their sound as "honky-tonk music." The term further expanded to include a genre of music that incorporates amplified guitars and Dobros, resonator guitars, played by country musicians who often sing sad ballads about drinking and social failures.[6] Within most Texas dance halls, honky-tonk remains just as popular as country, rockabilly, western swing, and roots music.

Dancers at the Broken Spoke move counterclockwise on the concrete floor to live music Tuesday through Saturday beginning at about 9:00 p.m. The tradition of dancing counterclockwise likely began because most people are right-handed and likely are right-footed.[7] The dance floor, divided into concentric lanes of movement, allows the slower dancers to dance closer to the center of the floor and the faster, more experienced dancers to pass to the outside. The "lead" dancers move forward by placing their right hand on their partner's waist while grasping their "follow" partner's right hand with their left. In this way, the lead dancers face forward and the follow dancers dance mostly backward in the counterclockwise direction. The best dancers move swiftly while using a variety of tiny steps within the boundaries of their own invisible circles of space. The experienced dancers twirl and dip their partners, never losing their place in the large flow as it moves across the dance floor.

In her book *Dance across Texas*, Betty Casey writes that after Texas won its independence from Mexico in 1836, the earliest settlers came from Germany, England, Ireland, France, and Spain on horseback after arriving by ship through the Gulf of Mexico. Each batch of arrivals brought the latest dances, including schottisches, waltzes, jigs, and polkas. People learned new dance steps by watching or by dancing. Casey refers to early Texas as "a bachelor republic" because "women were scarce in this man's world, and single women of courting size almost nonexistent."[8] Women were in such short supply that males danced with young girls half their age or with much older married women. The Texas male pioneers sometimes resorted to dancing with each other when there were no women available. These days it is not uncommon to see same-gender pairings—however, nearly all occur among women—at the Broken Spoke on Friday or Saturday nights. The more experienced country dancers often teach the beginners. Additionally, fathers dance with daughters, mothers dance with sons, and lots of folks sixty years and older step lively with much younger partners as they share their expertise on the dance floor. The dance most favored among the Broken Spoke's most experienced dancers, the western swing, may have originated in the 1920s in the Savoy Ballroom in New York City. However, nearly one hundred years ago East Coast swing dancers moved to the sounds of contemporary jazz orchestras, not country music.[9] The dance did not become a standard until Arthur Murray Dance Studio in Santa Monica, California, began teaching the western swing in 1951 from a syllabus created by teacher Lauré Haile, and it has undergone few variations since. The Broken Spoke supports the long-held Texas dance hall tradition.[10] Though more than one thousand Texas dance halls once existed between the 1920s and 1930s, fewer than half that number survive today, mostly in rural areas. An anomaly amid urban and contemporary neighbors, the Broken Spoke still remains one of the best dance halls in the state according to *USA Today*.[11]

CHAPTER 2

James White Receives His Honky-Tonk Education

Lena Fuchs grew up a country girl of German descent and lived in the rural Hill Country of Spicewood during the early 1930s. She loved music and she loved to dance, particularly at house dances. In those days, homeowners often hired a fiddler and a guitar player, rolled up the rugs, and put all the family's furniture on the front porch to make room for musicians to perform inside the house. People came from all over the Austin area to attend the house dances and usually stayed until the early-morning hours. Young women like Lena packed homemade suppers inside picnic baskets and brought them to the dances. To begin the festivities, the single men would bid on the meals as a chance to meet and to dance with the baskets' owners. Seventeen-year-old Lena happened to attend a dance one day just outside Austin's city limits in Oak Hill, a small community populated mostly by German immigrants who knew one another well.

Lena's half brothers, Carl, Robert, and Ernest Bauerle, together co-owned the most popular place in town, a lumberyard. Lena would meet her future husband there in 1932 at one of the biggest community events of the year, the annual Fourth of July picnic. Every year, Lena's brothers borrowed wood from their lumberyard to build a temporary bandstand complete with a railing and a wooden dance floor in the open-air lot. Once the dancing commenced, eighteen-year-old Bruce Lamar White made a beeline straight for Lena, the prettiest girl in attendance. After they made a few twirls around the dance floor, anyone with eyes could see the immediate attraction between them. Bruce courted Lena for nearly a year before asking for her hand in marriage. However, most of Lena's family and friends openly shared the opinion that the girl was too young to marry. So the two eloped to Bastrop County, where a justice of the peace married them on July 6, 1933.

The couple then moved into the Whites' family homestead in Oak Hill.

The simple log house built by Bruce's maternal great-grandfather, John Eaton Campbell, offered no indoor plumbing or sewer lines, but it quickly became a home. Lena's new mother-in-law, Rosa Patton-White, approved of the couple's marriage and embraced her new daughter-in-law as family. However, Rosa worried about Lena, who worked as an orderly at the Austin State Hospital, formerly known as the Texas State Lunatic Asylum. Nights at the asylum sometimes frightened Lena, especially whenever a patient suddenly turned violent. After one of the female patients attacked a nurse and administered a beating that left the woman bruised, Lena vowed never to return. Lena gave birth to her first son, Bruce Lamar White Jr., in 1935. As she recovered from childbirth, her husband barely scraped up enough money to feed his new family by working construction jobs. He began supplementing his income by selling home-brewed beer to residents in Oak Hill. Within months he found a more reputable part-time job working as a Travis County deputy constable, a position he liked because it allowed him to carry a pistol in the evenings. As part of his nightly rounds he frequented his favorite saloon, Moose Head Tavern, once located on the right side of the road just before US 290 West and State Highway 71 intersect at the "Y" in Oak Hill.

Lena gave birth to her second son, James M. White, in 1939 at the old St. David's Hospital in Austin. Within weeks she found a job working as a cashier at Crumley's grocery store, formerly located on West Mary Street. Her husband's sister, Margaret White-Grunewald, whom the family affectionately nicknamed "Nantie," served as a second mother to both James and Bruce Jr. during the days while Lena worked. Nantie Margaret and Lena shared a special unspoken sisterhood as they raised the White family's children. The family relocated several times, twice within the 1000 block of West Mary Street into houses that James's grandmother Rosa both owned and leased. They finally settled into a house in the 2300 block of Westway Circle in Barton Hills. During the day, James's maternal great-grandfather, James Andrew Patton, cared for him while Lena worked and Bruce Jr. attended elementary school.

Things began to change when Bruce Sr. joined the US Army and was stationed at Camp Wallace in Galveston County. The camp at one time served as a training facility for anti-aircraft units during World War II.[1] Bruce Sr.

worked as a military policeman at the camp, named for Col. Elmer J. Wallace of the 59th Coast Artillery.[2] For months Lena regularly made the 206-mile trek by car with her sons to visit their father. Once Lena found work at the PX, the family moved onto base. However, Bruce Sr. had a temper, especially when he drank, and he could be stubborn to a fault. Eventually Lena and Bruce Sr.'s marriage dissolved, and the two divorced in 1940.

Soon afterward while working at Camp Wallace, Lena met and married Sgt. Joe Baland. Bruce Sr. met his second wife, Lulu "Lou" LeBlanc, a pretty young Cajun woman, in 1942 on his way to pick up a prisoner at Camp Wallace. James recalled his father telling him the story years later. Soon afterward the army transferred Bruce to Salinas, California, and he and Lou married. Lena, Joe, and the two boys moved into Rosa's home in Austin. Lena and Rosa remained close; divorce had not succeeded in breaking up the female bonds within the White family. Whenever Bruce and Lou visited Austin, they also stayed at Rosa's house. James remembers the living room inside his grandparents' house as filled with laughter and joy. No one ever talked about the short marriage between Bruce Sr. and Lena all those years ago. When Lena took her two sons to visit their father or Nantie Margaret in California, all of them stayed at Bruce and Lou's house.

After the war, Bruce and Lou moved to San Diego. Lena's brother, L. J. LeBlanc, who had been stationed there in the US Navy, helped Bruce find work in security at the Convair Aircraft Manufacturing plant. Within months Bruce quit drinking; soon he and Lou settled into domestic life. Not long afterward Lou gave birth to a daughter, Cynthia Ann White-McCool.

All of the adults in James's young life enjoyed drinking and dancing in honky-tonks during the late 1940s and 1950s, so at seven years old, he began tagging along with Lena and Joe to bars throughout the Austin area. On the weekends James and his mother and stepfather often ran with a pack of Joe's friends, mostly construction workers, mechanics, and electricians who frequented Austin area drinking establishments. The places James remembers from childhood always had at least a three-piece ensemble consisting of a fiddle player, guitar player, and drummer.

Whenever he traveled to California to see Nantie Margaret or his father and Lou, James tagged along with them to visit their favorite drinking establishments. His father often told tales about the years he and his brother,

Dudley White, brewed their own beer in Oak Hill. James recalls, "They used to make it up in the barn until my grandmother [Rosa White] came in one day and all their home-brew bottles started poppin' in the heat. The heat popped the caps off, and the brew started seeping through the boards in the barn." Afterward, the White brothers stashed their bottles in a nearby cow pasture. "Come to find out, they buried it in a cow trail, and the cows all stomped on it and ruined their home brew. So they didn't have much luck in the home-brew department," James says. "My uncle Dudley used to have a little half pint under his coat with a straw, and he'd sip it out of that straw. He'd take a slurp from the straw and nobody would see him, even when he was dancing." During the time that James attended Becker Elementary and Fulmore Middle Schools, he began to receive his alternative education at the movies.

CHAPTER 3

Dance Hall Influences on James White

Saturday matinees at the Paramount or the State or the Queen Theater in Austin educated James White about western culture and Hollywood's version of the Texas cowboy. The Queen Theater opened in 1921 with the first electric sign in town at 700 Congress, which today houses the Contemporary Austin–Jones Center.[1] Both the Paramount and the State remain standing. Throughout its hundred-year history, the Paramount has hosted a variety of acts from vaudeville musicals to movies. The State Theater opened in 1935 as the fourth of the Interstate Circuit Theaters in Austin. Today both theaters feature refurbished marquees and vintage blade signs lit up in neon red on white outside with lavish interiors, including some original ceilings and walls. In these theaters James saw western film stars in person, who left firm impressions in his young creative mind. He also visited the Cactus Theater at Sixth and Neches Streets, formerly owned by Vaudeville star Richard "Skinny" Pryor, who starred in westerns and Spanish-language films in the 1930s and 1940s. Pryor's son Richard, nicknamed "Cactus," became a longtime and beloved Texas broadcaster and humorist. The Cactus Theater now houses the Velveeta Room.[2]

James also remembers as a boy paying only a nickel to see movies at the Capitol Theater where he saw his childhood hero, Woodward Maurice "Tex" Ritter, perform live. It was built in 1896 on West Sixth Street but was demolished in the 1960s. Ritter, a singing cowboy from Beaumont, starred in a dozen films and half a dozen television shows before he died in 1974. He represented one of the biggest names in country music throughout the postwar era.[3] "One Saturday I was at the Capitol Theater when in rides Tex Ritter on his horse, White Flash, onstage and shoots off his pistol and then rides off. Then they showed the matinee movie. That's the way they did things in those days. They'd get people who were in the movie to come out, especially if it was a western," James says. "I always loved Tex Ritter. He had that 'Rye Whiskey' song and 'High Noon' song and 'Hillbilly Heaven,' when he sang about all the greats of country music." James learned to sing the song's lyrics a cappella: "*I dreamed I was there in Hillbilly Heaven, oh what a wonderful sight.*" Ritter was one of the first inductees into the Country Music Hall of Fame in 1964, along with Ernest Tubb, and Bob Wills. All three hailed from Texas and would someday perform at the Broken Spoke.

Despite James's love for country music, his dream of building a honky-tonk had only begun to sprout by the time he turned twenty-one. Within a short time, James developed a fondness for local honky-tonks and created his own definition: "A honky-tonk is a place where you're feeling good, you're honkin' your horn, cuttin' up usually with your best girl or your wife. It's a place where you have a lot of beer and whiskey, you have a country music band, and you get out and dance and just have fun. You might get half-loaded drinking beer or alcohol. You get to honk and talk and pretty soon you're 'honky-tonkin.'"

One of James's favorite haunts had been his father's as well, Moose Head Tavern. Its fame grew less for a fascination about the actual moose head that hung on the wall inside the bar than for its large dance hall. On Saturday nights patrons could count on a fight. As the evenings grew long and the serious drinking began, James learned to keep away from trouble or from anyone who threw a bottle or a punch. "If a fight did happen, it was kind of like on cue; everybody just kind of stood up. If you weren't in the fight, you just kind of put your back against the wall and let 'em git after it," James says. "On a Saturday night, you could always kind of count on a fight at the Moose Head Tavern."

Now and then James drove to Pflugerville, just north of Austin, to Dessau Dance Hall to carouse. First built in 1857, the old Dessau featured a huge tree that grew out of the center of its sitting area beside the dance floor. People rested beside the tree or hung things on its limbs, but they also enjoyed the tree as a favorite spot to take pictures. Inside the Dessau, red velvet curtains draped its stage and a giant crystal chandelier hung from its rafters. When the place burned down in the late 1940s, fire took the tree along with the old Dessau stage. A second Dessau burned in 1967. A third version built in 1969 still stands. The current Dessau no longer has a tree in its center, but with a capacity for fifteen hundred it still provides the largest dance floor in the Austin area for private events.[4]

James also frequented Johnny's Place, a bar once located at South First and Barton Springs Road. He often sat at one of its unique round tables that featured a lazy Susan in its center that rose about three inches. Regularly, he and as many as twelve patrons sat at the round tables and took turns buying rounds of beer—Grand Prize, Falstaff, and Jax—until the bar closed. "They never let more than twelve people sit at the table because the number thirteen is unlucky," James says. He recalled the exact design of the tables years later when he and his stepfather created furniture for the Broken Spoke, but their smaller tables sit only eight to nine people.

In the summer of 1958, Bruce Sr. found his son a job in the plastic tooling department of the same airplane manufacturing plant where he had started his career in San Diego. James's job involved assembling parts for booster rocket missiles, including the Atlas, one of the first intercontinental ballistic missiles designed by the Convair Division of General Dynamics. James took pride in his work there, which later launched the Project Mercury missions, the first US manned space program. He worked on Atlas missiles likely used to launch *Friendship 7*, maneuvered by the famous astronaut John Glenn. They were the same style of missiles that made the first successful Earth orbits and later launched the first satellites into space.

After returning home to Austin one night, James drove his nearly new 1959 hardtop black-and-white Chevy onto the dirt parking lot of a dimly lit, thirty- by fifty-foot wooden-shingled building along a deserted stretch of rural road. A neon sign glowed like a beacon in the dark along that long lonely stretch of US 290 in Oak Hill, drawing James and other travelers inside searching for good times. Inside the Sportsman's Inn during the day, the jukebox played the top hits of country music. Those melodies would become familiar classics that resonated with James for years to come. One song in particular, "Wolverton Mountain," sung by Claude King, soon stirred feelings of homesickness. On Saturday nights, a cover charge at the door of the Sportsman's paid for a band. Any Sportsman's band often consisted of a six- or seven-piece ensemble: a piano player, an acoustic guitarist, an upright bass player, a fiddler, a steel guitarist, and a drummer, as well as a lead singer.

James and his friends preferred to sit closest to the sawdust-covered dance floor, a concrete slab. Tables and chairs situated along the sides of the dance floor provided the best views and easy access to dancers. The stage, built from wood paneling, rose just a half foot above the floor, extending its entire width. The ceiling fans gently whirled above patrons, providing small relief from the sweltering humidity and hundred-degree heat outside. After the sun fell well below the horizon, the atmosphere inside the roadside bar often remained muggy. In those days, James used extra care to comb back his hair on the top and sides and load it with Brylcreem, a product that created Elvis Presley's signature shiny, fixed pompadour, a favorite hairstyle of the times. After a few beers, James looked for the prettiest girl he could find to dance the two-step, a waltz, or the western swing. James could dance, and he quickly learned that most girls liked a man light on his feet.

PART II

The 1960s

CHAPTER 4

Origins of Country Music

In *The Handbook of Texas*, Gary Hartman writes, "Country music is rooted in the folk music of the British Isles. English, Irish, Scottish, and Welsh poetry, folklore, ballads, and sea chanteys form the basis for many of the early songs that came to be called country music in the United States."[1] Other ethnicities, including African Americans, Mexican Americans, German Americans, Polish Americans, and French Americans, also influenced country music over the years. As immigrants moved south, they adapted their traditional folk songs to fit their harsh environments, such as "Bury Me Not on the Lone Prairie," derived from an old English sailor's song, "Ocean Burial." Along the long cattle drives, cowboys wrote original songs such as "Home on the Range." One of the first composers to transcribe the American folk music classic, David Wendel Guion, also popularized the songs "Turkey in the Straw" and "Arkansas Traveler" during the 1920s.[2] At the time, Hollywood film producers launched a nationwide search for country singers and found many living in Texas, including Gene Autry, Dale Evans, and Tex Ritter. They also found Jimmie Rodgers, who hailed from Mississippi but soon joined the ranks of the singing cowboys of the American West.[3] By the 1940s, these country movie stars dressed well, rode horses, packed guns, and yodeled—all virtues that came to represent not real cowboys but those of the silver screen. Pretty soon the cowboy myth began to overshadow the reality.

At about the same time that the American cowboy received a do-over, a hybrid new style of country music—western swing—emerged from the Dallas–Fort Worth area that incorporated folk, blues, and big-band jazz, led by Bob Wills and the Light Crust Doughboys. W. Lee O'Daniel, then general sales manager of Burrus Mill and Elevator Company, hired Wills's band to advertise the mill's Light Crust flour at noon each day on radio stations in Fort Worth, Dallas, San Antonio, Houston, and Oklahoma City.[4] However, O'Daniel fired Wills in 1933 for drinking on the job. Within one year the bandleader had signed another contract to promote Crazy Water Crystals at KVOO in Tulsa. Thanks to the radio broadcasts, Wills's popularity grew so vast that his band made as much as eight thousand dollars each night performing in dozens of ballrooms throughout the Texas Panhandle. By 1946 after World War II ended, Wills's band drew as little as four hundred dollars a night because the era of television had arrived. People who remembered Wills's band and had danced to his music now stayed home to watch TV.[5] Wills and the Texas Playboys survived the 1950s from the sales of two top-ten hits, "Ida Red (Likes the Boogie)" and "Faded Love."

When Wills suffered two heart attacks in the early 1960s, the Texas Playboys temporarily disbanded. During a national tour, he suffered his first attack at fifty-eight years old in November 1962 on his way to a gig in San Antonio. By 1963 he and his band moved to Fort Worth. In 1964 he suffered his second heart attack. Following his recovery, Wills began to earn $150,000 a year performing what he called "The Bob Wills Show" in dance halls. Between 1965 and 1968 Wills, then known as "Mr. Western Showbusiness," recorded five albums for Kapp Records of New York, releasing fourteen singles that became some of the most popular in his career catalog, says his daughter, Rosetta Wills. Some of those singles included "Deep in the Heart of Texas," and "Kansas City," a cover song written by Jerry Leiber and Mike Stoller. During the time Wills spent performing in Texas dance halls throughout the late 1960s, he played at the Broken Spoke three times—beginning in 1966.

CHAPTER 5

The Broken Spoke Opens

One night in 1961 a pretty blonde girl wearing a red dress and dancing at the Sportsman's Inn captured James's attention. "That girl turned out to be the love of my life and my wife, Annetta Wells," James says. "People all the time ask me, 'Where did you meet your wife?,' and I always tell them, 'in a honky-tonk.' She . . . kind of caught my eye."

Annetta and James dated until he enlisted in the US Army on September 25, 1961, and he shipped overseas. Meanwhile, Annetta worked in the auditor's office for the accounting division at the University of Texas. James began his basic training at Fort Leonard Wood, Missouri. His previous job experience came in handy. He began his military career working on the Nike Hercules missiles at the Strategic Air Command (SAC) center where Westlake is located today. The SAC command guarded the Boeing B-52 Stratofortress, the long-range bombers used during the Cold War. James enjoyed his work and had hoped to stay assigned to American soil.[1] "My army recruiting sergeant had told me, 'Oh yeah, you won't go overseas. You'll probably be right here the whole three years that you serve in the army,'" James says. "Truth is, I wasn't in but just a few months before I was sent overseas; they sent me to Okinawa," where he served in the launch and maintenance crew for the Nike Hercules missiles.

Daily for eighteen months he assembled and loaded warhead sections of the missiles in their launch bays. He was sent to Bolo Point, which had once operated as a strategic training facility by the US military since being seized from the Japanese in 1945.[2] James learned to expertly attach nose sections that contained the guidance and flight controls on missiles. In October 1962, James and his crew prepared loaded missiles for launch and hid them beneath tarpaulins on base. They readied the weapons by aiming them over the East China Sea during the Cuban Missile Crisis. The crew waited thirteen agonizing days for an official word to launch from President John F. Kennedy as the United States prepared for nuclear war.[3] James says,

"I would literally sleep with the missiles when we had five-minute [launch] status during the Cuban Crisis, but most of the time we took turns on fifteen-minute [launch] status."

The crew coordinated launches from three trailers or vans with fuel-, generator-, electric-, or radio-powered systems.[4] "I just basically coordinated between our battery commander and launch crew about where the missiles were.... I got to fire one missile myself. It's kind of a power trip when you get to fire a big missile over the Philippine and China Seas," James says. On the weekends, James grew homesick. Whenever he and a few of his buddies left base for some R&R, they took a car called a *sukoshi*, the Japanese word for "small," into town.[5] Sometimes they ordered a larger cab called a *takusan*.[6] They frequented the local village bars, looking for the familiar "AAA" sign that designated the venue as friendly to anti-aircraft artillery soldiers seeking some American-style entertainment. "This one sake bar, as we called them, had a dirt floor, and the jukebox had one George Jones and one Hank Locklin record. So those are the ones we played, over and over again," James says. He played Locklin's "My Old Hometown" and Jones's "Window Up Above" as often as he could. "When you're overseas, you don't hear the country music and you get a craving for it," James says. "From that day forward I began to think to myself—'I've got to hear more country music.'" James also learned to appreciate the effects of Japanese sake while riding out the typhoons in Okinawa.

James returned to the United States in 1963 as a Specialist 4 in the Honor Guard, and before long the military promoted him to a Specialist 5 stationed at the Joint Base of Fort Sam Houston in San Antonio. The historic quadrangle had become famous because it once housed the Apache war chief Geronimo and thirty-two of his warriors captured alongside him in 1886.[7] The fort had also housed Gen. Frederick Funston during the Spanish-American War and Gen. John J. Pershing throughout World War I. James loved the history of the place. While there, James began to wonder about his future. "That's when I started wondering 'What am I going to do when I get out of the army?' And I thought to myself, 'Well, I'll just get me a place of my own.' I started havin' these wagon wheels spinnin' around in my head." Once on leave from the base, he saw the movie *Broken Arrow*, a western film that left a strong impression on James. He began to visualize a broken spoke inside a solid wood wagon wheel as a symbol of a cowboy's trial and triumph. James could not then have imagined how that image would serve him for more than half a century to come.

When he returned to Austin in 1963, James contacted a mutual friend to ask about Annetta Wells. Annetta recalls regularly visiting a roping arena in Oak Hill before going into the Sportsman's Inn. "We knew all the same people, but he had gone to California in '57, and that was about the time I got out of high school. Some of my best friends were Dewey and Sarah Cooper, and James was best friends with Dewey. We all went to the Sportsman's Inn."

Soon after she and James reconnected, Annetta learned how to gamble and to drink beer. "I was raised straight Baptist. I didn't gamble, I didn't drink, and I didn't cuss until I met James. He was raised wild and woolly," she says. "He said, 'If somebody wants to buy you a beer, you have to be social and accept it.' So I learned to drink beer, and I've been on a diet ever since." James also taught Annetta how to play cards. "James taught me how to put money on the table the first time when we went to Las Vegas and I loved it," she says. Their lifestyle offended some of her immediate relatives. "I am the black sheep of the family. My parents never blackballed us, but the rest of the Baptists in the family did."

One day as James drove his truck west along what was then Old Fredericksburg Road, he saw a "land for lease" sign posted in front of the defunct Al Ehrlich Lumberyard, where a large oak tree grew. James stopped and walked around the lot for a few minutes. What he saw convinced him that he did not want anything to do with the run-down lumberyard office. However, the land and the tree drew his rapt attention. He experienced what he called an epiphany. Immediately he jumped into his truck and headed for the nearest phone booth to call the number posted on the sign.

Jay Lynn Johnson Jr., the owner of a successful construction company and former city councilman, owned the land and lumberyard.[8] The two men met and within an hour Johnson agreed to lease James the land. As James recalls, "He said if you'll help me build the building since your stepfather is a carpenter, then I'll let you lease that land, and I'll lease the building to you, and you can stay there as long as you want to. So I signed a ten-year lease with an option to renew." James's stepfather, Joe, knew many of the city's plumbers, electricians, concrete workers, and construction workers on a first-name basis. "He knew every drunk in town. When I built the Broken Spoke, he got a bunch of our friends to come out and help me," James says. "People always ask me, 'Why didn't you ever buy that land?' I always tell them when Jay Johnson owned it, the land was not for sale." Johnson had received the land as part of a family trust that set conditions on the age at which he would be allowed to sell it. "Then after a while he didn't want to sell it. He told his kids the only way they could ever sell it was to sell it all together at one time; he said they could never divide up the land to sell it."

Johnson's daughter, Julie, remembers at seven years old tagging along with her father to the Broken Spoke's construction site all those years ago. "Dad taught me the name of every tool and every nail. He'd tell me, 'I need something,' and I'd go get it. I was his little gopher," Julie says. "It was mainly me; I just worshipped my dad. I was the oldest; the other ones [Jan, Jay, and Jim] weren't really old enough to go, so I followed him around like a little puppy." Julie's father kept his word to help James build the honky-tonk, although James paid for its construction.

The day James received his honorable discharge from the army, at twenty-five years old, he began building the one-room honky-tonk and called it the Broken Spoke. It opened November 10, 1964, about a mile outside what was then the Austin city limits. For the grand opening, guitarists Dave Perry and Johnny Rex performed. James paid the musician-singers in free beer and barbecue. He also gave away three hundred plates of brisket and plenty of cold beer that day to customers.

Joe's friends spread the word that the Broken Spoke had opened for business. In the days that followed Joe remained an ever-present and imposing force at the Broken Spoke, so much so that some patrons came to believe that he owned it. However, Annetta says that the Broken Spoke managed to stay open and operated on a shoestring budget only thanks to James's hard work and good credit. "We didn't have a dime to spare. When we sold one case of beer, we went and bought another case. We had ten dollars in a cigar box when we opened. We didn't have a cash register, and the one we got first didn't have a tape. We used two cigar boxes—one for incoming and the other one for outgoing," she says.

"We hadn't been in business long when we got a state audit; that's when our CPA told us to get a register with a tape." Because the Broken Spoke would not obtain a mixed-beverage liquor license until 1980, James sold "setups," such as 7 Up and Coca-Cola, and both bottled and canned beer.

The Broken Spoke opened on November 10, 1964, as a one-room saloon located about a mile outside the Austin city limits. Courtesy of James White.

Patrons also brought in bottles of liquor wrapped in brown paper sacks, a practice they referred to as "brown baggin.'" "Guys got drunker then, because they looked at their bottle and figured that they'd only had a couple of inches left and they might as well drink what was left rather than cart the bottle home," he says. James recalls that he sold beer for twenty-five cents a bottle or premium beer like Schlitz, Budweiser, or Miller High Life for thirty cents. He sold setups with a glass of ice for thirty cents each. "Basically we had to sell four beers to make a dollar, and we didn't clear that much because of the price of our beer; our overhead cut into everything," James says. "I used to bartend sixteen to seventeen hours a day out here. I learned to pop two beers in each hand, and I could pop beer as fast as I could sell it." On busier nights, thousands of beer-bottle caps littered the floor.

Soon news about the place spread; before long the Broken Spoke filled to capacity nearly every night. Doris Gerald "D. G." Burrow and the Western Melodies often played a Sunday gig at the Broken Spoke.[9] James paid the band thirty-two dollars a night, which amounted to quite a bit of money back then. James asked customers to donate to a band fund by passing around a tip jar that he called "passin' the kitty." James seldom collected more than twenty dollars, but the tips offset his costs to hire a band. His first mistake was allowing band members and waitresses to drink all the beer they wanted. "Come to find out, the waitresses were getting too drunk, so I had to start charging them. I had one girl who just made a hog outta herself like an old sot; she just drank all the free beer, and toward the end of the night she wasn't worth a flip," he says. "So I just had to start charging the help. Even today, we charge what we call 'an employee price,' which is a little bit less than what the customers pay. They still do a lot of drinking on the side or buy their friends drinks. It's still hard to try to control that."

James soon began hiring bands to play Fridays, Saturdays, and Sundays. He paid Travis and the Western gentlemen twenty-five dollars to play every Friday; on Saturdays Bill Dorsey and the Melody Drifters played for thirty-five dollars. "We would pack them in. It was just solid wall-to-wall people. I would pop beer as fast as I could—four for a dollar, and we'd sell setups. It was just really a big crowd. It was so busy that folks would dance into the dining room and out the front door, right out into the parking lot and then turn around and come back inside dancing," he says. "Back in those days a lot of people would dress up more than what they do today, as far as wearing a coat and tie. They would want to look their best—shine their shoes and put on their dancing shoes."

Even back then stepping into the Broken Spoke often felt like a flash out of the past—it looked like the dance halls of the 1940s and 1950s that James remembered visiting as a boy. James built a place that people would always remember for its appearance, its live music, and its good food. Joe worked as a cook, but not for long. "I had to learn to cook because my stepfather would get so drunk that he couldn't cook," James says. "He'd go to cook a hamburger, and people might tell him to leave off the pickle and onion. He'd yell back, 'Damn it, you're gettin' it all the way or nothing; rake off what you don't want.' Or if he was drinkin' a beer at the time when someone came in to ask him for a cheeseburger, he'd tell them, 'McDonald's is down the road; go get you a burger down there.'"

The first night that James learned to cook, a customer asked Joe for a steak and hash browns, he recalls. "My stepfather had been drinkin' all day, so he just took the spatula and he slammed those hash browns against the wall and left. So I told the guy, 'I'll finish cookin' your meal.' The guy said, 'I didn't know I was gonna cause a family argument; all I wanted was a steak.'" James began working in both the bar and the kitchen as Annetta waited tables. After several cooks left the Broken Spoke in the middle of their shifts for one reason or another, James learned how to cook, a skill that would come in handy. "I had my aunt help me, and a lot of different relatives would come over," James says. "It was one big family and friends I had known all of my life." James and Joe had installed a black stainless-steel four-burner and double-oven Garland stove in its kitchen that finally quit working in March 2015, so Annetta had to buy another. The Whites custom-built kitchen today strangely resembles the set for the vintage television sitcom The Adventures of Ozzie and Harriet.

However, life for the Whites became anything but idyllic. On August 1, 1966, Charles Joseph Whitman opened fire from the twenty-eighth-floor observation deck inside the clock tower on the UT campus, killing fourteen people and wounding thirty-two others.[10] That day Annetta still worked in the auditor's office inside the main building below the tower. She recalls, "It was about quarter to twelve, and our auditor came in; he locked that double door, and he said, 'No one is to leave this office.' We heard banging and stuff going on outside, but we thought they were just working on the building by sandblasting it. So we didn't really pay it any mind." The building had been undergoing renovations for months. "Then the auditor said, 'Somebody is up in the tower shootin' people.'"

"So I immediately tried to get hold of James on the phone," Annetta says. She remembers her co-workers also began dialing family and friends. "I finally got hold of James at the Spoke. I told him to turn the TV on. Watching the news, he could tell me more about what was happening on campus than we knew." James instructed Annetta to hide under her desk. She recalls, "I told him, 'He [Whitman] can't get inside,' but James said, 'Get under that desk anyway.' We could see people fall outside the windows, and there were a lot of windows in that office." The auditor's office had been inaccessible by elevator; it did not open on the first floor. "Everybody just crowded around my desk because I could tell them what was happening as James told me what he saw on the TV. We knew that if we could see that tower, he [Whitman] could see us."

Much of the Austin Police and Travis County Sheriff's Department arrived on the scene, including APD officers Ramiro Martinez and Houston McCoy, both of whom fired fatal shots that struck their target that day.[11] Police released Annetta and other UT office personnel about 2:30 p.m. "As I walked across the area from the main building to Guadalupe Street and across to the University Co-Op, I could see blood all over the sidewalks where people had been shot. By the time I got to my car, I was almost running," she says. "I went straight to the Broken Spoke and I had a beer." The Associated Press and United Press would later rank the event as one of the most important stories of 1966, second only to the Vietnam War. Annetta continued to work weekdays in the auditor's office; meanwhile she also worked evenings at the Broken Spoke.

Annetta usually went to work at the Broken Spoke about 5:30 p.m. and often worked past midnight in the dining room or the kitchen. On weekends she also trained Broken Spoke cooks to prepare two of her specialties, the chili and the chicken-fried steak with its white gravy, just as her mother, Maxine Wells, had taught her. From the very first day the Broken Spoke opened, the most popular item on the menu has been the chicken-fried steak with french fries or a baked potato and a small salad served with rolls and butter. Annetta learned about commercial cooking from the Broken Spoke's first night cook, Lee Ballard, who taught her how to make homemade salad dressings and barbecue. Within fifteen years, both *Texas Highways* and *Texas Monthly* magazines would name the Broken Spoke's "the best chicken-fried steak in town."

In its early days, nearly two hundred people ate lunch daily at the Broken Spoke. By 2015 that same number would come to represent the plethora of restaurants surrounding the Broken Spoke within two square miles, providing testimony to its staying power in the South Lamar business district. "We'd run out of prepared lunches. I used to make a five-gallon pot of chicken and dumplings for Thursday lunches. I'd cook eighteen fried chickens on Tuesday for the 'blue plate special lunch,' and we'd sell out by two p.m. It was a ton of work, but I was young and had a strong back then," Annetta says. Annetta prepared the lunches with the help of an Italian cook, Luciana "Lou" Norman. However, Norman took a vacation for two months every summer to visit her family in Italy. As a result, the entire extended White family began working at the Broken Spoke, including James's mother, Lena, who prepped in the kitchen while Nantie Margaret washed dishes.

James's namesake and uncle, James "Doc" Campbell-White, often stopped by to entertain the family with stories about his rough days working as a Texas law enforcement officer. Before Campbell-White had retired as a Texas Ranger and an FBI agent, he had made news headlines for assisting in the FBI raid on Ma Barker and her son in a shootout in Ocklawaha, Florida. Campbell-White helped capture kidnapper George "Machine Gun" Kelly and his wife and made friends with Texas Ranger Frank Hamer, once credited as the special investigator for the Texas prison system and responsible for the ambush that killed notorious bank robbers Bonnie Parker and Clyde Barrow.[12] James recalls that his uncle loved visiting the Broken Spoke and would talk about how he had assisted during the FBI's killing of notorious bank robber John Dillinger in Chicago in 1934.[13] "In the last year of his life when he was at the rest home, he would come down to the Broken Spoke on Wednesdays and Sundays. He always ate two poached eggs with toast with the crust cut off," James says. "He always drank two Falstaff beers. He would top it off with a slice of apple pie with a scoop of vanilla ice cream on top." Before he died in 1967, Campbell-White deeded James his ranch of more than two hundred acres just eleven miles west of the Broken Spoke's front door. James's uncle always seemed to James like the grandfather he never knew, John Dudley White, who had been shot and killed by an army deserter while serving as a Texas Ranger in 1918.[14] The White family ranch soon became an extension of the Broken Spoke. The ranch became a special place where James and Annetta entertained country stars and friends on Sundays and Mondays when the Broken Spoke closed to the general public.

Although James and Annetta had worked side by side both personally and professionally as partners for two years after the Broken Spoke opened, they did not marry until September 15, 1966. They held their wedding at the Central Presbyterian Church in downtown Austin. Two receptions followed that day, one at the church for Annetta's Baptist family members and another at the Broken Spoke for everyone else. At about 11:30 p.m., they left town on a two-week honeymoon and drove nearly five thousand miles across the southern United States. First they drove to Memphis to see Elvis's Graceland and then to Nashville to see the Grand Ole Opry, which at the time occupied the old Ryman Auditorium. From there they drove to Washington, DC, to see the Smithsonian Institution, the Washington Monument, and Arlington National Cemetery. Afterward they drove to Miami, Florida. They visited New Orleans before heading for home.

The first chairs the White's ever bought were wooden chairs that they spray-painted orange. "I don't know why we decided to paint them orange—

probably because we loved UT—but they looked awful," Annetta says. "We went back over them and lightly sprayed them brown, which made them look antiqued, so it turned out pretty good, but I think those eighty chairs lasted about two weeks."

Over the next few years the Whites tried to create a family-like atmosphere at the Broken Spoke for their eldest daughter, Terri. However, Terri's unconventional childhood growing up at the Broken Spoke provided her with plenty of life lessons. As Terri recalls, "I went to bed in the office. The next day I'd go to school. You had a bar life as your home life, and so the Broken Spoke is our second home." When patrons drank too much beer, bottles often flew. The White family considered the fights that followed just part of the territory while managing the ups and downs of a honky-tonk and its most colorful characters. "Oh boy," James recalled. "My daughter Terri loved to watch the fights in the parking lot from the front window of the Broken Spoke. We would tell her, 'Get away from there,' but she couldn't help herself; she would get all excited watching the action." James often found himself caught in the middle of fights while trying to break up the action. "We had some rednecks who had been at a wedding elsewhere show up. Someone called them 'monkey suits,' and they got into a fight," James says. "I had a can of mace and a pile of people higher than the tables. My mother fainted. Then I grabbed one woman who was foul-mouthed and telling me 'what-for,' so I took that can of mace and I sprayed it right into her mouth. I filled her mouth up with mace until it foamed out."

People often tell Terri how lucky she is to have James White as her dad. "I've heard it a thousand times: 'You have the greatest dad. I wish he was my dad.' Yes, well, my dad is the king," Terri says. James has always doted on her. "He was a good dad. He was a great dad. When I was growing up, I'd wanna go a different way to school every day or to the baby sitter's, which was my aunt Margaret's. He'd sing songs every mornin,'" Terri says. "Yeah, the Broken Spoke is its own life, for sure. It's very nostalgic. It reminds you of your very good heartfelt days, when you're young, when things really meant so very much to you." As a youngster, Terri learned to dance by taking impromptu lessons from one of the Broken Spoke's cooks, Rosemary Hallmark. "I loved her. She taught me, and then a whole bunch of hairy-legged farts taught me." As a young woman, Terri would also enroll in ten years of formal dance lessons. However, that training did not prepare her to teach dance lessons at the Broken Spoke. "I have to take somebody with two left feet and teach them how to get confident and apply it," Terri says.

By the year 1969 Annetta had quit her job at UT, but their lives soon took on a hectic pace when the Whites opened a second business, the Fortress Steak House. James's great-grandfather, James Andrew Patton, had overseen the construction of the building, Patton Rock Store, on US Highway 290 West in 1898. After operating as a general store and post office for several years, the building had served as a lodge for the Woodmen of the World. After Patton died, the building's title passed to James's Nantie Margaret, who then deeded it to James. When James took over its ownership, the building possessed only one electric light bulb and no running water.[15] The Whites installed 220-volt electricity and Annetta's brother, Gene Wells, added indoor plumbing. Soon afterward they built an addition onto the back that James named the Red Dog Saloon. Annetta paid for the improvements at the Fortress with money she had received as a pension after leaving UT's accounting department. She began working eighteen-hour days at the Fortress.

Managing the Fortress, the Red Dog Saloon, and the Broken Spoke quickly became too much for the Whites. On July 20, 1969, when US astronauts landed on the moon, James White remembers standing in front of the Fortress restaurant and making the decision to take a few giant steps backward as a restaurant business owner. Armstrong proclaimed those now famous words, "That's one small step for man, one giant leap for mankind."[16] James recalls that the statement moved him. "I walked outside that old rock store in Oak Hill and looked up at the moon and the moon was full, but I couldn't see him [Armstrong.]" The Whites felt overworked and missed domestic life. "It got to where I never got to see my daughter and my wife, so I decided to lease it [the rock store] out to several people," James says. It later housed several businesses, including Cowboy's restaurant run by Willie Nelson's daughter, Lana Nelson, and the Natural Gardener. Today the Whites still own the building, but they lease it to the manager of Austin Pizza Garden. After stretching his business interests too thin, James learned a valuable lesson. From that day forward James made a note to his future self to focus all of his energy on the Broken Spoke. James learned to rely on his common sense. Meanwhile, James recalls, his stepfather continued to suffer from a lack of that particular attribute.

One day late in 1969 a customer sitting at a round table at the Broken Spoke with James's stepfather said he had a spider monkey that he no longer wanted. Joe told the man he would take the monkey, build a cage for it, and keep it at the Broken Spoke. Joe and the Whites called the pet monkey "Skeeter," and for a while they kept him in a cage on the patio. Every now and then that monkey escaped his cage. Sometimes Skeeter escaped out the front door of the Broken Spoke and climbed up on top of the power lines along South Lamar. Or he climbed into the big oak tree in front of the Spoke. Skeeter liked to just sit out in that tree for hours chattering away. Whenever he came down from the tree, his favorite thing to do was to pee on the top of someone's head.

One day a bunch of drunks at the bar started talking about buying Skeeter a girlfriend, James recalls. "So they bought a monkey girlfriend for Skeeter and they put 'Mrs. Skeeter' in the cage with him. Skeeter chased her around the cage for three days until he caught her and she beat the hell out of him. She even pulled some of his hair out," James says. Then one day "Mrs. Skeeter escaped and jumped up on top of a Coca-Cola truck in the parking lot, and she rode it all the way downtown to the Coca-Cola warehouse. Someone at the Coca-Cola warehouse called me and said, 'We have your monkey down here,' and I said, 'You can have her.'" Skeeter lived a solitary life for the remainder of his days until a tragedy occurred at the Broken Spoke in 1968; an electrical fire destroyed the game room. "After the fire, we cleaned up the building, and we found Skeeter in one of the booths—B-2, in the back where the game room is located now," James says. "The smoke must have killed him." Not long after, James and Annetta reopened the Broken Spoke for business, but they retired Skeeter's cage. "Annetta never liked Skeeter. She used to throw things at him," James says. "But Lee Ballard, our cook, liked to feed Skeeter bananas."

CHAPTER 6

First Performers Booked for Dancing at the Spoke

Austin grew until the city boundary line stretched all the way to the Broken Spoke's front door. As soon he could manage it, James asked Mayor Lester Palmer for access to the city's water utilities. James slyly obtained the city's water lines by telling Palmer and Austin City Council members that his horses lacked sufficient water. Actually, James sought the city's sewer lines because his septic system had failed when a beer truck driver one day sunk a wheel into it. Soon natural gas lines also reached the Broken Spoke, followed by cable television service. The upgrades paid off as the number of Broken Spoke patrons increased. "People sat on beer cases when the place got packed," James says.

James needed to expand the Broken Spoke in 1965 because his building could no longer hold the crowds. A friend, Chuck Cook, poured the concrete slab for a ninety- by sixty-five-foot dance floor that today still holds up after use by thousands of dancers. Back in the day, if bands could not play well, they played loud. Regardless of their talent, band members dressed like stars in elaborately embroidered and rhinestone-studded western suits. Patrons also dressed well. Male dancers wore western slacks or Wrangler jeans, a dress shirt with a wide embroidered yolk, and either a tie or a bolo, along with their best cowboy boots and hat. The women wore peasant-style blouses or shirts similar to the men's with either Wrangler jeans, knee-length square-dance circle skirts or shorter rockabilly skirts with full layered petticoats and boots or dancing shoes. The Whites passed the kitty two or three times a night to pay the band members fifteen to twenty dollars each; James's costs had begun to more than double from the days when he had paid thirty-five dollars for an entire ensemble. After James added the dance hall, he began booking bands. He paid Dave Perry and the Texas Swing Boys, and Damon Meredith and The Western Caravan sixty dollars to play on a Friday or a Saturday. At times, James sponsored "a battle dance" featuring two bands. "One band would play an hour; then another one would jump up and play right after that one got through. They called them 'battle dances' back in them days," James says. "That was back in the days when they hadn't even started to do the Cotton-Eyed Joe."

Broken Spoke dancers then enjoyed dancing in a partner-changing mixer round of dance called the "Paul Jones." The women danced clockwise within an inner circle while the men danced counterclockwise in an outer circle to a fast fiddle song.[1] Most often the dancers at the Broken Spoke requested the "Orange Blossom Special," a bluegrass song long considered "fiddle players' national anthem," written by Ervin T. Rouse and recorded with his brother, Gordon, in 1939.[2] The song has been rerecorded at least a half dozen times, from the legendary Johnny Cash in 1965 and most recently by the Charlie Daniels Band in 1974.[3] At the Broken Spoke, when James blew the whistle or rang a bell, the dancers stopped dancing the Paul Jones to grab the first person standing opposite in the second circle. "So sometimes, you'd end up with a pretty nice-looking gal, and maybe the next time she wasn't quite as pretty," James says. "Same with the men; I mean the women might end up with some older guy, or they might end up with a young handsome fella also. It was a fun dance."

Soon people also began dancing the Cotton-Eyed Joe and the Bunny Hop at the Broken Spoke. Though it predates the Civil War, the Americanized instrumental version of "Cotton-Eyed Joe" may be derived from a Scottish mountain song known as "General Burgoyne's March."[4] The fiddle piece has been recorded by dozens of performing artists over the last two centuries, including most recently by the Swedish popular combo Rednex in 1994.[5] The song's lyrics vary considerably, but its refrain remains pretty much the same: "*Cotton-Eyed Joe / where'd you come from / where'd you go?/ Where'd you come from Cotton-Eyed Joe?*" Some say the song tells the story of a man who suffered blindness by drinking methanol or wood alcohol. Others claim the lyrics began as a rhyme about a lovelorn slave who once lived in the Deep South.[6] Singer and author Dorothy Scarborough wrote in her book *On the Trail of Negro Folksongs* that slaves working on a Texas plantation shared the song's original lyrics with her sister in 1925.[7] Regardless of its origins, "Cotton-Eyed Joe" remains a folk classic throughout Texas. During the early 1970s younger audiences who had just received their license to drink at eighteen years old changed the line that follows the refrain to *"whup, whup."* Bandleaders today follow each refrain with the words *"what you say / bull sh*t"* on the hard-hitting beat of the song, James White says. It remains one of the few dances technically categorized as a line dance, but still allowed on the Broken Spoke dance floor.

The Bunny Hop may have been derived from a Finnish style of dance known as a "jenkka," although Balboa High School students in San Francisco debuted similar novelty steps in 1952 to the tune of Ray Anthony's hit "Bunny Hop."[8] Duke Ellington also popularized the conga line-style party dance when he released a salsa instrumental version, the "Bunny Hop Mambo," in 1954. This energetic dance incorporates steps that have influenced countless others in pop culture. Ironically, the song "Hokey Pokey" appeared on the flipside of Anthony's 45-rpm vinyl "Bunny Hop" single. Folks danced to the "Bunny Hop" for more than a decade at the Broken Spoke before James put a stop to it. "I don't let 'em do the Bunny Hop no more 'cause they were hoppin' from the dance floor up onto the wooden porches along the dance floor at the Broken Spoke. There would be more than one hundred of them hoppin' up and down, and one of them busted through the floor," James says. "The Bunny Hop then was outlawed out here—just for safety reasons. . . . Other modern western line dances are not considered country—they began in Nashville, Tennessee—not Texas in the 1980s. No one can line dance on our dance floor while folks are country dancing because they'd run into each other. Therefore, we don't allow no line dancing at the Broken Spoke," James says.

In 1966 the king of western swing, fiddle player and bandleader Bob Wills, became the first legendary star to grace the Broken Spoke's bandstand, although a few other somewhat contemporary performers had headlined in the previous two years. "All the drunks at the bar said to me, 'Oh hell, he'll be drunk; he won't show up, he'll be chasin' some woman somewhere,' but Wills opened the door and he was all by himself," James says. "He had his cigar in his mouth, a cowboy hat on, and his fiddle up under his arm. All the old drunks at the bar just about fell off their bar stools. They started whistlin' and they said, 'Man, that's Bob Wills over there.' It was a really exciting time for me to be able to book a childhood hero of mine." James today performs an accurate imitation of Wills's famous line "Take it away boys—San Antonio Rose—Ah, ha." "It was a great magical moment—a proud moment for me. I got to walk Bob Wills up on the bandstand." James booked Wills again in 1967 and 1968.

Fans always acted like they knew Bob Wills, but they really did not know him like James claims he did. Before Bob Wills passed away in 1975, James had the opportunity to get to know Wills well. "I have a lot of fond memories because he was a household word around my family when I grew up, a legendary guy," James says. He arranged the bookings through Billy Western, a one-time promoter located in Granger, Texas, who paid Wills just four hundred dollars to perform. "The car they traveled in wasn't air-conditioned. The band members would just go to sleep in the back seat. They didn't have none of those tour buses," he says. Wills set new standards for country music both as a performer and as a recording artist. He became the first musician allowed to perform at the Grand Ole Opry with a full drum set onstage, James says. "Bluegrass bands don't really have drums,

James White stands beside the king of western swing, fiddle player, and bandleader Bob Wills, who first graced the Broken Spoke's bandstand in 1966. *Courtesy of Annette White.*

but Bob Wills knew that the drums get your feet movin.' He liked the drum beat, and he brought the drum beat to western swing. Then when he got to feeling good, Bob Wills would shout out 'Ah, ha.'"

Also in the late 1960s, James booked stars like Roy Acuff, Bobby Bare, Jim Ed Brown, Henson Cargill, Little Jimmy Dickens, Tillman Franks, Jack Greene, David Houston, Claude King, Charlie Louvin, Willie Nelson, Bashful Brother Oswald, Tex Ritter, Shoji Tabuchi, Ernest Tubb, the Geezinslaw Brothers, and Charlie Walker. Back when James first started booking Willie Nelson at the Broken Spoke, he paid him eight hundred dollars to play. San Antonio or Nashville promoters arranged Nelson's bookings; they often stopped by or sent letters to James in advance. "Once those booking agents talked to each other about where their musicians played, everyone found out I had a new place to play," James says. Nelson also performed at the Skyline Club or Gil's Club in Austin.

James soon began booking Hank Thompson through promoters located in Oklahoma City. Pappy Hal Horton, Dallas disc jockey for KRLD, helped to make Thompson and The Brazos Valley Boys regional favorites with their honky-tonk and western swing music from the 1940s until the 1970s.[9] Throughout the 1960s, the band was the first to travel the Texas-Oklahoma dance hall circuit by bus; it did not take long before James booked them at the Broken Spoke. "Back then it was a simple contract. There wasn't no rider contract. Nothing fancy. They didn't demand hotel rooms. They didn't demand anything like they do today. I never signed a rider contract," James says. "I've always signed a basic contract that says 'you're gonna play so many hours; the cover charge is going to be this, I'm gonna guarantee you this, or you'll recoup a percentage at the door of the Broken Spoke at this address.'" James says nowadays bands often request contracts with "a rider" that might include towels, a dressing room, free drinks, coffee, snacks, and a bottle of whiskey for the band or a case of iced-down beer. "They might want me to buy their supper and I just don't do it. The way I see it, they should buy my damn supper," James says. "So I stopped booking bands with too many demands. The way I see it, they need me more than I need them."

Thompson and The Brazos Valley Boys performed at the Broken Spoke during the peak of their popularity after Thompson in 1965 recorded the first live album by a country band.[10] Thompson dressed in the popular western suits of the times, encrusted with rhinestones. His band members always looked like stars when they performed onstage. Early in his career Thompson wrote love songs around nursery rhymes. His first song, "Humpty Dumpty Heart," became a national hit after he recorded it on a magnetic tape recorder. He had played the southern and western circuit of US dance halls during the late 1950s. The Waco native would become the subject of a novel by Thomas Cobb in 1987 and the movie *Crazy Heart* in 2009, starring Jeff Bridges. Thompson enjoyed being a flashy dresser and wore lots of gold: gold buckles embedded with gold coins and gold coin–encrusted necklaces, watches, or bracelets. Thompson's wife, Ann, often dressed like an Indian princess in a costume that consisted of a beautiful ceremonial buckskin dress. "Both of them were really good people, and I enjoyed having them here," James says.

Thompson's steel guitar player, Bert Rivera, who had attended school with James at Travis High School, also performed solo at the Broken Spoke with his own band, the Night Riders. James remembers Rivera as a good South Austin kid whose father worked in a brewery and often bought his friends

Hank Thompson and The Brazos Valley Boys, dressed in western suits encrusted with rhinestones, performed at the Broken Spoke at the peak of their popularity in 1967. Courtesy of Rick Henson.

beer at the Broken Spoke and at other bars in town. Rivera would receive several awards throughout his career, including induction in the Texas Western Swing Hall of Fame in 2001 and the Austin Latino Music Association Award in 2006.[11]

James booked the Geezinslaw Brothers at the Broken Spoke in 1964, who remained its longest-running act until just a decade ago. For more than forty years, Sammy Allred fronted the famous comedic country band known worldwide from 1961 until 2005 as just the Geezinslaws. They included Dewayne "Son" Smith, no relation to Allred. Together they recorded twelve albums on various labels and appeared six times on the *Austin City Limits* and *The Texas Connection* TV shows. The band toured with trumpet player Herb Alpert and his Tijuana Brass, who created five number-one albums and earned five Grammys. The Geezinslaws also toured with Roger Miller, who popularized the hit song "King of the Road," and 1950s crooner Perry Como, who made the *Chesterfield Supper Club* radio show famous. The Geezinslaws also appeared on Ralph Emery's *Nashville Now* once a month in 1986.[12]

James White booked Sammy Allred and the famous comedic country band known as the Geezinslaws, including Dewayne "Son" Smith, from 1961 to 2005. Courtesy of Rick Henson.

The Geezinslaws began their career as a duo and ended it as part of a six-piece band, playing at the Broken Spoke for the last time in 2005. "We called Dewayne 'Son.' We used to have an older guy who played the fiddle and people would ask, 'Is this y'all's dad?' We used to joke around and say, 'Yes, this is the dad and this is the son,'" Allred says. However, the two performers ranged no more than nine years apart in age. Today when Allred's memory and patience often run thin, his friend and former keyboard player Larry Telford fills in by recalling stories from the good old days. Telford played with the Geezinslaws beginning in 1988 and also performed separately for Richard Samet "Kinky" Friedman and country singer-songwriter and guitarist Lee Roy Parnell. The Geezinslaws played the last Saturday of every month for twenty-nine years at the Broken Spoke. Telford says that Allred's comedy material, as well as their great country music, established them. "There's a lot of bands that don't have an identity," Telford says. "The Geezinslaws had an identity. They knew who they were." While appearing at the Broken Spoke, the Geezinslaws never knew what to expect in the way of an audience.

"There was always an element of surprise," Telford says. "We never knew who would show up—who would walk in the front or the back door." Also, you never knew if it was going to be a packed house or a light crowd. One regular fan would come to include Earl Campbell, a University of Texas football player who later earned the Heisman Trophy and became a number-one draft pick for the Houston Oilers. The former running back used to show up to sing "You Never Even Called Me by My Name," a song made famous by David Allan Coe. Singer-songwriter and film director Dwight Yoakam once stopped in to perform "Honky-Tonk Man," a remake of the Johnny Horton song that marked the first country music video ever to broadcast on MTV. Sonny Throckmorton stopped by once to sing a few of his 150 hit songs recorded by great country artists like George Strait. Cast members from the reality TV show *The Housewives of Beverly Hills* also showed up one night.

Allred created the Geezinslaws' song set lists. "Sammy would call the songs," Telford says. "We had a large list of songs that we would play. We never had a song set list per se. Basically, we shot right off the hip." The Geezinslaws did not call themselves a dance band, but people danced to their music just the same. "Actually, we had songs adapted from show tunes. The Geezinslaws might play the song in double-time and change the lyrics," Telford says. "'Til There Was You' was a crowd favorite that the Geezinslaws performed often with their own versions." Allred's repertoire included three hundred to four hundred versions of other people's songs. He created his own signature look, a stereotypical representation of an American male tourist on vacation. At the Broken Spoke, Allred often wore a Hawaiian shirt and his trademark sunglasses along with a deliberately tacky straw hat. "Inside his hat, he kept a list of jokes. He would remove his hat and look inside the brim of the hat to pull out different joke titles. That would help him to remember his line of jokes," Telford says.

People who sat in onstage included West Texas oilman Clayton "Claytie" Williams, who stopped by once to sing "El Rancho Grande." Williams owned Clayton Gas Company, at one time the largest individually owned gas company in Texas.[13] A lot of regulars often came by the Broken Spoke to hear the Geezinslaws because they also heard Allred, a regular radio personality, as one-half of the Sam and Bob in the Morning show on country radio station KVET. For many years, Allred served as an icon at the station until Clear Channel corporate managers fired him for using racially offensive language while broadcasting live on the air in 2007.[14] "Sammy would pump up the Broken Spoke on the radio, and a lot of people would hear him and come in to hear the Geezinslaws," Telford says. Allred's great comedic skills as a frontman led to the band's success at the Broken Spoke. "He would always say, 'It's time for our twenty-nine-dollar light show.' The band would do a drum roll, he would flip a switch, and the lights on the ceiling over the stage would come on. He used to jokingly refer to it as his 'light show,' but they were just Christmas lights," James says.

"He brought Ralph Emery out here a couple of times. Sammy would tell jokes and the band would play and then he would tell more jokes. They won more awards than anybody." James had heard the duo perform on the radio show *Louisiana Hayride*, and Bob listened to Allred's and Cole's syndicated morning radio program. An old sign hanging on a wall at the Broken Spoke reads "All Drinks Free" and serves as a reminder to James for the night when Son Smith performed solo and he paid for everyone's drinks to help promote the show. The plan could have gone south fast, but it didn't. "I don't know how in the hell I pulled that off," James says.

In 1967 James began booking a little-known band, Willie Nelson and the Record Men, who had just released a local hit song, "Mr. Record Man." Nelson wrote the song while working as a Texas deejay during his early career at radio stations in Pleasanton, Denton, and Fort Worth. He had become popular locally playing both his instrumental and lyrical music in nightclubs while also writing songs for other famous performers.[15] By the time Nelson turned eighty years old, he would become a legendary icon with an impressive portfolio of sixty-eight studio, ten live, thirty-seven compilation, and twenty-seven collaborative albums. In the 1960s Nelson played often, and he always arrived early at the Broken Spoke, clean-shaven with short hair and sometimes wearing a turtleneck sweater with a vest or a sports coat. An early picture of a young Willie Nelson standing beside James hangs on the wall across from the bar at the Broken Spoke. "He was always polite and always had a great smile. He could always pick the guitar great," James says.

Legendary singer-songwriter Ernest Tubb first performed at the Broken Spoke beginning in the late 1960s and continued to make regular appearances throughout the 1970s. The singer, known as the "Gold Chain Troubadour," recorded more than 250 songs, including top-ten hit favorites

Keyboard player Jimmy Day, drummer Paul English, and singer-songwriter Willie Nelson, 1969. Courtesy of Annette White.

In 1967 James White began booking a little-known band, Willie Nelson and the Record Men, who had just released a local hit song, "Mr. Record Man." Courtesy of Annette White.

"Walking the Floor over You" and "Waltz across Texas." The Country Music Hall of Fame inducted Tubb in 1965. Always well-dressed in a tailored Western suit and his ten-gallon hat, Tubb helped erase the hillbilly stigma from country music performers of his day.[16] James recalls that Tubb always took the time to meet his fans and signed autographs during his breaks. The star of the Grand Ole Opry during the 1940s and 1950s had sold more than thirty million records; he also helped the Everly Brothers and Elvis Presley jump-start their careers with his radio program *Midnight Jamboree*.[17] James recalls, "He never hid from his fans; he never ran out to the bus like some of them do." Neither Tubb nor his band members ever drank onstage, and they wore matching western suits. "When he wasn't onstage, he liked to drink; he liked to gamble—he liked to shoot dice," James says. "I liked him. He was solid country, playing about three hundred dates a year across the country. He always remembered where he came from and he kept country music goin.'" Tubb had written the words "thanks" on the back of his guitar, and after ending each song, he flipped the instrument around so that the audience could see his message. "He called his band members 'Billy Bird' or 'Butter Bean.' He came from just a different generation. Today he wouldn't put up with none of this rockin' country music," James says.

Jack Henry Greene also appeared as a solo performer at the Broken Spoke in 1967. He had previously played drums and toured with Ernest Tubb's band during the mid-1960s.[18] Greene, who also played guitar, was known as "The Gentle Giant" for his height and deep voice. He had performed with Tubb's Tennessee Mountain Boys on their hit single "The Last Letter" in 1945, and more than twenty years later recorded "There Goes My Everything" in 1968.[19] Greene and his band, the Jolly Giants, performed at the Broken Spoke after releasing five number-one country hits. "He practiced two days back in the back of the Broken Spoke getting his Jolly Giants ready," James says. "He couldn't call them the 'Jolly Green Giants' because the name was copyrighted, and the Green Giant folks [at General Mills] would get onto him. So he just called them the Jolly Giants. They had a new motor home when they played here; it wasn't nothin' fancy—I think maybe it was a Winnebago." After their show, James gave the band a gift that featured a General Mills product logo with the official image of the Jolly Green Giant. "I was at the grocery store, and I talked the manager out of an advertisement sign that the grocery store used to sell Jolly Green Giant food, and so Greene and his Jolly Giants were tickled about that. They stuck the sign on the dash of their motor home."

James "Little Jimmy" Dickens performed at the Broken Spoke only once in the late 1960s, seemingly the one night that he wasn't performing at the Grand Ole Opry in Nashville. The Country Music Hall of Fame inducted Dickens in 1983 for performing at the Opry regularly for more than sixty years.[20] "He's one of the last of the old-school old-timers. He had a lot of old comical country songs like 'May the Bird of Paradise Fly up Your Nose' and 'A Sleepin' at the Foot of the Bed,'" James says. He can still break into Dickens's 1967 song "Take an Old Cold Tater (and Wait)" a cappella. The lyrics begin, "*Taters never did look good when you're hungry for a steak.*" When Little Jimmy Dickens performed at the Broken Spoke, its street address had changed from Old Fredericksburg Road to South Lamar.[21]

When Jim Ed Brown performed his "Pop a Top" song after it hit number 71 on *Billboard* magazine's Hot Country Singles chart in 1967, the song helped

First Performers Booked

promote the sales of canned beer with pull tabs at the Broken Spoke.[22] "Up until then, we would open them with what we called 'a church key,' a can opener, but the women didn't like them [pull-tab beer cans] because they thought the tabs would cut their lips," James says. Brown's country music solo career followed the breakup of one of America's favorite country singing groups, the Browns, which had included his sisters Maxine and Bonnie. The trio performed together for eleven years before releasing their biggest hit, "The Three Bells."[23] James first met Jim Ed Brown backstage at the Austin Auditorium following a concert. Afterward James invited Brown and his family out to the Broken Spoke. "They all came up here and ate, and then later on I was able to book him and his band here," James says. "They were really nice people."

James also booked singer-songwriter Claude King five years after his big 1962 hit, "Wolverton Mountain," followed by twenty-seven other chart singles, including "The Comancheros," a song that reached Billboard's country top-ten list.[24] King, with chiseled good looks and an athletic build, started his career as one of the original members of *Louisiana Hayride*, the show that also started Elvis Presley's career. "He had a wonderful voice. 'Wolverton Mountain' was always one of my favorite songs," James says. "I knew of him before I even went into this business. That's another hero of mine that I got to book right here at the Broken Spoke."

James also booked Adolph Hofner, then known as "the Bing Crosby of Country," and the Pearl Wranglers. A Czech musician and western swing bandleader, Hofner grew up in Lavaca County and settled in San Antonio. Pearl Beer Company sponsored Hofner's band locally to play a variety of polkas.[25] Hofner had earned a following after recording the minor hit "Maria Elena" in 1940. Some say that he became the first person to record "Cotton-Eyed Joe." Broken Spoke patrons often bought Hofner and his band members beers all night long. At the end of the night, the band members took every beer bottle or can of beer left on the tables and poured them all into a giant storage vessel that they loaded onto their tour bus. "They would drain every drop; it didn't matter who had drank out of it before," James says. Charismatic and well-dressed, Hofner sported a lock of curly hair. Often his good looks and charming ways made him fast friends. He died of cancer in 2000.[26] "If he didn't know your name, he'd say, 'Hey good buddy, how are you doin'?' and he'd say to the women, 'Hello, my little pearl'—that kind of went along with the Pearl beer theme," James says.

Roy Claxton Acuff, once known as the "King of Country Music" and his Smoky Mountain Boys performed at the Broken Spoke on April 1, 1969, before he quit touring to hold court permanently at the Grand Ole Opry. Acuff had grown up singing in a Church of God choir. In 1940 his recording of "The Great Speckled Bird," an old gospel standard, had made him an overnight sensation in Tennessee. He also imitated the sound of a train whistle to entertain crowds and used that talent in the recording of two songs, "Steamboat Whistle Blues" and "The Wabash Cannonball."[27] As a boy, James remembers first hearing Acuff sing on the radio. Acuff's well-known hits "It Won't Be Long" and "Tennessee Waltz" joined the canons of classic country music in 1947. It gave James a particular thrill to be able to book Acuff at the Broken Spoke. "When I was a boy, Acuff would always perform live from Nashville, Tennessee, on Saturday night, and we'd listen to *Louisiana Hayride* on Friday. We'd always hunker down around the radio and we'd always talk about Roy Acuff and the Smoky Mountain Boys. I never dreamed that I would be able to book him here at the Broken Spoke. That was the last tour that he ever made—though he didn't know it at the time."

James recalled the day that Acuff's two four-door traveling cars pulled into the dirt parking lot in front of the Broken Spoke. Acuff's tour had stretched from Nashville to Anaheim, California, where he had performed in Disneyland and drove back again. On his return trip home, Acuff stopped by the Broken Spoke to perform. Acuff had possessed little dance hall experience until he and his band performed at the Broken Spoke. Until then he had preferred to perform two-hour shows in auditoriums or theaters.[28] He often balanced his fiddle bow on his nose and walked around performing tricks with a Duncan yo-yo before he sang. "Up until that time, people just looked at me and said, 'You don't know what you're talkin' about. Roy Acuff ain't going to play no honky-tonk dance hall. His daddy was a hard-shell Baptist preacher,'" James says. He had persisted and surprised patrons when Acuff arrived at the Broken Spoke. "Sure 'nuff he came driving up in those two four-door cars and piled out. . . . Roy Acuff said, 'Darn, we haven't got any speakers.' I had to call up real quick and get a sound system out here. I talked him into doing a couple of long sets because he was used to doing like one set. Everybody was wantin' him to sing that song. Acuff said, 'I don't know if [my dad would] approve of me singin' this in a dance hall,' but then he said, 'I'm gonna go ahead and do it for y'all as long as you don't clap and cheer at the end of the song.'"

People in the audience that night listened intently to give Acuff all the proper respect he deserved. "A lot of those old-timers had tears in their eyes because a lot of them were born and raised back in the Great Depression, and they knew what hard times were," James says. "The one thing you never could take away from them was their love of country music." Beecher Ray Kirby, better known as "Bashful Brother Oswald," also performed that night with Roy Acuff. Brother Oswald sang high harmonies and played Dobro, guitar, banjo, and a jug while performing comedy with Acuff beginning in the 1930s. During the 1960s he also launched a solo career that continued well into the 1980s.[29] Brother Oswald wrinkled up his eyebrows and clowned around a little bit onstage during the Broken Spoke show. He wore overalls, which for most folks who lived in Tennessee at the time, were not really a fashion statement. People wore them because they did not own many nice shirts or pants. The night Acuff performed at the Broken Spoke, James stood at the bar drinking straight whiskey when Brother Oswald approached him. "I asked him, 'Do you want a drink?' He says, 'What is it?' I told him, 'Straight whiskey,' and he says, 'That's the only kind I drink.' So he kind of wiggled his eyes up and down and threw himself back a double shot." Before the two left, the Whites bestowed them with gifts. "We gave Roy Acuff the walking stick with a hidden whiskey flask, and gave Brother Oswald the big oversized pocket watch. We'd see him [Brother Oswald] on TV flashing that watch. We should have given the walking stick to Brother Oswald because Roy Acuff didn't drink."

James also booked Bobby Bare in 1969, nearly ten years after the song "All American Boy" hit number 3 on the country music charts and just before the US Army drafted the star.[30] Bare and Willie Nelson had been roommates before Bare toured with other pop music greats such as Roy Orbison and Bobby Darin. Onstage the military veteran wore his hair a bit longer than most country stars of his day; he sported more facial hair, primarily lamb chop–style sideburns. "He was a good person, and I was really glad to get him," James says. "He's another one I liked when I was overseas. I thought of his song '500 Miles' when at the time I was probably seven or eight thousand miles away from home. I heard that song just about the time my airplane was pullin' out of Kadena Air Base and heading for stateside USA and California. It was really one of the greatest feelings I ever had to leave 'the rock' there as we used to call it—Okinawa—and head back to the United States."

David Houston, one of the most successful country singers of the 1960s, performed at the Broken Spoke three years after releasing his first major hit, "Mountain of Love," and winning a Grammy for the song "Almost Persuaded" in 1966.[31] That song set a record for its nine-week run on *Billboard's* Hot Country Singles chart, a record until Taylor Swift's "We Are Never Getting Back Together" surpassed it after ten weeks at number 1 in December 2012. Houston possessed a versatile voice and often performed duets with popular female singers, including his number-1 hit with Tammy Wynette, "My Elusive Dreams," in 1967. He recorded the album *A Perfect Match* with Barbara Mandrell in 1974, which included two major hits, "After Closing Time" and "I Love You, I Love You." "There's an old picture taken of me and David Houston and Terri [White] on our Broken Spoke bandstand back when she was a little girl," James says. Houston's manager, Tillman Franks, became good friends with James. Franks also managed a tall Japanese American country fiddler and singer with a bowl-cut hairstyle, Shoji Tabuchi, whom James booked at the Broken Spoke. Tabuchi later started his own club, the Shoji Tabuchi Theatre, in the 1980s in Branson, Missouri, where he still performs.[32]

Ottis Dewey "Slim" Whitman, the high-pitched yodeling country crooner who recorded the famous songs "Indian Love Call" in 1952 and "Love Song of the Waterfall" in 1954, had nearly faded from the public limelight until his 1965 comeback song, "More Than Yesterday." Twenty-two other hits followed before James White met Whitman at the Broken Spoke.[33] In 1975 he became something of an advertising sensation with a successful television mail-order campaign to sell 1.5 million copies of his compilation album *All My Best.* "One time back in the sixties I fixed ol' Slim up. He really wasn't that slim when I met him—but I fixed him up. He was a pretty stout-looking guy when I knew him, but he was a great yodeler and a great-lookin' guy," James says. "He could sing those good ol' cowboy songs and love songs. So I hooked him up with one of the Broken Spoke waitresses."

James also booked Charlie Walker, who had scored a minor hit with the song "Pick Me Up on Your Way Down."[34] In 1967 Walker released another hit, "Don't Squeeze My Sharmon," inspired by the Charmin toilet paper advertising catchphrase.[35] Two years later he performed at the Broken Spoke and, like other country stars who had performed there, asked James to arrange a golf game with Coach Darrell K. Royal. The Austin icon coached the Longhorn football team for twenty seasons from 1957 until 1976 and earned a 167–47–5 record. The University of Texas later named its stadium after him.[36] Walker, the first to ask James to arrange celebrity golf games, started a trend among other Broken Spoke performers who later also asked for private rounds with both Coach Royal and country stars Willie Nelson and George Strait. Walker also played the field a bit. "Charlie got up onstage at the Broken Spoke, and in between singing his songs, he'd notice a blonde-haired girl he said he'd like to meet. 'Have her meet me out there by the barbecue pit and the walk-in cooler on the patio,' he told me once. So I had her out there waitin' for him on his break," James says. "They got to knowin' each other, and they spent a lot of time together over the next two or three days at the Spoke."

Throughout the late 1960s, whenever the Texas legislature met in session, lawmakers visited the Broken Spoke to party once a week, often on Tuesdays. The event quickly earned the name "Legislators' Night."[37] State Representatives Peyton McKnight from Tyler and "Jumbo" Ben Atwell became regulars.[38] "Jumbo was a character. He had his medicine wagon parked out in front of our big oak tree for a long time; he was in all the chili cook-offs. He'd always want me to come down to the [Terlingua] chili cook-offs, and I took him huntin' a few times at my ranch," James says. Atwell, named by *Texas Monthly* magazine as "one of the 10 worst Legislators" in 1973, died in 1998.[39] "On his headstone is a granite map of Texas that says 'I raised taxes in Texas,'" James says. "He got defeated because his district was in Dallas, but he campaigned mostly here at the Broken Spoke in Austin." During his career, McKnight served as both a state representative and a senator best known for his public service; he supported Texas prison reform, helped establish a highway safety code, and devoted much of his career to improving education.[40]

James also booked Charles Elzer Loudermilk, better known as Charlie Louvin, who had become popular on Chattanooga's radio station WDEF after winning a singing contest. Loudermilk and his brother, Ira, became

The late Longhorn football coach Darrell Royal frequented the Broken Spoke from the 1960s through the 1990s and became James White's friend. *Courtesy of Don "Winker" Emmons.*

the Louvin Brothers and had performed traditional gospel shows after World War II and released more than twenty songs that topped the country music charts.[41] One of the Louvin Brothers' hits, "When I Stop Dreaming," featured harmonies that would someday influence Emmylou Harris, Gram Parsons, and the Byrds. After Ira's death in a car accident, Louvin began a solo career that earned him numerous appearances on the Grand Ole Opry before his death in 2010.

One of the greatest games in Longhorn football history also led to one of the most historic parties at the Broken Spoke; it occurred the day after UT beat the Arkansas Razorbacks 15–14 in Fayetteville in 1969. The media dubbed the game "The Great Shootout," or "The Game of the Century."[42] ABC telecast the game live into the homes of fifty million fans to celebrate the one hundredth anniversary of college football. Team members who had played in the National Championship later came out to the Broken Spoke following a big reception at Robert Mueller Municipal Airport. However, the Longhorns' party followed a day later at the Broken Spoke. Coincidentally James had previously booked that Sunday for a private birthday party for Leo Brooks, the defensive tackle for the Longhorns. James had hired a band led by Henson Cargill, who at the time was a one-hit wonder after releasing "Skip a Rope."[43] "I didn't realize it at the time that it was gonna be 'the game of the century,'" James says. The whole senior class of the Longhorn football team visited the Broken Spoke that Sunday night in December 1969 except the starting defensive safety Freddie Steinmark, who had been injured during the game. His injuries later led to the discovery of a cancerous bone tumor in his left leg, which had to be amputated. Just twenty days later, the Longhorn football team would dedicate the Cotton Bowl game to Steinmark as he sat on the sidelines to watch them beat Notre Dame. A year later he accompanied Royal to the White House to meet with President Richard M. Nixon to mark the annual fund-raiser for American Cancer Society.[44] In April 1971 Steinmark published his autobiography, *I Play To Win*, with help from Blackie Sherrod, sports editor for the *Dallas Times-Herald*, but two months later the disease would claim his life.[45]

Before the football team arrived at the Broken Spoke, one of James's bartenders, Bob Turner, offered to pay for everyone's drinks. "So that's what I did. I let the whole team in, and he bought all the beer." Bartenders back in those days made only about ten dollars a night, but Turner paid the tab. James claims Turner more or less worked free for several years while he found other sources of income. "He was the kind of guy who built an airplane inside his mother's garage over in north Austin, but then he had to take out a whole wall to get the plane out. He forgot that one minor detail, you know?" Midway through the night of Brooks's birthday party, things turned a bit dicey. James recalls, "Everybody was getting kind of rowdy drinkin' all that free beer. Somebody said, 'James Street would like to sing,' and I said, 'Okay. Let's let him sing.'" At first Cargill liked the idea. However, when Street invited the whole senior class of football players onstage, a few of them started banging on the drums while another attempted to play Cargill's guitar. As Street began to sing, the team refused to leave the stage. The antics of the football team worried Cargill, who feared someone might damage his expensive musical equipment. "These were big ol' boys back in them days. Cargill says to me, 'You gotta get all those guys off the stage.' There were about twenty of them up there," James says. "I was real serious when I looked at him and said, 'Well, you're the one who invited them up there; you get 'em off.' Anyway, he looked at me like 'Duh.' He said, 'That's my ten thousand–dollar guitar they're droppin' up there.'"

Also in 1969 Louis Marshall "Grandpa" Jones performed at the Broken Spoke after having enjoyed limited success with his remake of the Jimmie Rodgers song, "T for Texas," which had hit the top five on the country music charts in 1962. It became the first of several of Rodgers's songs that Jones rereleased over the next decade.[46] At the time Jones dressed in khaki pants and an ordinary shirt; he had not yet begun wearing his signature suspenders. He had not yet been recognized for his cornball comedy and banjo picking on the popular television show *Hee Haw*. "Right before he'd go onstage, he would go back in my office and put on his big ol' boots that he stomped when he played the banjo. He played some good ol' bluegrass tunes like 'Old Rattler' or 'Mountain Dew' or 'Rollin' in My Sweet Baby's Arms,'" James says. Jones hung around Austin for a couple of days afterward, and the Geezinslaws opened a few of his shows.

Also about that time, the son of legendary singer-songwriter Buck Owens, Alvis Alan "Buddy" Owens, performed at the Broken Spoke after singing for the first time at one of his father's Christmas concerts in Austin.[47] Buddy's first hit single, performed as a duet with his dad, "Let the World Keep on a Turnin,'" had climbed to the top-ten list in 1968. Buddy made several appearances on *Hee Haw* beginning in 1970 and achieved moderate success over the next eight years after releasing a few singles on the Capitol Records label. He eventually left the music business in 1978 to take a job as a program director at a local radio station in Tempe, Arizona.[48]

PART III

The 1970s

CHAPTER 7

The Progressive Country Movement

Austin's bar business boomed after Congress enacted the Fair Alcohol Consumption Act in 1973, a law that allowed states to permit alcohol sales to people as young as eighteen years old.[1] The city's bars soon began to draw a mixed bag of clientele, from rednecks to hippies, a trend that quickly established itself as the new normal around town. Venues like the Armadillo World Headquarters, Vulcan Gas Company, and Threadgill's helped to establish new music that questioned authority with more intellectual and liberal song lyrics. Waylon Jennings, Willie Nelson, and Billy Joe Shaver defied Nashville record company control over their original music and soon earned the nickname "outlaws." Their albums sold both to the established core country market and to non-country fans. These artists and others who followed performed crossover music that incorporated honky-tonk, rockabilly, and the Bakersfield, California, sound with the attitudes of the 1960s counterculture movement. Suddenly a seminal figure in the development of Austin's music scene began promoting a compelling mix of Texas musicians.[2] When Austin radio station deejays Joe Gracey and Rusty Bell at KOKE-FM began calling this new genre of music "progressive country," Billboard magazine in 1974 declared it "the most innovative station in the United States."[3] A multitalented musician and writer, Gracey also wrote rock reviews for the Austin American-Statesman, marketed advertising for Armadillo World Headquarters, and worked as the original talent coordinator for the Austin City Limits television series before he died in 2011.[4] Austin City Limits, the brainchild of director Bill Arhos, producer Paul Bosner, and director Bruce Scafe, began broadcasting on PBS in 1974 with a diverse mix of country, blues, and folk artists from a small stage in Austin. The pilot was shot on October 14, 1974, featuring Willie Nelson. Today the show remains one of the longest continuously running music television programs nationwide.[5]

Smaller local venues followed the progressive country trend by sharing some of the same artists: the former Castle Creek; Split Rail; IL Club; and One Knite Saloon, which became Stubb's Bar-B-Q, as well as bars that still exist today, such as the Victory Grill. Even smaller and more obscure venues such as Soap Creek Saloon and Bevo's started offering performances by folk musicians. Club owners who bucked the local trend by refusing to play anything but rock and roll suffered financially.[6] Austin's music scene, an amalgamation of classic country, folk, honky-tonk, rockabilly, and rock music, began to broadcast its good vibrations by radio and television nationwide. No one sensed the impact of these changes better than the Broken Spoke's proprietor, James White.

Meanwhile, Townsend Miller, a local stockbroker who also wrote a twice-weekly column for the *Austin American-Statesman*, became a leader in the local music scene, a position of power that he held for more than ten years. Miller played an extremely influential role in persuading James White to hire Freda and the Firedogs to perform at a local political fundraiser for Congressman Lloyd Doggett held at the Broken Spoke in 1973.[7] Miller had not only mentioned Freda and the Firedogs several times in his columns, but his devotion for the band went further; he loved lead singer Marcia Ball's singing. Every year Miller compiled his list of favorite singers, both male and female. Waylon Jennings nearly always topped Miller's list of favorite male country singers; however, Marcia Ball's name never wavered as Miller's favorite female vocalist. "Townsend Miller, unbeknown to me and to the band, had actually gone to the Broken Spoke himself to ask James White to book Freda and the Firedogs. He [Miller] wrote in his column that 'Freda and the Firedogs was a natural fit for the Broken Spoke,'" says the Firedogs' former bassist Bobby Earl Smith. Miller died in a car fire in 1989 before being inducted into the Texas Western Swing Hall of Fame.

CHAPTER 8

The White Family Expands

Annetta gave birth to the Whites' youngest daughter, Virginia ("Ginny"), October 15, 1975. Ginny received her name from her paternal great-great-grandmother, Virginia Bishop. A photo inside the dining room features a portrait of Ginny at just eleven days old in the arms of the legendary Ernest Tubb. James recalls, "Whenever he performed, Ernest Tubb would always make a point to say, 'This song is going out to little Ginny. She's one year old.' Or two years old—whatever it was." Tubb liked to say that Ginny was born "smack dab in the middle of country music month—October 15." "I always refer to Ginny as 'Daddy's lil' darlin.' We nicknamed Ginny 'the little boss,'" James says.

Across from the bar hangs a 1976 photo of Willie Nelson holding Ginny when she was about six months old. Over the years Nelson would also stop by to perform with other country stars onstage and to take an updated photo with members of the White family. "Willie likes playing here," Ginny says. "He likes my dad. Whenever he plays here, he calls my dad 'Mr. White' and 'Papa White.'"

The Broken Spoke became Ginny's "second home." As a toddler, she often tagged along with her parents whenever they went to work. As she grew older, because they did not have nine-to-five jobs, other family members cared for her after 9:00 p.m., took her to school in the mornings, or picked her up in the afternoons. Ginny never rode the bus. She also grew up with all the love and attention of three sets of grandparents: her dad's mom and stepfather; her dad's father and his wife; and her mom's parents. Another regular caregiver included her paternal great-aunt Nantie Margaret.

Ginny remembers often falling asleep beneath a table in the dining room at the Broken Spoke while lying on two or three chairs pushed together by her mom. At times the dining room became a makeshift romper room for Ginny and all of her adolescent friends. "My girlfriends and I would bring all our toys up there," she says. "One of my best friends, Michelle, and I would play [with] My Little Ponies, and we would play Barbies in the booths." She also remembers riding her tricycle around the dance floor. As a preteen she celebrated her birthday in the dance hall, which had been transformed into a roller-skating rink.

As she became a teenager, the Broken Spoke began to lose its appeal. "When I was probably about sixteen or seventeen, my mom says it went all downhill from there; they gave me a car." James and Annetta attended every home football game at Toney Burger Stadium to watch Ginny perform at halftime with the James Bowie High School marching band until she graduated in 1994. "My dad even gave me a marching lesson in our driveway," she says. Just as her father taught his daughter how to march, Annetta taught Ginny the merits of a strong, unconditional work ethic. "She will do anything up there—she will plunge a toilet, she will cook, she will bartend all night long, and she's seventy. If there's a job she has to do, then she does it," Ginny says.

After high school Ginny studied business management by day at Southwest Texas State in San Marcos, now known as Texas State University (TSU), and worked nights at the Broken Spoke. In the meantime, she continued to play hard. Annetta often served as the family's disciplinarian and rule enforcer. "She was the type that would dump out my purse," she says. "She would clean my room and find a wine bottle. Nothing was private."

Ginny remembers a regular group of male customers who used to visit the Broken Spoke every Friday night for years. The men sat at one of the round tables in the front dining room. They were friends of her late stepgrandfather and they "talked up a storm." Ginny can still quote verbatim what her paternal grandmother used to say to that table of loud talkers. "My grandmother [Lena] used to tell them . . . , 'Y'all made too much money for this little table. You need to move over to the big table with all these big ideas you have going.'" "[Joe] seemed to always come up with these crazy ideas, and he used to drink quite a bit of beer."

She feels that the Broken Spoke represents her past, her present, and her future. Its unchanging nature has become a touchstone, not only for her and the entire White family but also for some of Austin's longtime residents. "People love taking their pictures out front. Another thing they love is bringing their kids up to the Spoke and saying, 'This is where I met your mom,' or 'This is where I met your dad and we danced here.'" Her parents "keep rollin' like a wagon wheel," Ginny says. Like others of their generation who grew up at end of World War II, the Whites have a work ethic that refuses to quit. "You don't spend a day at home when you're sick. Mom says 'sleepin' makes you lazy,' and if you're up here at the Broken Spoke working with her, you work all day until the work is done," Ginny says. She admits, "I'm a daddy's girl. There's never going to be anyone else like him to me." Whenever James and Annetta babysit her two boys, Jackson and James Lamar, their grandfather often takes photos of them with his iPhone and later texts the images to Ginny. Becoming a parent has helped Ginny understand the significance of the Broken Spoke. "I was naughty when I was growing up, but I've made up for it in my older years."

Ginny does not like to think about a future without her dad living in it. "I hope that the Spoke stays as popular as it is, and I hope that I honor him. It's very important. I want it to keep going for a long time. It's a big legacy." She does not take the Broken Spoke for granted. "It's allowed me to have a very nice life." As for the future of the Broken Spoke, Ginny plans to keep her promises. "There will never be any rock bands at the Broken Spoke and no rappers. I'm not saying they're bad; I used to love rock and roll, but that's not what Dad wants. He wants the Broken Spoke to stay country."

Ginny hopes to introduce new generations of country music fans to the Broken Spoke. "I hope maybe someday one of my sons will take it over when I'm not around." She also hopes the Broken Spoke will remain standing for another fifty years. "As long as we can keep it in one piece, that's what we're going to do; we're going to keep it going."

Celebrities have joined the extended White family over the years. Ginny recalls visiting Willie Nelson's seventy-six-acre ranch near Lake Travis with her parents years ago right after the birth of her oldest son. Both Lana Nelson and her dad greeted the Whites. Everyone noticed that James and Willie had dressed in the same shirt. "Lana says to my dad, 'You need to change your shirt for the photo.' So Dad changed his shirt." Both White and Nelson had received matching shirts as gifts after playing poker one night with the late blues bar entrepreneur Clifford Antone. The shirts featured an image of an ace on a sleeve embroidered close to the cuff and easily concealed by rolling. "You know the saying in poker: 'You've got an ace up your sleeve?' Well that was the idea." James and Antone had also shared a special friendship. "Clifford looked up to my dad I think; he was more like a role model. They were both mavericks in town. Antone enjoyed being around my dad because he was a good guy." Beginning in the mid-1970s, the Whites' extended family also began to include Alvin and Stephanie Crow. Ginny feels especially close to Alvin Crow, godfather to James Lamar. Crow has performed at least once a month at the Broken Spoke since 1974 with his band the Pleasant Valley Boys. In its early days, the band featured Alvin's brother, Rick, on lead guitar, Bobby Earl Smith on bass, Roger Crabtree on harmonica, and Herb Steiner on steel. Alvin recalls those days.

"I can remember showing the place to my parents right after I moved here. In the light of day, it had swingin' flaps over the windows, and it didn't have air-conditioning. Real similar to how Gruene Hall is now. So I played all over town for maybe about two years before I got my first job playing here," Crow says. "There was kind of a gap between the hippie bands and the redneck bands at the time, and I was kind of straddlin' the middle."

These days Alvin's son, Josh, plays bass for the Pleasant Valley Boys. Former Texas Playboys' guitar player Jesse Ashlock also performed on the band's self-titled album in 1976. Other members of the Pleasant Valley Boys have at times included the late Pete Mitchell, who had played guitar with Ernest Tubb's Texas Troubadours for ten years; former Texas Playboys' piano player Al Stricklin; and vocalist Leon Rausch. The latter two also appeared on Crow's 1977 *High Riding* album. For a brief time in the 1970s, James also performed sets with Crow's band in the Broken Spoke's dining room as part of what they called their "Hardcore Country" show. The shows began with Crow playing his fiddle and singing classic songs made famous by the late great Jimmie Rodgers. The two also performed a sort of historical country review of the music made famous by Roy Acuff, Bob Wills, and Hank Williams. People began to call Crow "Mr. Jukebox" because he has a broad working knowledge of some six hundred melodies from the country classics music canon. Whenever he can remember only a line or two of a song's famous lyrics, he improvises.

Since then Crow has recorded ten albums in the western swing style of Milton Brown, Pee Wee King, and Bob Wills. Crow also has appeared in a few movies: *Roadie* (1980), *Endangered Species* (1982), and *Friday Night Lights* (2006).

Alvin's wife, Stephanie Geller-Crow, first began visiting the Broken Spoke in 1978 at just fifteen years old with a group of local girls. Today she admits to disguising her age as a teenager after falling hard for her future husband. "As soon as I was old enough to get in the door, I was in the door. We took pride in being backstage at every bar in Austin—including *Austin City Limits*, the Frank Erwin Special Events Center, and the [Austin] Opry House." James and Annetta often allowed underage kids inside the Broken Spoke during the 1970s. "We had access and it was awesome," Stephanie says. "It took me a couple of hours to put my makeup on so that I would pass for a grown-up, but I was good at it." Soon she and her friends began showing up at all of Alvin's gigs in town. "It was a very elite, super secretive, select few. There were only four of us. We often made up stories as to why we left early from high school football games, parties, et cetera," Stephanie says. "We did not want anyone to know where we were or where we were headed." Their mission remained unflappable—to hang out with the band backstage. Once inside the Broken Spoke, she and her friends sat as close to the stage as possible to catch glimpses of Alvin and his band. Between sets, Stephanie hung out behind the Broken Spoke, partying outside with the musicians. "James and Annetta still to this day don't go back there. They know what goes on, but they never ever go out there. A lot of pot was smoked back there. All kinds of people would wander back there bearing 'gifts' for Alvin." The only structures that existed at the time behind or beside the Broken Spoke were the Woodmoor apartments and a little house where Joe Baland lived. "Nobody ever came back there," she says. "If they did, you could see the [dirt] smoke come up, or you could hear the rocks movin' under car wheels."

As if James and Annetta did not have enough to do with running a family, two businesses, and a ranch, they began showing quarter horses at shows throughout the South. At one time the Whites owned twenty quarter horses that they either showed or bred and kept on their ranch. One of the Whites' prized mares, Munchkin, won dozens of trophies throughout the 1970s, 1980s, and 1990s.

In their "spare time," the Whites also painted landscapes in oils on canvas and sold their artwork at art shows, at auctions, or at the Broken Spoke. Some of their original art still adorns the walls of their home, though many of the larger pieces sold years ago. When Ginny was born, both James and Annetta found their hands too full to continue painting.

CHAPTER 9

George Strait, Alvin Crow, Jerry Jeff Walker, and the Wheel

Immediately after Texas legislators lowered the legal drinking age to eighteen, both legal and underage teenagers alike flooded the Broken Spoke several nights each week. James recalls, "We just had to watch the minors when they came in. We had a whole stack of fake ID cards that my wife, Annetta, collected at the door when we were taking the cover charges. They would cry and moan to get that fake ID back because it probably belonged to one of their friends, or brothers, or whatever, but we wouldn't give them back. We had such big crowds. It was really great, but there were a lot of minors in bands. They would try to break the rules, and a lot of times they would get into fights." If James caught minors fighting or drinking, he barred them for a couple of weeks. "All the high school students came out here on Wednesday nights."

Musical tastes had long polarized the hippies who liked rock and roll and the rednecks who liked classic country music. However, music recording stars such as B. W. Stevenson, Rusty Wier, Ray Wylie Hubbard, Jerry Jeff Walker, and Steve Fromholtz began to forge a popular hybrid country sound, and a few of Austin's local bands introduced the trend to the Broken Spoke.

Marcia Ball, who had formed friendships with young Democrats working in the state capitol, first performed at the Broken Spoke in 1973. Her band, Freda and the Firedogs, performed at US Representative Lloyd Doggett's fund-raising party when he began his first run for the Texas Senate. More than five hundred people packed Doggett's private campaign party at the Broken Spoke, a group made up in large part by hippies, either barefoot or wearing moccasins or tennis shoes. Few knew the traditional two-step, so they improvised by dancing what James called "the hippie hop." "We were a little hippie country band," Ball says. "We were pure country then, but we just didn't look the part so much. We were playing some of the most classic country in town of anybody. We weren't playing radio country even then; we were playing older stuff—Merle Haggard and George Jones." Back in those days, Ball sang a lot of Tammy Wynette and Loretta Lynn hits, and she also yodeled a bit. "We were singing 'Don't Come Home a Drinkin' with Lovin' on Your Mind' and stuff like that," she says. "I remember how happy we were that first night that we played there at the Broken Spoke, standing on the old loading dock hauling our stuff in. We thought we had made it; we really thought we had."

During those days, Joe and Lena often helped manage the Broken Spoke. Joe enforced strict dress-code rules. "I remember that you couldn't wear a hat on the dance floor," Ball says. "Joe would come out and tap you on the shoulder and make you take your hat off. It was like it was impolite to wear a hat on the dance floor; it also started fights." Performing at the Broken Spoke had been the ultimate goal for Freda and the Firedogs. "Playing the Broken Spoke legitimized us in a way that we were aiming for," Ball says. The band's other original members included Bobby Earl Smith, who sang backup vocals as he played bass; lead guitarist John X. Reed; drummer Steve McDaniels; and steel player David Cook. The Firedogs played together from 1972 until 1974, when Ball left. However, their friendships endured. Ball began a solo career singing rhythm and blues. "I have to say if anybody has held the line on being the same club, doing the same thing he was doing the day he opened his doors, it would have to be James White at the Broken Spoke," Ball says. "The Broken Spoke is a little bit like the Alamo now. The Broken Spoke draws tourists to town, to Texas really." As Ball recalls, "James White weathered all of the competition that ever existed in this town. In the late 1970s when Austin was overrun by pre-fab metal buildings pumping out *Urban Cowboy*–type country music, James White just stayed there in his little spot and kept it real." The former competition has vanished, and "James is still here and it's still real," she says. The Whites have helped nurture a generation of musicians, songwriters, and singers. "What Clifford Antone was to the blues here, James White is to country music in Austin," Ball says.

After playing in the Firedogs' band, Bobby Earl Smith continued to perform and to record with some of Austin's other equally talented musicians throughout the 1970s, including Alvin Crow and the Pleasant Valley Boys and Kimmie Rhodes and the Jackalope Brothers. "I have nothing but great mem-

After Freda and the Firedogs disbanded, singer Marcia Ball and steel player Jimmy Day sat in onstage to perform with Alvin Crow and Gary P. Nunn in the late 1970s. Courtesy of Rick Henson.

ories of playing the Broken Spoke. It was bridgewater in a lot of respects. It was a very important gig for us to get, and it opened up a number of other purely country venues. Once other area clubs found out we were playing at the Broken Spoke, it opened other doors."

Music writer and author Joe Nick Patoski recalls that during the 1970s the progressive country music revolution found a new and inviting audience with the tried-and-true two-steppers at the Broken Spoke. "The Spoke was a lot like Austin and more like the rest of Texas in that there was a lot of unease about long hairs and all things alternative. In a lot of joints, including the Broken Spoke, long hairs were not welcome." However, after James White and Joe Baland saw the writing on the wall, things changed. "They would have been fools not to welcome those folks in. Look what they did, and look what they brought," Patoski says. The Broken Spoke began to be identified as a new hybrid venue and as a game changer for Austin. Game-changing bands included Ray Benson and Asleep at the Wheel, who had relocated from Berkeley around 1974, and Alvin Crow and the Pleasant Valley Boys, who moved here from Amarillo at about the same time. Both bands revived the western swing music of the 1930s created by Bob Wills and the Texas Playboys. One of the original Texas Playboys, Jesse Ashlock, also began playing regularly in Alvin Crow's band. Patoski recalls, "Jesse, when he came down here from Oklahoma, couldn't believe all these young bands playing Texas Playboys' music. Then Jesse began playing a lot with Alvin Crow. Al Stricklin, Bob Wills's piano player, started sitting in with the Wheel, so these new bands combined with these old-timers brought the music full circle. So these young bands that played old-time music—Freda and the Firedogs, Asleep at the Wheel, and the Pleasant Valley Boys, as well as Buckdancer's Choice—became accepted by the Spoke."

Because they had become accepted and could play often at the Broken Spoke, they also began to attract hardcore country audiences. They soon played residence gigs at the Broken Spoke previously held only by Willie Nelson and Jerry Jeff Walker. "What the difference was in Austin as opposed to everywhere else was all these hybrid country rock venues for the 'Jerry Jeffs' and all that were complemented by these old traditionalists who came in and

Rusty Wier and Jerry Jeff Walker stand in the bar at the Broken Spoke on the legendary night when the Texas Playboys performed, September 17, 1975. Courtesy of Rick Henson.

Freda and the Firedogs reunited March 22, 2015, at the Broken Spoke and included John X. Reed on guitar, Bobby Earl Smith on bass, and Marcia Ball on keyboard.

embraced the old ways," Patoski says. "It definitely wasn't just a Michael Murphey, or a Jerry Jeff, or a B. W. Stevenson, or even a Freda and the Firedogs venue." Freda and the Firedogs looked different and they acted different. They may have smoked pot, but James welcomed them into the Broken Spoke because the band showed an eagerness to perform in front of a traditional audience.

For Patoski, the Broken Spoke represents more than a honky-tonk music venue. He met the love of his life, Kris Cummings, there while she worked as a waitress. The Fort Worth native first wrote about the Austin music scene for *Texas Monthly* in 1975 and then at *Rolling Stone* magazine. In Patoski's 1977 article for *Country Music* magazine, he prophesied that Alvin Crow would some day spend most of his time playing at the Broken Spoke and hanging out with James White. "I moved to Austin specifically because I saw the music scene and I wanted to write about music—and boy, it turned out to be right," he says. "There was a music scene developing here. I was different; I had long hair. I was probably one of those people who couldn't have walked into the Broken Spoke at one time without getting threatened or [someone] getting out the sheep shooters." He began to chronicle Austin's two very different cultures—the hippies and the cowboys—as well as the mixing and the mingling. These crossovers into enemy territory surprised Patoski, who quickly discovered bigger and more diverse audiences. "People began to say, 'You know, my parents are into those old rednecks, and a lot of them like to smoke pot as much as we do,' and the rednecks were saying things like, 'Them old hippies might smoke their pot or do whatever, but they drink beer like we do.' You know, that didn't happen in San Francisco," Patoski says. "One big difference about Austin's hippies compared to hippies elsewhere is that they liked beer and country music. Beer was not considered cool, and country music wasn't considered cool in San Francisco. Merle Haggard was considered the enemy, yet here in Austin these [traditional country] people were embraced. That period of time was critical, and the Spoke's role in how all this all happened is as significant." Austin helped change the public's perception with the amalgamation of local country and rock-and-roll bands.

Steve Wertheimer, current owner of the Continental Club, a mecca for roots, rockabilly, country, and western swing music, first began visiting the Broken Spoke in 1976 while attending UT. Wertheimer developed an appreciation for live music venues at the Rome Inn, where Jimmie Vaughan used

Alvin Crow performs a western swing duet on fiddle with Johnny Gimble, one of the original members of the Texas Cowboys, 2010. Courtesy of Rick Henson.

to perform with feature guest performances by his brother and blues guitarist Stevie Ray Vaughan. Wertheimer reopened the Continental in 1987, a retro Austin relic that dates back to 1957, and became friends with James White. The Broken Spoke has always reminded Wertheimer of home. "It's very similar to the places where I grew up in Rosenberg. There were dance halls in Rosenberg and East Bernard and all the surrounding small towns," Wertheimer says. "Where there was an American Legion hall or a Knights of Columbus, or something like that and they had bands very much like those that James White books at the Spoke. You know, I've grown to fall back in love with it."

Some of the same bands that have performed at the Broken Spoke have also played at the Continental Club over the years. "There seems to be some sort of—I don't know what you call it—compatibility between that club and this club here. It doesn't hurt us that Dale [Watson], Jesse [Dayton], and the Derailers play down there and they play here on a weekly basis. What I see sometimes is a totally different crowd at both places." As Wertheimer recalls, relationships among club owners in Austin never returned to the level they once enjoyed while Clifford Antone lived. "The three of us—Clifford, James, and myself—would often run into each other at any one of these three places. They were here if there was some show here they wanted to see, and I would run into those guys down at Antone's, and I would see Clifford out at the Broken Spoke." Wertheimer says that the three formed a "brotherhood" before Antone died. "As a club owner, if you do it long enough, the others take you under their wings and induct you. [White and Antone] must have decided 'he's here to stay; he's ok,'" Wertheimer says.

One of the Broken Spoke's main competitors for many years, the now-defunct Armadillo World Headquarters (the Dillo) was co-owned by a group of music partners including Eddie Wilson, Spencer Perskin, Jim Franklin, Mike Tolleson, and Bobby Hedderman.[1] The converted National Guard armory opened in Austin in 1970 and closed down on New Year's Eve in 1980. Wilson had also operated the Raw Deal, a tiny bar and restaurant, which became a watering hole popular among a more sophisticated crowd, mostly local politicians and news reporters until 1976. He sold the restaurant, but the same year Wilson closed the Dillo, he bought Threadgill's original old filling station on North Lamar from Kenneth Threadgill. The diner had drawn in all kinds of performing artists for twenty years, including the late gritty rock-and-roll singing star Janis Joplin. Wilson spent a year remodeling the historic landmark before reopening it in 1981. Fifteen years later he opened Threadgill's World Headquarters on West Riverside Drive.

Today Wilson and James White share a similar music history and common friends. Wilson says his favorite memory of visiting the Broken Spoke involves Clifford Antone. "[Guitar player] Billy Campbell used to call Clifford 'Abdul the Dancing Bear,' and I'm talkin' ballroom, not boot-scootin' and swing dancing. Most people do the two-step, but I'm so limited that I call mine 'the one-one, one-one,' but Clifford danced like he weighed ninety pounds and was full of helium. I mean he was the smoothest dancer you ever saw. He just glided around the dance floor and did little tricky spins with his dancin' partners." Wilson says that he and others who saw Antone dance could not believe their eyes: "He was just Gene Kelly, just amazingly smooth."

Wilson says food played an important role in making the Broken Spoke

Country singer and bar owner John Kenneth Threadgill visited James White at the Broken Spoke in 1969, a year before Congressman J. J. Pickle declared him "The Father of Austin Country Music." Courtesy of Annetta White.

Claudia Alta "Lady Bird" Johnson visited the Broken Spoke during the 1990s with her daughter Lynda Johnson-Robb and grandaughter Jennifer Robb. Courtesy of Annetta White.

popular as both a restaurant and dance hall over the years. The Broken Spoke serves a hot meal five days a week Tuesday through Saturday, whereas most dance halls, honky-tonks, lounges, and clubs do not open until "happy hour" at the earliest. The Broken Spoke, as a hybrid, provides a restaurant, a saloon, and a dance hall all under one roof. The dining room greets visitors in the front, and the bar draws them toward the dance hall in the back. These days, Wertheimer, Wilson, and White—"the three Ws"—consider themselves to be some of the last of the longtime bar owners in town. Wilson says he has never felt any sense of competition with either James White or Wertheimer. "We don't know who liked who first, but they've always just treated me so well," Wilson says.

The president of Waterloo Records, John Kunz, first ventured into the Broken Spoke in the early 1970s looking for a good time, a beer, and a few spins around the dance floor. He had no idea that one day he would be married there. Enjoying a somewhat altered state of consciousness, Kunz visited the Broken Spoke to hear Alvin Crow and the Pleasant Valley Boys perform. Kunz later met his future wife, Kathy Marcus, in 1973 and they started dating in 1975. The couple married in 2006 during a surprise ceremony held at the Broken Spoke. They initially camouflaged the event by calling it "Waterloo's 33 and $1/3$ anniversary party" in Austin. Famous media speechwriter and political humorist Liz Carpenter, Clifford Antone, and blues piano player Joseph "Pinetop" Perkins all attended the event with several hundred other guests.[2] Few guests suspected that the event would host a wedding, including famous singer and musician Joe Ely. Kathy Marcus revealed her secret wedding agenda to Ely when the bandleader seemed insistent on performing nonstop onstage that night. "We said, 'Joe, you can't tell anybody, but we're getting married,'" Kunz says. "'So you have to take a break.' So he took a break. A lot of people had thought we were already married." Perkins somehow never noticed the wedding ceremony under way as he sold his CDs onstage, and he stood right in front of the couple. The thought did briefly occur to Kunz to stop the ceremony, but he resisted out of concern that he might make a scene.

Afterward, Ely sang a song that he once sang with the Clash at Armadillo World Headquarters. Ely headlined the Broken Spoke on May 21, 1992, and later often appeared onstage as a guest with other bands. Kunz created Waterloo Records with Louis Karp in 1982 and became the sole owner in 1987, using the slogan "Where Music Still Matters." He also cofounded the Watermelon Records label. Over the years some of the Broken Spoke's performers have also appeared in showcases at Waterloo Records. The Kunz and White families have enjoyed a long history of mingling both work and personal interests. Kathy Marcus formerly served as photo editor for *Texas Monthly* and photographed the Broken Spoke for the magazine. She also served as the art director of Watermelon Records and photographed Don Walser for one of his CDs at the White Ranch. "Fifty years is a big deal," Kunz says. "James might have another thirty years in him. At least, I hope so. James has a lot to look forward to. He always has; he just always has the biggest smile on his face, and he has the best attitude about everything."

Grammy-nominated rockabilly guitarist, singer, and songwriter Bill Kirchen began performing at the Broken Spoke sporadically during the

1970s after leaving Commander Cody and His Lost Planet Airmen. Kirchen, a Bridgeport, Connecticut, native, together with George Frayne and the band recorded seven albums, including *Live from Deep in the Heart of Texas*, listed among *Rolling Stone* magazine's "100 Best Albums of All Time."³ Kirchen's genre often blends the best attributes of country, rockabilly, bluegrass, western swing, R&B, and truck-driving music. He became known for his guitar licks and onstage persona while playing his 1959 custom sunburst-finish Fender Telecaster, or "Tele." The world's first commercial body, single cutaway electric guitar configured with a dual pickup transducer captured mechanical vibrations and produced a revolutionary sound. The Tele set trends in both the music industry and in electric guitar manufacturing. *Guitar Player* magazine nicknamed Kirchen the "Titan of the Telecaster" after he released his 2006 album, *Hammer of the Honky-Tonk Gods*. Kirchen has recorded and performed with a long list of celebrity musicians. Today he lives in Austin and collaborates musically with his wife, Louise, and their daughter, bass player–songwriter Sarah Brown.⁴

Professional photographer Rick Henson began taking photos of James White and Alvin Crow and other stars at the Broken Spoke in the mid-1970s. He met White in 1975 when Henson visited the Broken Spoke to photograph Ernest Tubb. "James was a celebrity there. I would just follow him around, and that's how I got photos of the stars," Henson says. Over the next decade, Henson also photographed such other stars as George Strait and Elvis Presley at other local venues.

James White began booking George Strait and his Ace in the Hole Band in 1975, a gig they held until 1982. Courtesy of Annetta White.

Thanks to Alvin Crow, country singer George Strait and his Ace in the Hole Band began performing regularly at the Broken Spoke from 1975 until 1982. One night Alvin made a phone call to James White to ask if Strait could fill in for him at the Broken Spoke until he arrived. Strait had been recently discharged from the army and sang lead for a band made up of college friends from TSU.[5] Lead guitarist Ron Cabal, steel guitarist Mike Dailey, bass player Terry Hale, and drummer Tom Foote renamed the band the Ace in the Hole after Strait joined. Strait eventually was inducted into the Country Music Hall of Fame. When Strait retired from touring in 2014, he fondly remembered Austin's famous honky-tonk as one of the places where he began his music career forty years ago: "When you talk about a honky-tonk, you come up with all kinds of images of what it may look like. Especially, I guess if you've never been in one. I've played a bunch of them in my life, and there are some classic ones that, if you've never been and would like to see what it's like, you should go to. There are three that really stick out in my mind, and one of the best is the famous Broken Spoke in Austin, Texas."[6]

Strait recalled specific details about the inside of the dance hall: "It's the classic low-ceiling, big dance floor, tables on the sides with longnecks being sold by the dozens," he says. "You better have your stuff together, too, when you play one of these great honky-tonks or the folks are going to let you know about it and will leave. Filling the dance floor is a must. You dance—you get thirsty, right?" Strait says that the Whites have helped keep country music alive in Austin. "It also gave us some great experience that we used throughout the years when things started to get big. I really appreciate the fact that Mr. White is dedicated to keeping the tradition alive. Young bands need a place to play live, and I can't think of a better spot to do it than the Broken Spoke. I'm just an old honky-tonker at heart, and I'm proud to say that I cut my teeth in one of the greatest honky-tonks on earth, the Broken Spoke." A few of his band members continue to perform with other groups at the Broken Spoke. "Although I haven't been there in many years, I hear from friends that it's still the same and I hope it stays that way. I'm sure Mr. White will make sure of that. He gave me and the guys a chance to play there in the seventies, and I'll never forget the good times we had on those nights."

Tom Foote, the original drummer for Ace in the Hole who later became Strait's tour manager, also fondly remembers performing at the Broken

Spoke during the mid-1970s. Foote had just earned a college degree and had become certified to teach history. As he recalls, "We were the opening act for Alvin Crow. We were big fans of Alvin. We just loved everything he did and loved the music he played. The Spoke was always the place we aspired to play at in Austin. We never were an Austin band; [we were] from a much smaller music scene in San Marcos. The Broken Spoke was a place I used to go to before we played there. I used to go to the Spoke to go dancing. Mr. White realized we were playing traditional country music with an edge." Meanwhile, Strait wrote songs for the band, and local radio stations began to play them. "We weren't Texas country music like Jerry Jeff Walker, but there was the Country Music Revue playing the top-forty country music. It was a great response. George has always been a distinctive vocalist and a good-looking guy, so Mr. White asked us back."

The band also played at the Broken Spoke a couple of times after Strait released his first hit single, "Unwound," in 1981. Foote remembers feeling challenged to fit all of the band's members onstage. "It was kind of a tradition to stick your drumstick in the ceiling," he says. "When we first started, it wasn't so much about the people reaching out and touching you. You knew you were accepted because people were on the dance floor. It wasn't a concert situation when we first started." Foote still enjoys the Broken Spoke's chicken-fried steak and says he will be forever grateful to James White. "I do remember vividly opening for Alvin and what a big deal it was and how important it was. Later on we had a lot of success and Mr. White was always a booster of ours. He always supported us on a personal level. I think he recognized George's talent. That's why we still go there today and remember him so fondly and enjoy watching his kids grow up."

James White recalls that George Strait eventually became too expensive to book. As James recalls, Strait "was still playing here when he was recording up in Nashville and becoming real famous and I kept on bookin' him. He jumped up from four or five hundred dollars a night to I think thirty-five hundred dollars. Then he jumped to twenty thousand dollars, and I couldn't afford him anymore. Then he went to one hundred thousand dollars—or whatever it was—it was a lot of money." Strait's name soon drew more crowds than any other band James booked. "On the calendar at first I just called them 'The Ace in the Hole band,' and then later I added 'Featuring George Strait.' Then I got to where I just put 'Tonight we're having

George Strait,'" James says. "Then I started booking George Strait for a percentage of the door. Then one night I was talking with his drummer, Tom Foote, and Tom says, 'George isn't going to be here tonight because he's up in Nashville recording.'" James knew plenty of musicians who had performed at the Broken Spoke and who had gone to Nashville to record, but none of them would ever achieve Strait's status.

"I always remember those seven years that he played out here—1975 through 1982. We were good friends and we're still good friends. He's the best country music singer in the business as far as I'm concerned. He's got a great voice, a wonderful voice. He sings a good solid country song." Because members of the original Ace in the Hole still perform at the Broken Spoke occasionally with other bands, the friendships have endured. "We still get invited to different things for George Strait. We always get a good seat in any one of the auditoriums that he performs in. We saw him at the Erwin Center when we went backstage during his 'Farewell Tour' Austin concert," James says. Strait's piano player, Ronnie Huckaby, joined the Ace in the Hole long after the band had stopped performing at the Broken Spoke. However, Huckaby still performs there often as a member of his own Texas Jamm Band.

The Broken Spoke's most profitable night of the year often fell on the Wednesday before Thanksgiving, James recalls. "Because they [teenagers] didn't have any school the next day, the dance hall door would just be lined up with people, a big mob. We could always expect some type of a problem because there were so many people and they were [mostly] underage." Tommy Hill and the Country Music Revue began performing on Wednesday nights and always drew a young crowd. The band never made it to the big time, but Hill enjoyed a limited career as a successful songwriter creating hits for other country artists and became a producer of albums for MGM and Starday Records.[7] After the Country Music Revue became popular at the Broken Spoke, their manager mistakenly decided to take the band on tour. Band members planned to return to the Broken Spoke within a year or so bigger and better than ever, but that never happened. Instead, they had lost so much of their local following that the bar receipts at the Broken Spoke dipped when the band returned. Because James has always booked bands that drew big crowds—especially those that spend a lot of money at the bar—he stopped booking the band. However, James's brief success with advance advertising for the Country Music Revue had taught him a valuable lesson about how to drum up customers and how to match the local bar competition.

Sometimes late at night, James drove past the Vulcan Gas Company or by Armadillo World Headquarters. "I saw that the cowboys were beginning to grow their hair long and started looking like hippies themselves. I remember those days; it was a good time, but a competitive one," James says. So in 1973 he began creating monthly calendars with the scheduled performances of all of his bands listed in chronological order to boost weeknight beer sales. At the entrance to the dance hall, James distributed the catalogs as flyers on blank sheets of paper that Annetta had prepared using a manual typewriter and later mimeographed. "I had some of my most successful nights during 'Ten Cent Beer Nights,'" weekly events until the 1980s, when the drinking age was raised. "I would get like six hundred people on Wednesday nights. I wasn't making a lot of money, but it seems like we had a whole hell of a lotta people out here. The young people liked it and the band, People's Choice." On those nights, James offered Falstaff, Jax, Lone Star, and Pearl beers for ten cents a glass but charged regular prices for premium beers such as Schlitz, Budweiser, and Miller High Life. He also charged extra for draft beers. When James and Annetta shortened the Wednesday-night special promotion to two hours from 8:00 to 10:00 p.m., beer sales often broke records, especially if People's Choice performed. "We would pop those beer caps just as fast as we could sell them," James says.

Beginning as early as 1976, People's Choice played private wedding receptions, reunions, proms, birthdays, conventions, and political gatherings nearly every Wednesday night and maintained the standing house gig for about twenty years. Howard T. Levine joined People's Choice as lead guitarist and vocalist, replacing Doug Hughes. Today the sixty-five-year-old Levine still performs with the band, but People's Choice no longer plays at the Broken Spoke because its members' musical preferences have changed. In the old days, the band never charged more than two dollars per person cover charge. "Every time we went up a dollar, we thought it would ruin us," Levine says. "I remember when we went to five dollars. We thought, 'No. We can't go to five dollars. No one is going to pay.' These days we charge ten or twelve dollars at venues."

He recalled when the band performed on the Wednesday nights before

Thanksgiving: "They just stood on the dance floor—as we would use the expression—'elbow to elbow or as*hole to belly button.' That's the way people talked about it. They just stood there. Once we began to play, then they all began to move. Then when the song ended, everyone would stand on the dance floor again. It was really strange." Perhaps that is why to this day a sign hanging over the dance floor reads "No Standing on the Dance Floor." People's Choice members early in their careers also performed what Levine calls "mostly Texas music"—cover songs by Johnny Bush, Darrell McCall, Randy Cornor, and Frenchie Burke.[8] Before the People's Choice lead singer Stacey Poole retired in 2001, the band and the Whites reached an end-of-contract agreement, Levine says. "We had the best years of our lives playing at the Broken Spoke. Whenever we talk about it, it's almost like it was another era and another life." One of Levine's fondest Broken Spoke memories involves Earl Campbell, nicknamed "the Tyler Rose," who used to sit in occasionally onstage with People's Choice to sing "Silver Wings."

When western swing frontman Ray Benson and Asleep at the Wheel came to town in 1973, they soon sought out the Broken Spoke. The long, tall transplanted Texan with a ponytail has been wearing his trademark white Stetson hats for more than forty years, about as long as he has been performing with his band at the Broken Spoke. The Wheel first performed there the same year they released their first album, *Comin' Right at Ya*. Benson's original Asleep at the Wheel band came together in Paw Paw, West Virginia, and included keyboard player Floyd Domino, pedal steel guitarist Reuben Gosfield "Lucky Oceans," rhythm guitarist and vocalist Leroy Preston, guitarist and vocalist Chris O'Connell, and bass player Gene Dobkin. After the band began to earn a steady gig at Berkeley, California's, Longbranch Saloon, Van Morrison mentioned the band as one of his favorites in a *Rolling Stone* magazine interview, and the band landed a contract with United Artists before relocating to Austin on the advice of Willie Nelson.[9] "What we had come to Texas to do was to play Texas dance halls, and at that time there were a lot of them," Benson says. "We had finally learned what we needed to play in these places—you have to play a waltz, a two-step, the Cotton-Eyed Joe, and a polka." Ray and the Wheel have performed together more than forty years, earned nine Grammy awards, and released more than twenty-five studio albums. The group revived western swing with their 1993 album, *A Tribute to the Music of Bob Wills and the Texas Playboys*.[10] Benson also co-wrote with Ann Rapp the script for the Broadway musical *A Ride with Bob*, which enjoyed a limited nationwide run in 2005 to commemorate Wills's one hundredth birthday.[11]

Austin in the early 1970s supported a tremendous number of venues that catered to folk or country and western. "We just loved the early 1970s. In the 1960s, if you had long hair and were a hippie or whatever and you went into a Texas dance hall, you got your hair cut or beat up or both. The Broken Spoke was the first place that I know of where the two got along—cowboys and hippies," Benson says. "As long as you were playing music, they were like 'we don't care who you are.' The music is what they cared about." Some might argue which venue officially began the amalgamation of music genres in Austin, but no one can argue that when the Wheel performed at the Broken Spoke, the dancing never stopped. In between making albums, receiving Grammy awards, and touring throughout the world, the band has managed to come home to perform a show at the Broken Spoke every year, usually in January.

The Wheel also has traditionally backed up Willie Nelson at private parties at the Broken Spoke, especially those held annually in February provided by Robert and Bettie Girling, who founded Girling Home Health Care. When Benson did not tour with Asleep at the Wheel, he often sat in onstage at the Broken Spoke to perform with other well-known musicians and singers, including Dale Watson, Jerry Jeff Walker, and Townes Van Zandt. "There was a picture someone sent to me of me and Townes Van Zandt performing together at the Broken Spoke at one of the private parties there. I played guitar for Townes. That stands out as a big memory for me." Benson says the Broken Spoke has since served as a home to his most enduring friendships that span more than forty-five years in the music business. He also considers the Whites' ranch an extension of a home away from home in Austin. "I used to go out to their ranch and ride horses—when I used to ride. I don't ride anymore, but they have a gorgeous ranch out there."

Country singer-songwriter, guitarist, and drummer John Bush Shinn, otherwise known as Johnny Bush, began performing at the Broken Spoke beginning in the mid-1970s.[12] Bush had played in Willie Nelson's band and with Ray Price and the Cherokee Cowboys before beginning his solo career. He had earned the nickname the "Country Caruso" but lost most of his voice in 1972 because of vocal chord spasms, just after the top-ten song Bush penned, "Whiskey River," hit the country music charts.[13] By 1985 about 70 percent of Bush's voice returned long enough for him to front a San Antonio band and release the album *Hot Texas Country*. By 1994 Bush hit his stride to release more than a dozen albums in as many years, and his autobiography was published in 2007.[14] James recalls their friendship also has stretched for more than thirty years. "I'd met Johnny Bush years ago when he played with Willie and he played with Ray Price. He had a beautiful voice. He could really hit those high notes. He sings some real good drinkin' and dancin' songs. He gave me his hat and a pair of boots that he wore the first time he recorded 'Whiskey River.' I have those patent leather boots." White cherishes a vintage photo of the two men that hangs at the Broken Spoke. In one picture, James White hands Bush a gun. "I was handing him this ol' rusted-out shotgun, and he's got it in one of his display cases in San Antone," James says. "A lot of times he would come in and sit in with another band. Other times, he might sit in and do a show with Cornell Hurd or maybe Al Dressen. Seems like he could hardly talk at one time, but he could still sing. It's been very hard for him over the years." Bush also underwent heart surgery in 1998.

The late Bill "Billy" Clayton, the first person in state history to serve four terms as Texas Speaker of the House, founded "Speaker's Night" at the Broken Spoke in 1975. The Republican farmer and rancher from Springlake earned the title "country slicker," a moniker he kept until retiring from politics in 1983 to become a Democrat and a lobbyist. In 1975 during the middle of his third term as Speaker, he became the subject of an FBI sting and was indicted on charges of accepting a bribe from a union leader; he was acquitted in 1980.[15] On the nights after Clayton dismissed the Texas legislature, he often adjourned to the Broken Spoke to eat a chicken-fried steak, drink some cold beer, and do some dancing—often in that order. "We used to kid to say, 'There are more bills passed at the Broken Spoke than on the floor of the capitol,'" James says.

When Clayton retired, Gibson D. "Gib" Lewis became Speaker of the House in May 1983. The Mexia native surpassed Clayton's term record in both the House and at the Broken Spoke. He became the first to serve five terms as Speaker, a seat he held until he retired in 1993, when he became a lobbyist and consultant. Under Lewis's tenure, Speaker's Night attendance among legislators at the Broken Spoke reached an all-time high despite a controversy regarding his campaign finances and a 1992 conviction on misdemeanor charges that he violated the state's disclosure laws.[16]

In the mid-1970s Willie Nelson performed fewer live concerts at the Broken Spoke, but he still visited unexpectedly, played for a private party, or appeared in a TV event such as taping a segment of TNN *Live*. When Willie returned to Austin after touring Europe, he immediately came to the Broken Spoke to practice his segment for TNN. The following night he performed the show live there. "That night there were wall-to-wall people, and it was like eight miles deep with cars all the way down Lamar with folks who wanted to see Willie," James says. "Those who couldn't get in that night had to watch the show live on the TV sets out in the parking lot; one of the TVs was in the back of my truck. A great time was had by all."

Beginning in 1975, long before the late Ann Richards served as Texas' forty-fifth governor, she began frequenting the Broken Spoke as a Travis County commissioner, a practice she continued when she became state treasurer. Brassy and bold with a shock of white hair, Richards's big personality often overshadowed her politics.[17] James recalls that Richards had a great sense of humor. "One Halloween she came out to the Broken Spoke dressed like Dolly Parton. She had real big boobs on, and she was all made up with long blonde hair. She told me, 'Don't tell anybody who I am.' So, I didn't. Afterward, she always brought it up and she'd say, 'Oh yeah, I used to love it out there.' She would come out on Speaker's Night and she was always a good person to talk to." Richards possessed a rich Texas twang and a wit that allowed her to deliver memorable remarks with skillful compression and a twinkle of her eye.[18]

The late Darrell Royal also began visiting the Broken Spoke regularly in the mid-1970s. "One night he says, 'I want to meet Willie Nelson tonight.' So I went over and got Willie and took him over to Coach Royal's table. That night after the show here at the Broken Spoke, Coach Royal and Willie went out together to listen to music and to talk and I imagine have a few drinks. The next day Coach Royal's wife, Edith, told me, 'I guess they had a good time. They didn't get home until six o'clock in the morning.'"

Doug Sahm, the late multitalented musician who founded the Sir Douglas Quintet in 1965, also performed incognito with the Texas Tornados and other bands at the Broken Spoke in the 1970s.[19] The long-haired San Antonio native had an appetite for more than Tejano and country music, James recalls. "If he came in to eat here, he ordered the chicken-fried steak and the Mexican plate—both." Sahm experimented with several genres of music, from rhythm and blues to country, over the span of sixteen years following his 1965 chart-topping song, "She's About a Mover," that he recorded with Bob Dylan in 1965. His infatuation for conjunto music would earn him the nickname "Doug Saldana," in the late 1980s.[20] He occasionally sat in with Alvin Crow's band, often using a pseudonym. Sahm had been identified as a child prodigy in the 1950s at just eight years old and nicknamed "Little Doug Sahm" after appearing on Louisiana Hayride country radio program. His performances with the late greats of country music Webb Pierce, Hank Thompson, and Faron Young became legendary.[21] He released several singles during his teen years and earned a spot in the Grand Ole Opry but turned it down because his mother wanted him to finish high school. In 1973 Sahm began recording with such notable artists as Dylan, Dr. John, David Bromberg, and Flaco Jiménez. He also started his own record label, Tornado Records, and enjoyed a short career as a movie actor before he died of a heart attack in 1999.[22]

The Country Music Association of Texas held its awards show at the Broken Spoke in 1975 to honor B. J. Thomas, Gene Watson, and Red Steagall.[23] Thomas crossed genres of pop, country, and gospel; his biggest hits include "Raindrops Keep Fallin' on my Head," "Another Somebody Done Somebody Wrong Song," and "I'm so Lonesome I Could Cry."[24] The seventy-two-year-old Gene Watson wrote two dozen top-ten hits after releasing his first single, "Love in the Hot Afternoon," in 1975.[25] Songwriter, recording artist, television personality, and movie actor Red Steagall wrote more than two hundred songs that he or others recorded, including "Here We Go Again," "Party Dolls," and "Wine."[26]

The late Waco radio personality Bud Fisher cofounded the CMA in 1972 and held its annual awards programs at the Broken Spoke well into the 2000s before relocating the show to the Woodlands. James White received the Bud Fisher Lifetime Achievement Award at the CMA of Texas gala in 2015 at a venue in Spring, Texas, and former president George W. Bush proclaimed the day "Country Music Day in Texas."[27]

Many of the original Texas Playboys performed at the Broken Spoke in 1975, the year that Bob Wills passed away. "Sleepy" Johnson, Jesse Ashlock,

Many of the original Texas Playboys performed at the Broken Spoke in 1975, the year Bob Wills passed away. Leon Rausch sang while Alvin Crow performed on fiddle. Courtesy of Rick Henson.

and Keith Coleman all played fiddle; Smokey Dacus played drums; Leon McAuliffe performed on steel guitar; Al Stricklin played piano; and Leon Rausch sang with guitarists Tommy Allsup and Bob Kiser. James, Bobby Earl Smith, and Joe Gracey played a significant part in organizing the Texas Playboys' appearance in Austin at both ACL and the Broken Spoke. Many of its members had suffered financially in the year following Wills's death; they had performed few steady gigs since, so James helped raise the funds necessary to bring them to town and put them up for a couple of nights in a local hotel. "They could have never played the Austin City Limits if there wasn't guaranteed money to pay for their motel rooms and their gas getting here. Because they didn't have CEO jobs; they had jobs working in service stations, mowing grass for the county, and one of them was a disc jockey," James says.

The night after the Texas Playboys performed for an episode of ACL, they played at the Broken Spoke. The band used Marcia Ball's piano; as she recalls, "The place was full, and people were sitting on the dance floor. That was something I had never seen—it was weird to see people sitting on the

Broken Spoke dance floor; people usually danced. Everybody had packed in there that night to see the Texas Playboys. As I walked in, they were playing the song 'Maiden's Prayer.'" Ball recalls that she had heard earlier in the day how well the Texas Playboys had performed the night before at ACL. "I thought that perhaps they had exaggerated. When I saw them perform that next night at the Broken Spoke, it was just better than I could have imagined. It brought tears to my eyes; it was just wonderful."

Outlaw country singer-songwriter Jerry Jeff Walker recalls first stepping inside the Broken Spoke with Joe Ely to hear Ernest Tubb perform one night in the 1970s. "We were right in front of him, and Tubb says, 'A couple of young boys want to come up and sing "Waltz across Texas" with me.' We got a big kick out of that," Walker says. A photo of Walker and Ely performing onstage with Tubb hangs at the Broken Spoke. Walker, born Ronald Clyde Crosby in upstate New York, first recorded with Circus Maximus in 1967 before hitchhiking to Austin. The inspirations for his songs most often have been real people he has met on the street.[28] Fans have associated Walker with the progressive country music scene for more than forty years. After writing the song "Mr. Bojangles," Walker recorded his first gold album, ¡Viva Terlingua!, in 1973 in the tiny Texas town of Luckenbach and helped make it famous. The stories Walker began to tell in the lyrics of his songs often germinated inside the Broken Spoke kitchen, which served as

Jerry Jeff Walker and Joe Ely perform
with Ernest Tubb, 1975. Courtesy of Rick Henson.

James's makeshift office at closing time. In the old days, after closing up at the Broken Spoke, Walker and White often sat in the kitchen drinking and strumming guitars while singing songs. Other nights after Walker and his band finished performing at another gig in town, he headed over to the Spoke. "It was a good place to go after we'd played someplace else, to wind down a little bit," Walker says. "It was kind of what we did. It was that down-home feeling."

Sometimes Walker stopped by to sit in onstage with his friend Alvin Crow. White would also sing a song or two onstage. The trio performed old traditional country tunes, though Walker admits that those performances blur a bit in his memory today. "I had periods when I was really 'plugged into the scene,' and then I would go away for a while. I don't know what I'd call it. I'd be running, jogging, and eating well; then all of a sudden I'd be honky-tonkin' and touring again." Sometimes he imagines a future as a bar owner like James. James also appeared in one of Walker's music videos, driving up in his vintage Cadillac and offering Walker a ride to an unknown destination. Walker gets into the car and they drive away together. Over the years, that scene has played out often in real life without any cameras present. "I think James drove me home a couple of nights in his old Cadillac," Walker says. In the early days of his career, Walker drank a little too much, and when he did, he found it difficult to leave the Broken Spoke. Someone sober would usually volunteer to take Walker home, a practice that James affectionately named "Jerry Duty."

Walker, who has recorded thirty-four albums, shares James's love for life in general, and music has been a staple for them both for more than forty years. Walker's late grandfather served as a square dance drummer, and he grew up listening to Waylon Jennings's music, a tradition he has passed along to his son and musician Django Walker, who also would perform at the Broken Spoke in the 2010s. Jerry Jeff, a master storyteller, began his career writing songs in Greenwich Village in the 1960s, telling stories and setting the tales to acoustic guitar music at the height of the counterculture movement with the likes of Bob Dylan. He played crossover country music because that type began to draw more than just one kind of music fan—including patrons of country, rock, blues, and folk. The Whites have kept the country tradition alive so well and for so long that Jerry Jeff still feels like he's visiting a neighborhood bar when he steps inside the Broken Spoke. "It feels down-home and comfortable like an old slipper." Jerry Jeff toured up to three hundred days a year in the late 1970s and started his own production company, Tried and True Music, in the 1980s. James recalls that some of the Broken Spoke's biggest crowds gathered for Walker's belated birthday parties over the years.

For the past forty years, Al Dressen has performed at the Broken Spoke by fronting one band or another. He performed there with the Sunset Riders throughout the 1970s and later the Super Swing Sausage Revue. Legendary steel guitarist Jimmy Day also performed with Dressen for five years before returning to Nashville to play and record regularly with country singer Ray Price. Dressen remembers performing at the Broken Spoke in the days before the Whites installed air-conditioning. James often took the stage to sing "Mountain Dew" with Dressen's band. In August 1982 Dressen would begin giving away smoked sausages at all of his shows at the Broken Spoke and would continue doing so for two years until changing the band's name to the Super Swing Revue. Dressen recalls that in all the years he performed at the Broken Spoke, a fight never broke out during any of his sets or breaks. "But I was here one night when a fight happened," Dressen says. "Aubrey Lowden's band was playing—Aubrey 'Blue' Lowden. He was a well-known fiddler back in those days, and he's still around. Lowden's wife at that time often sat in the audience when he performed, and she sometimes got a bit jealous." He says a woman came up to talk and flirt with Lowden, and his wife had had enough. A girl fight ensued that entertained patrons for the next several minutes until even the men started fighting and Broken Spoke personnel broke it up.

People respect the "authenticity" of the Broken Spoke, Dressen says. As an example, Dressen cited the dance hall's unique restrooms. Decorative plastic shower curtains—often with a Texas theme—hang on metal rods in front of each of the toilet stalls in the women's restroom. The curtains provide an illusion of privacy unless the fans inside the room blow too fast; this causes them to billow outward two or more feet. People waiting in line often have to avert their eyes to avoid getting an eyeful. The Broken Spoke still possesses likely the oldest urinals in Austin. The vintage six-foot-long rusted receptacle in the men's restroom offers no privacy whatsoever when three men stand side by side. James admits that the unit remains in bad shape: "Annetta had seen somewhere that this person advertised that he could reporcelain anything. So I got him to take a look at our men's urinals. He took a look at them and said real quick, 'I can't do a thing for you.' Then he left." Dressen says some patrons may make fun of the restrooms, but others have said, "'That's what I expect a Texas bar to look like.'"

Percussionist Bear Eagle, a Mescalero Apache from Ruidoso, New Mexico, has played a handmade washboard at the Broken Spoke for over thirty-five years with an assortment of musicians and singers. Bear Eagle plays a vintage board used to hand-wash clothes at the turn of the century. He plays his instrument with a glove on each hand fitted with stainless-steel sewing thimbles attached to the fingertips. He creates different rhythms and sounds by rubbing his thimble-tipped fingers against the wavy metal rows of his modified instrument. The sheet-metal board hooks over his shoulders like a vest that hangs to his waist. Performing first with Gary P. Nunn in the 1970s, Bear Eagle has since played onstage with the Derailers, Alvin Crow, and Cornell Hurd. "So technically I went from being someone who plays a rubboard to 'a rubboardist.' That's what they're calling me now." Bear Eagle began playing the rubboard as a child after finding an old piece of tin on the side of the road near a New Mexico reservation where he once lived. "My grandmother took it and began cutting potatoes with it sideways," he says. "Something happened where it made a noise and I kind of liked it, not knowing then what I could do with it. Then I took nickels or knives and started playing it with them. The next thing I knew, it developed into spoons." When Bear Eagle left the reservation, he visited Louisiana and discovered zydeco, a style of French creole music. "The old folks there that I met playing zydeco music taught me the steps to play zydeco on a rubboard and then they made one for me. Then I was hooked."

James recalls several colorful characters who regularly visited the Broken Spoke in the 1970s. Anyone who has ever played the jukebox in the dining room has likely wondered about the mule deer head with the nine-point antlers that hangs just above the game room door. William "Grouchy" Egardner Tatsch used to regularly sit and drink at a table next to the big-game trophy, no matter the time of day. He also occasionally fronted Grouchy and the Texas Pioneers band.[29] Tatsch claimed to have shot the deer (actually it was his friend Harold Short who fired the gun that killed it). Grouchy tried to sell the deer head for one hundred dollars. Throughout the 1970s Tatsch also parked his car and temporary trailer home beside the Broken Spoke. "He made the mistake of tending bar out here and while he worked, he would often try to take bets behind the bar," James says. "I told him, 'Grouchy you can't take bets behind the bar—it's illegal.' I told him, 'You're either gonna have to quit yer gamblin' or I'm goin' to have to fire you.' He told me, 'James, you know I can't keep from gamblin.' So I fired him." Before Grouchy died, he told the Broken Spoke waitresses he had hidden gold and diamonds in his trailer home. "As soon as he died, those waitresses went into Tatsch's trailer to search for the gold and the diamonds," but they found nothing but a bunch of junk and old clothes. "Ol' Grouchy could exaggerate."

John "Bunky" Grumbles liked to haul a horse around in the back of his pickup truck and park it out front of the Broken Spoke, James says. Grumbles claimed to have worked at the former Travis County dump off Highway 71. "I never let him ride his horse inside this bar, but it was something he did at other bars in town. I made him tie it up out front or leave it in his pickup," James says. Frank Otto "Dutch" Glauninger also often visited the Broken Spoke in the 1970s, James recalls. Glauninger owned the Western Inn and Circle G Construction company in Oak Hill for many years.[30] The two men came to the Broken Spoke either separately or together often with another friend, Charles Knutsen. His friends called him "the Naughty Norwegian." "One night, all three of them—Grouchy, Dutch, and Bunky—were all in here together drunk, and Bunky and Dutch decided to run a foot race. So we all went out on the south side of the Broken Spoke and each bet one hundred dollars on the foot race," James says, but the race ended up in a fight. After three races, Dutch was announced the winner, but Bunky could not afford to pay up on the bet. Instead he ended up painting the porch at Dutch's home as payment.

James White says another patron, who went by the nickname "Stinky," also used the alias Dave Chapman. No one ever learned his real name. He wore khaki pants with a belt buckle that always faced sideways on his waist, a loose-fitting shirt, boots, and a fisherman's cap. Stinky often slept outside the Broken Spoke in his truck, and he liked to gamble at pool. "One time I saw him playing pool in his socks here at the Broken Spoke. He had bet his boots and lost them. Then he bet his pickup truck and lost it. Then he lost his false teeth playing pool," James says. "Another customer, James 'Bubba' Bryant, one time won Stinky's false teeth playing pool and hung them on his rearview mirror inside his car. I played Bubba at pool to win those teeth back for Stinky." Terri White used to kid Stinky about his habit of flirting with female dancers at the Broken Spoke. Stinky liked to pull his false teeth out of his mouth and make faces by expanding his lips and revealing a mouth of toothless gums. Because Stinky considered this facial feat attractive to women on the Broken Spoke dance floor, Terri began to call him "Don Juan."

James says another couple of regular Broken Spoke customers during the 1970s, "Preacher" Dill and his wife, "Maggie D" Dill, had managed a bar in Oak Hill known as Maggie D's that went out of business. "One time Maggie D wanted to get Ernest Tubb's autograph. She was wearing a pair of white short shorts and went backstage at the Broken Spoke. She put those white shorts right in Ernest Tubb's face, and he wrote an 'E' on one cheek of her shorts and a 'T' on the other," James says. Preacher Dill had a gravelly voice and liked to drink. "If you asked him if he wanted a beer, he'd always say, 'It's a beer joint, ain't it?'"

Also in the 1970s the Whites hired a bouncer always only referred to as "Whitey." His real name was Whitey Whiddon. To this day Whitey remains legendary among longtime Broken Spoke patrons. "We paid Whitey ten dollars a night. If there wasn't a fight, he would start one just to earn his money. He was a character." James also recalls two former Broken Spoke waitresses that he identified by just their first names, Patty and Judy. Austin police threw the two women into the city jail one night after they got into a fight in the parking lot. "They were wearing the Broken Spoke T-shirts the night that they got thrown into jail. They raised a ruckus all night long in that jail and wouldn't let nobody get any sleep," James says. When friends bailed the two out of jail, everyone behind bars shouted their good-byes, referring to the women as "those Broken Spoke bitches."

Former representative Harvey "H." Hilderbran from Kerrville has remained a faithful patron of the Broken Spoke for forty years—since the day he turned sixteen during the summer of 1976. Hilderbran fondly remembers competing in Austin's junior rodeo and visiting the Broken Spoke when People's Choice performed. He moved to Austin in February 1986 as a lobbyist for the Farm Bureau. "I would go to these 'Speaker's Nights.' Not that I had big expense accounts to be a sponsor for Speaker's Nights," he says. At the time, he befriended Gibson "Gib" D. Lewis, then Speaker of the Texas House. Hilderbran moved into a bachelor pad that stood just a couple blocks north of the Broken Spoke's front door. Hilderbran and his friends used to walk their dates over to the Broken Spoke most Friday and Saturday nights. After his election as a Texas legislator, Hilderbran teamed up with Lewis to promote Speaker's Nights. "Speaker's Nights were big, and people looked forward to them," he says. "It wasn't just one event back in those days; it spanned six to eight weeks." The Speaker's Nights continued during every session of the Texas legislature. Hilderbran says that the Broken Spoke became the place to be on Tuesday nights, partly because its members did not have to pay cover charges. Speaker's Night continued through the 1990s.

In 2003, Hilderbran began celebrating "Chairman's Night." "I was chairman of Culture, Rec, and Tourism, what we nicknamed 'the Bubbas and ballet committee.' It was huntin' and fishin' and the arts. Me and Ray Benson [bandleader for Asleep at the Wheel] became pretty good friends, working together on the Texas Music Museum," Hilderbran says. "The format was, we had a band. If you were part of the capitol community, you didn't have to pay a cover to get in. You would either identify yourself as a sponsor or working at the capitol." Both Speaker's Nights and Chairman's Nights generated enough legislators that the beer sales at the Broken Spoke helped underwrite the costs of hiring a band. "There were some great crowds on Chairman's Night that were reminiscent of the old Speaker's Night. The trick was to find out how many people had time and the desire and were motivated enough to come. That was how you decided how long to keep it going," he says.

Both Democrats and Republicans enjoyed fellowship after hours at the Broken Spoke. "That was my scene. I'm a country and western guy, and I was single as a lobbyist and single as a member of the legislature for two terms. I enjoyed going to the Spoke," Hilderbran says. Hilderbran still visits the Broken Spoke to dance, even though Legislators' Nights, Speaker's Nights, and Chairman's Nights have long since ended. "I think the Broken Spoke is a legend," Hilderbran says. He and his older brother, Jody, together with Representative Richard Raymond saw Ernest Tubb perform at the Broken Spoke in 1982. He remembers Tubb's band put the country star in a chair that looked like a throne to sign autographs. Once when Hilderbran and his wife, Tracy, went to the Broken Spoke, Gary P. Nunn asked an old friend from the audience to join him onstage. The friend turned out to be singer B. W. Stevenson, who performed a ten-minute rendition of "My Maria" about one month before he died on April 23, 1988.[31]

John Kelso, a humor columnist for the *Austin American-Statesman*, jokes that he and the Broken Spoke represent two of the oldest landmarks in this town. For the past thirty-eight years Kelso has written more than a dozen articles about the historic honky-tonk and James and Annetta White. In the mid-1970s Kelso first visited the Broken Spoke to research where the legislators went to drink, and he showed up for Speaker's Night. "James White wasn't even there as far as I know, but Joe Baland was. That night he was running the show. I told him what I wanted to do with the story. He got kind of chapped and he says something like, 'Well if you want, you can sit there and talk to me like a man.' Then he stomped off," Kelso says. After Baland snubbed him, Kelso decided to stick around for a bit longer. When he looked to his right at the bar, he saw Nat Henderson, a former writer for the *Statesman*. Henderson held a bottle of whiskey in a brown bag and offered Kelso a drink. "As soon as Joe Baland saw me being accepted by Nat Henderson as an actual human being, he came over and put his hand on my shoulder and says, 'Son, let me introduce you to Senator Peyton McKnight,' who was in the Broken Spoke at the time." McKnight, an oil businessman from Tyler, became a legislator at twenty-three years old while still attending UT law school.[32]

In one of Kelso's later columns, he wrote about the owner of Dance Across Texas, a club on East Ben White Boulevard, who lodged a complaint against the Broken Spoke for violating the city's fire code: "Rumors Spur Trouble between Rival Country and Western Clubs," ran July 20, 1991, in the *Statesman*. "Dance Across Texas became popular really fast. I wrote about how the owner of that place had a flap with Annetta," Kelso says. Friend and attorney David Walter represented the White's. Dance Across Texas consisted of a huge, sprawling warehouse with a pseudo-western storefront and cowboy paraphernalia. In essence, it represented the mirror opposite of the Broken Spoke before it closed. A code inspector gave the Whites just ten days to comply with city code and required them to spend more than eight thousand dollars to upgrade with emergency lighting and safety exits. The honky-tonk added eight new signs with red arrows that pointed to exits. James worried that too many exit signs might ruin the club's country look. "I told him, 'Look, I don't want people to think the name of this place is 'The Fire Exit,'" James says. Throughout the building they added fire extinguishers. "Now we've got fire extinguishers hanging from every post out here."

Kelso also has held family celebrations there, including his sixtieth birthday party ten years ago. "One of the guys who came was Rich Oppel, the former editor of the *Statesman*, who catered the barbecue. So they had this barbecue line and Oppel tried to go through the line twice," Kelso says. "Annetta said, 'No. You can't have second helpings. You can only go through the line once.' So she turned back my boss and she wouldn't let him go through the line again." Kelso says that he has enjoyed writing stories about the trials and tribulations of the White family for three decades. Kelso also wrote about how the construction of The 704 apartment complex severely limited access to the Broken Spoke's parking lot. That story, "Honk If You Like Valet Parking," published in the *Statesman* on February 10, 2013, revealed that Transwestern hired valets to temporarily park cars for patrons. He wrote that not many other businesses on South Lamar today have survived since the 1960s. A mural just outside the northern wall of the Spoke and visible along South Lamar depicts some of the Broken Spoke's most famous celebrity performers over the years.

Two longtime friends, Bobby Dan Woods of Sweetwater and Chris Baumann of Albuquerque, found their "favorite place in the whole world" at the Broken Spoke during the 1970s. The buddies have continued to visit the honky-tonk regularly for the past forty years although they live out of state. Woods discovered his future haunt while attending college in nearby San Marcos in 1975. "I had heard about this regional band called Alvin Crow and the Pleasant Valley Boys, and I'd heard about the Broken Spoke and what a neat place it was," Woods says. Soon afterward, Woods met James White. "He's such a nice guy, and he's one of those kinds of guys that can make friends with people real easy. He's made friends with presidents of companies, governors, celebrities, and on and on, but he's also made friends with goofballs like me and Chris. Baumann, who hails originally from Quakertown, Pennsylvania, and another friend, Jack McAuliffe, used to save up their money to fly to Austin, rent a Cadillac, and visit the Broken Spoke. Baumann moved here for a while in 1989, but McAuliffe stayed behind. "At various times we both bartended there whenever we were in between jobs," Woods says. "We asked Annetta which one of us was the sorriest bartender, and she says, 'Oh, you were. Chris was much better.'"

For a while after Baumann landed a full-time job elsewhere in town, Annetta continued to call him when she needed backup help in the bar.

Ringing the bell that hangs over the bar became Baumann's favorite part of bartending at the Broken Spoke. These days, the old bell attracts only dust. "I rang that bell. I complain nowadays that nobody rings that bell anymore. With that bell we used to ring in the old days all the time—ding, ding, ding—if somebody played a good song, or anything," Baumann says. "Jerry Jeff or Gary P. Nunn would play a good song and I'd ring the bell. Nobody rings the bell anymore. So I would show it to the young bartenders and say, 'You see that thing up there? It's an instrument. It's part of your job to ring the bell.' We had a good time doin' that." Baumann says that he first heard about the Broken Spoke while still living in Philadelphia where fans had mythologized stories about the country music scene in Austin. He fell in love at first sight with the red, rustic old building and then embraced the Whites. "If you befriend James and Annetta, they have this unique deal where if you're a part of their lives and they meet somebody, they want you to be friends with their friends," Woods says. Recently he discovered that name-dropping helps when renting Austin's hotel rooms. "All the motels in town were booked. Then the desk clerk says, 'If you're going to Mr. White's birthday, y'all come on. We'll get you fixed up.' It's not what you know, but who you know I guess."

PART IV

The 1980s

CHAPTER 10

Urban Cowboy, Dallas, and South by Southwest

In the 1980s country suddenly became cool with the release of the movie *Urban Cowboy*, starring John Travolta and Debra Winger as a star-crossed couple searching for love in a East Texas dance hall. It spawned a pop culture that transformed discos nationally into country and western clubs complete with mechanical bulls.[1] However, in Austin, patrons of the Broken Spoke had known all along where to find the best live music and the best dancing, says country singer Cornell Hurd. "The Broken Spoke is absolutely the epitome of all the good stuff about Texas music. The dance tradition never left Texas. The dance tradition was different as it spread across cultures: the Germans, the Spanish, and the Czechs. Everybody did it; everywhere else it may be nearly all gone now. This is where it remains. The Texas dance tradition is still alive here, and this is just one of the places keeping it alive." Hurd says all of the country music stars that he grew up listening to either hailed from Texas or they performed at the Broken Spoke regularly. Thirty-five years ago, every bar or lounge in Texas had a dance floor. Today the Broken Spoke's astounds visitors from anywhere outside Texas.

Austin calls itself "the live music capital of the world"; however, Hurd claims the genre of music performed at the Broken Spoke makes the city renowned worldwide. "Austin's not the rock capital of the world, not anywhere even close. It's not the blues capital of the world; we haven't been a blues town in a long, long time. It isn't the reggae capital of the world, and it isn't the jazz capital. Classical music?—No. It's none of those things. What are we the capital of? We are the capital of Ameripolitan music," Hurd says. "People come from all over the world to hear us do that. There are people who take their vacations here so that they can come here to the Broken Spoke." Ameripolitan, coined by country singer and entertainer Dale Watson, refers to the genres of country, rockabilly, honky-tonk, western swing, outlaw, and roots music.[2]

The prime-time television soap opera *Dallas*, starring Larry Hagman as the oil baron J. R. Ewing, cast a strange spell over viewers, intensifying the world's fascination with Texans.[3] The series, which ran fourteen seasons from 1978 through 1991, provided a surprising ripple effect within this state's live country music venues, including the Broken Spoke, as Americans became further engrossed in Texas culture from its music to its fashions. James White recalls that the dancers at the Broken Spoke as a result began dressing more the part of country dancers and often left their former hippie threads at home.

At the same time in the 1980s, a small group of people began to envision ways to expose Austin's live music community to the world and to bring other bands from throughout the world here to perform. Their efforts led to Austin's first South by Southwest (SXSW) Music Festival in March 1987, with seven hundred registrants.[4] Soon SXSW festivalgoers and performers started showing up at the Broken Spoke, and word spread fast internationally that James's place offered a once-in-a-lifetime experience. That's about the time when people started adding a visit to the Broken Spoke to their bucket lists.

CHAPTER 11

"The Broken Spoke Legend" Song

James and Annetta self-published a 1,029-page book specifically about their White family ancestors in 1980, *They Came to Texas: Patton-White-Campbell Families and Connecting Branches*. James had spent most of his life living and working in Oak Hill as a member of one of the area's oldest founding families. The Whites spent seven thousand dollars and ten years researching the White family tree, tracing its lineage from Texas to Virginia. Their decade of research had helped the Whites obtain a Texas Historical Marker in 1970, presented by Governor Preston Smith for their family's Patton Rock Store at 6266 US Highway 290 West. The Oak Hill landmark had been built under the supervision of James's great-grandfather James Andrew Patton in 1898.[1]

John Eaton Campbell, a county surveyor, married Lavina Davidson and they came to Texas in 1851. When he died, the Masons buried Campbell, the first rancher to run cattle on Barton Creek, in the Masonic Cemetery in town. The Campbells' daughter Maggie married Robert Emmett White, and they had four sons and a daughter. James White's namesake, his great-grandfather James "Jim" Andrew Patton, born January 12, 1853, in Lockhart, became a community leader in Oak Hill. Patton served with the Texas Rangers under Capt. Alexander "Buck" Roberts, and his Minutemen Company fought Comanche on land near where the Broken Spoke stands today. Patton later donated the limestone to build the old Oak Hill School and original Patton Elementary. Patton was involved in changing the local subdivision's name to Oak Hill when he became its unofficial mayor and served as the area's first postmaster.

In the 1980s at the Broken Spoke, James began drinking a lot of Colorado Bulldogs, a popular drink at the time made with Kahlúa liqueur, vodka, cream, and Coca-Cola, especially when he and his friend Don Green took road trips across Texas with Annetta. The drink tastes like a dessert but provides a kick that lasts for hours and delivers a whopping 250 calories. In 1989 Alvin Crow and the Pleasant Valley Boys traveled with James White to the nation's capital at the invitation of US Representative Charlie Wilson. They performed one night for the Texas State Society (TSS) of Washington, D.C., one of the largest groups on Capitol Hill. Wilson would later become famous for his involvement in a CIA operation known as "Operation Cyclone" that organized and supported Muslim rebels fighting the Soviets in Afghanistan.[2] Members of TSS then invited Crow and his band to play at the Washington, DC, Sheraton during George H. W. Bush's presidency. James says that they attempted to decorate the stage like the Broken Spoke, but the backdrop looked more like a fake barn. About fifteen hundred people attended the event. "When I got up onstage and said, 'You all act like you're in Austin, Texas, at the Broken Spoke,' it made a whole lot of people from Texas proud, including myself, and we made them homesick for Austin. I sang 'The Broken Spoke Legend' song, and Alvin Crow kicked off the dance. It was a great time, a fun time. I really enjoyed that trip."

The next day the Whites visited the Smithsonian Institution together with Alvin Crow's wife, Stephanie, and Don Green. James recalls that TSS paid for everything. Green worked more than thirty years in various state government jobs and today serves as the chief financial officer for the Teacher Retirement System of Texas. He frequently also served as the unofficial travel coordinator for Alvin Crow's tours in the 1980s. To this day he remains a huge Broken Spoke fan. Green and his father, who had connections with Delta Airlines, helped coordinate travel for the group's trip to Washington. "Dad got our Delta pilot to make an announcement that James White and Alvin Crow were on the plane flying with us to Washington, D.C.," Green says. While attending the University of Texas, Green first started visiting the Spoke and at one time lived in the Woodmoor Apartments located just behind the honky-tonk. He recalls when James White first began his "BSU speeches." "James used to say, 'I graduated from BSU—Broken Spoke University,'" Green says.

James began writing the lyrics to the song "The Broken Spoke Legend" in the mid-1980s with Alvin Crow. James recalls, "We would be back there in the kitchen drinkin' and talkin' about different things and singin' old country songs. So my wife, Annetta, said, 'Why don't you sing Alvin that song you wrote called the Broken Spoke Legend?' So I sang it as a waltz tune.

Afterward, Alvin said, 'Why don't you write one more verse and then we'll record it.'" It took James a little longer than he expected to finish writing the song. "I can't do it like James Hand does it or Chris Wall or Dale Watson does. I kind of get a hook line and then I get kind of a melody goin' around in my brain. I tend to write a song a lot better when I'm out on the road just drivin' by myself down the highway. It's probably better out in West Texas where there aren't a whole lot of distractions like traffic in Austin."

Soon the songwriting muse began to visit James whenever he least expected it. "When I get a tune in my head, I know I should get on my recorder and sing that tune back into it along with the words of the hook line, or whatever I want to use," he says. "Sometimes, after I have laid in my bed and I've woken up, I've thought 'this is a good line for a song,' but if I don't immediately get up and write it down or hum into a microphone and record it, I'll forget how it goes." Early one morning in 1988, after he locked up the Broken Spoke for the night and headed for home, his song's remaining lyrics came to him. "I was fixin' to get in my truck in front of the Broken Spoke and I thought, 'Well, hell, this is just a red rustic old building with a dirt parking lot, and there's a big old oak tree by the highway that means quite a lot.' It all rhymed with my waltz tune, so I had my song finished," James says.

Meanwhile, Crow began playing more often than any other performer at the Broken Spoke. "Alvin played a lot of our New Year's Eve dances out here; he has just been a family friend of ours for a lot of years," James says. Crow and James recorded his song "The Broken Spoke Legend" for Crow's CD *Pure Country*, released in 1988. "So I sang it to Alvin, and he says, 'Well, good, let's sing it tonight on the bandstand.' So I sang it up there and everyone loved it. Alvin recorded it, and for the first time I sang on a record. I sang the very last part of 'The Broken Spoke Legend,'" James says. Soon afterward James wrote an additional six country songs and would produce his own album in 2005. "It's an accomplishment and I always have a lot of fun doing them. Getting up onstage and singin' with the different bands is a lot of fun and I really enjoy it."

Terri White gave birth to her daughter, Ashley Carey, on December 16, 1982. Ashley had always hoped to meet a man like her "Poppy" James White. She plans to marry Stephen Dutton on October 30, 2016. Currently Ashley works as a hairstylist not far from the Broken Spoke and often asks her grandparents for advice on business matters. "I trust them. Obviously they're doing something right, to own their own business for fifty years; not a lot of people can do that." The Whites working together as a team has made all the difference in their personal and business success. Ashley says that her grandmother "loves to be the supportive one and always wants to step out of the way and let [James] shine. She loves that about him—she's proud of him." Ashley described her grandfather as a humble man. When he talks to someone, that person, no matter who he or she is, feels like the most important person in his universe at that moment. "I just can't fathom a life without him in it," she says. "Part of what people love about the Broken Spoke is that they love him. He's just a nice man and he's friendly to everybody. He will remember somebody's name from I don't know how long ago. He knows everybody." When Ashley took college classes a few years ago, she helped the Whites out by working nights as a cocktail waitress or a bartender at the Broken Spoke. She still occasionally helps out when needed. Always, Ashley enjoys witnessing firsthand her grandfather's knack for treating everyone with dignity and respect. "They don't make 'em like him anymore," she says. Ashley also has two children of her own, Alexander and Brenn.

CHAPTER 12

Mixed Drinks and Loyal Customers

Because Ginny had become so fond of watching the TV series *Dallas* with her stepgrandfather Joe Baland, James took the entire White family on a quick road trip one Sunday in 1980 to see Southfork. Also about that time, during the downtime for the production of the 1980 movie *Urban Cowboy*, John Travolta stopped by the Broken Spoke. One of his bodyguards came with Travolta that day, as James recalls. "I am just sorry that I didn't have a camera. It wouldn't have been no problem because it was just me and John Travolta and his bodyguard in the dining room. The bodyguard told me, 'I wanted him to see what a real honky-tonk looks like.'" Travolta also politely thanked James for giving him a grand tour.

Despite the *Urban Cowboy* craze, James and Annetta did not give in to whimsy; regardless of the popularity of line dancing, the Whites would not allow it on their dance floor. Always the honky-tonk's unofficial disciplinarian, Annetta politely tapped dancers on the shoulders to tell them they could not line dance. For years she also has had no qualms about telling men they cannot wear sleeveless shirts or asking women to buy a Broken Spoke T-shirt to pull over whatever attire she deems to be too revealing. Unlike some local discos and Austin clubs, the Broken Spoke never installed a mirror ball above its dance floor, nor is there a mechanical bull anywhere. As James recalls, "I even had some band members of the People's Choice band tell me, 'You need to get a big ol' ballroom globe with spotlights on it and spin it around and spin the glow from mirrors all around.' That's about the time I added to my Broken Spoke Speech the phrase 'I ain't changin' nothin,'" James says. James believes his resistance to change remains one of the main reasons that the Broken Spoke has stayed open for more than fifty years. "The backbone to our success is never changing anything or making the Broken Spoke rock and roll. We didn't want disco out here. We want to keep it country and as true to the roots as we can get it," he says. "I told the bands, 'I'll let you sing "Woolly Bully" [the 1965 song made famous by Sam the Sham and the Pharaohs] out here one time a night, but don't ask me for no more.'"

James did make one obvious change to the Broken Spoke's appearance. He allowed former cooks Ron Karow and George Freeman to paint its rustic gray exterior barn door red in 1980. However, the two men did a messy job, James recalls. "It was like a cartoon. They were both kind of goofy-looking people. Ron was on a scaffold and George was kneeling down below, when suddenly George had this waterfall of red paint coming down upon him. The two of them suddenly were covered in red paint. They had more paint on them than they had painted on the building."

The Whites dragged their feet for ten years before making the decision to sell mixed drinks at the Broken Spoke in 1980 after business had waned. However, obtaining the license allowed their business to boom once again. A 1970 amendment to the Texas Constitution gave counties the option by election to permit the sale of mixed drinks in bars.[1] Annetta recalls the difficult transition: "At first our old customers just threw a fit when we first started offering mixed drinks." Some of the occasional patrons seemed offended by the amount of alcohol being consumed by the more serious ("bring your own booze," or BYOB) drinkers, who frequently left the premises early in the evenings. Annetta recalls, "Brown baggin' really hurt our business, and we just weren't having anybody at night after a couple of years. We just said, 'You know what? We appreciate your business, but this is what we have to do.' So we added mixed drinks."

The Whites also used a little ingenuity to improve their bar service. James physically removed half of the beautiful vintage twenty-four-foot, hand-carved oak bar banister from the Fortress Steak House, sawed it into two pieces, and installed them inside the Broken Spoke. He handmade a matching twelve-foot bar banister and placed it in the dividing wall between the dance hall and the dining room. The configuration allowed bar service on three sides: in the dining room, in the dance hall, and in the room between them. However, beer remained by far the most popular drink. "We sold a lot of beer at the Broken Spoke and we had a lot of loyal customers come in every day," James says. "The ones that didn't drink beer liked to mix their own drinks and bring their own brand of whiskey in to 'brown bag' it. They'd usually set the bottle on the floor, although other times they'd set it on the table. They wanted to be able to mix the amount of liquor that they liked, and a lot of them liked pretty strong drinks."

James admits he put off applying for the mixed-beverage license with the Texas Alcoholic Beverage Commission (TABC) to avoid increasing his state sales tax from 8 percent to 14 percent. Today for every one hundred dollars the Whites earn in liquor sales, the Broken Spoke gives the state of Texas nearly fifteen dollars, James notes. "That's why you never want your bartenders to overpour their drinks. The TABC takes inventory when they come out here; they make sure that if we're selling whiskey, they are getting their money from it, which is fine. That's just business. We don't do anything illegal; that's why we stay in business. We pay our taxes and run an honest business." Obtaining a mixed-beverage license restricted him from selling six packs of beer to go, which happened to be a popular practice among his clientele at closing time. As forty-year patron Don Green recalls, "James had a little microphone located behind the bar, and he would announce, 'Last call for alcohol and six packs to go.'"

James paid three thousand dollars for his initial mixed-beverage license in October 1980 and had to install soda dispensers and a "speed railing" for pouring drinks at the bar. "It meant an outlay of cash which we didn't have, but somehow or another we found the money like we always do—we find the money somewhere. We got it and I'm glad we did. Here lately, for the last two years anyway, you can have a license and renew it every two years. I always hand-carry mine to the TABC office like a trophy because I have the oldest mixed-beverage permit in Travis County." However, the Whites continued to offer Ten-Cent Beer Nights until the People's Choice band came up with "Nickel Beer Night" to promote the sale of ales only. Selling keg beer offered a much more generous profit margin than bottled beer, but the inventory process presented problems for James. "I had to figure how much a keg of beer cost or how many cups in a keg of beer. We had a lot of math going on—a lot of adding and multiplying." The chore of calculating became even more challenging on nights when the Broken Spoke staff members drank throughout the evening or suffered from a hard day's work.

Fans of the Broken Spoke often tell James that they remember Nickel Beer Nights fondly. "They'll say, 'Aw hell, I remember when I came out here in high school for Nickel Beer Night. We'd go into the restroom and somebody would have a pitcher of beer in there they were sellin,'" James says.

James soon discovered that folks sold beer secondhand illegally to minors at the Broken Spoke on those nights. The resellers made more money than James did at the bar because they bought pitchers of beer for a dollar each, which they resold for five dollars a glass. As James recalls, "We had to cut out all that really low-priced beer and really tighten up on all the minors before we got into trouble. We still allow minors to come in, but we watch them, especially when they're a certain age—around fifteen, sixteen, or seventeen. That's when they want to get a beer and you really got to watch them."

In the 1980s James created the room between the dining room and the dance hall and officially nicknamed it the "Tourist Trap." On one wall hangs a 1980 photo of James and Willie Nelson standing together. Professional photographer Rick Henson took the photo the same year Nelson starred in the movie *Honeysuckle Rose* and wrote the film's song track, including "On the Road Again." To this day it remains Nelson's most recognizable song; it reached number 20 on *Billboard*'s Hot 100 music chart and earned a Grammy Award for "Best Country Song." Director Jerry Schatzberg filmed scenes from the movie at the Broken Spoke with Willie Nelson, Dyan Cannon, Amy Irving, Slim Pickens, and Nelson's band, as well as James White. James recalls that he enjoyed show business. "There was a lot of time spent sittin' around visiting with the different movie stars. We all had a great time," James says.

The Tourist Trap museum features a glass case filled with the former personal belongings of famous men throughout country music history. Hats on display include those worn by Willie Nelson, Alvin Crow, George Strait, President Lyndon Baines Johnson, Ray Benson, members of Asleep at the Wheel, the Geezinslaws, Jody Nix, Gary P. Nunn, Don Walser, and Bob Wills. The Tourist Trap also displays a clean plate once used by country singer Randy Travis. "Randy Travis was eatin' a chicken-fried steak and he was in a hurry to leave. His limo driver kept tellin' him, 'Hey, we gotta go; we gotta make another stop.' So my wife says to Randy, 'Why don't you just take that plate with you and keep on eatin'?' And he did," James says. "So anyway, about two weeks later from Nashville I got a package and inside was the plate with a note that says 'great chicken-fried steak—Randy Travis.' He'd cleaned it up and wrapped it up and sent it back, which I thought was pretty neat, 'cause I never thought I'd see that plate again."

Rosetta Wills, the daughter of Bob Wills, gave James her father's half-smoked cigar to display in the Tourist Trap nearly thirty years ago. "The cigar made the newspaper. There was an article [in the *Austin American-Statesman*] and a picture of it and everything," Rosetta Wills says. "Actually, the cigar was smoked back when my father was courting my mother in 1938. He left the cigar in an ashtray, so my grandmother saved it and wrote a little note on it that says, 'This was one of the first dates they had.'" Rosetta Wills later sent James a copy of a photograph of her mother as a seventeen-year-old standing beside Bob Wills. The couple married in 1939 within a year after meeting inside a dance hall where he performed. Rosetta thought it unusual that her grandmother saved Wills's cigar and gave it to her granddaughter. Her parents divorced before Rosetta turned two years old. Afterward her grandmother took Rosetta to visit "Daddy Bob" only a few times. Though Bob Wills and his music became famous, his daughter hardly knew him until years later when the two finally reconnected. When Rosetta and her mother first heard Wills's music performed live by other artists at the Broken Spoke, it inspired Rosetta to write his biography in 1998, *The King of Western Swing: Bob Wills Remembered*. Rosetta claims to possess no musical talent whatsoever; no one in her extended family inherited Wills's musical abilities or interests.

Living in Turkey, Texas, where her father grew up, keeps Rosetta connected to her father's legacy and his fans. Since 1970 Turkey has celebrated an annual Bob Wills Day during the last weekend in April. Every year except 2014 the emcee has been West Texas A&M University history professor emeritus, Charles Townsend. The US Postal Service also added Wills's image to a postage stamp on September 9, 1993. A giant poster replica of the stamp hangs on the wall behind booth B-4 in the dining room at the Broken Spoke. Whenever she visits the Broken Spoke, Rosetta often runs into old friends. Willie Nelson became one of the Wills's favorite performers at the Broken Spoke. "We used to go out to the Broken Spoke nearly every weekend, and of course we've been back there a few times to visit since we moved, but not regularly like we used to do," she says. Her husband, bass player Michael Grace, has performed with several bands throughout Texas over the years, including some at the Broken Spoke.

Music writer and former director of the Austin Music Awards Margaret Moser started writing about the Broken Spoke in 1981 for the *Austin Chronicle*

Rosetta Wills, daughter of Bob Wills, and her daughter, Renee, stand with James White at the Broken Spoke, September 9, 1993. Courtesy of Rick Henson.

and continued to do so for thirty-eight years, during which time she developed a relationship with the Whites. She remembers often interviewing musicians behind the Broken Spoke. "We would often go out back where there was less noise, but more privacy too. Or sometimes we would sit out in the restaurant," she says. "Then we would stay for the show. That was always the greatest thing for me—the full package. I would get my personal time with the musicians to get the story and then get to see the show. It was so much fun over the years." She still loves people watching there. "This is a place for older people too," she says. When Moser moved to Austin in 1973, she immersed herself in the music scene. She had previously lived in San Antonio, Denton, and Seattle. "None of those places seemed to have what Austin had. In 1972 in Denton, I kept hearing about all the people who would drive down to Austin and come back to Denton just raving about it and with these little music flyers," she says. "I thought, that's where I want to be, that's what I want to be doing." Moser dropped out of high school and headed to Austin. She authored three books and worked as a music reporter for the defunct *Austin Sun* and then the *Austin Chronicle* from 1981 until 2014, when she retired.

Her fondest memory surrounds the night in 2006 when one of the Rolling

Stones crashed the Spoke. "When the Rolling Stones came, boy, you couldn't set foot in this town without hearing rumors about where the Stones would go. Hubert Sumlin and Blondie Chaplin were playing at Antone's, so I had a pretty good idea that would be where Keith Richards would hang out," Moser says. "I got a call from James White, who says, 'Margaret, the club is packed down here. We've got one of the Rolling Stones here.' I thought, 'Oh wow. This is great.' Then I asked, 'Who's there?' James hesitated for a minute, and then he said, 'It's Chuck—Berry.' I just burst out laughing because of course I knew it wasn't Chuck Berry. I knew that it was Chuck Leavell, the Rolling Stones' keyboard player." When Moser arrived, she saw Leavell holding court at a table located alongside the porch that faces the dance floor. "You couldn't really get anywhere near him because people were kind of crowded around just trying to get a view of the Rolling Stones' keyboard player. This was neither Mick nor Keith; this was just Chuck Leavell. Yet here he was—he was a rock star to the 'umpteenth degree' and James was so proud. James was on the dance floor doing his usual thing where he greets everybody who comes in. He'd shake your hand and say, 'One of the Rolling Stones is right over there.'" For years Moser stood her ground as the only female music writer in Austin. In retirement, she leaves somewhat of a gender gap.

Native Oklahoman Gary P. Nunn and his current band, the Sons of the Bunkhouse, known as "SOBs" for short, began performing at the Broken Spoke in 1983 at the start of his solo career when he was thirty-eight years old. He used to play at the Broken Spoke at least once a month before he moved to Marble Falls; these days he performs at the honky-tonk several times a year. James particularly likes Nunn's songwriting. "Nunn takes a great saying, and he makes it into a song. He'll get everyone singin' along with his songs when he's here. He loves Texas history, and he is part of a horse-riding *vaquero* organization. He fits in with the ranching crowd too—he ranches horses and cattle and he's smart." Governor Rick Perry once declared Nunn an ambassador of Texas music, and Nunn's name hangs on the wall at the West Texas Walk of Fame in Lubbock, along with those of Buddy Holly, Waylon Jennings, Bob Wills, and Roy Orbison. Nunn's music career began with the rock-and-roll band The Sparkles. Later Nunn joined up with the late great, Rusty Wier to perform with the Lavender Hill Express, a group that had been popular during the 1960s. Their group effort was well received.

A pivotal moment in his career occurred while on the road touring Europe with Michael Martin Murphey. Lonely and homesick for Texas, Nunn wrote the now legendary tune "London Homesick Blues." Nunn soon met a music publisher at Abbey Road Studios in London and felt inspired to write songs for artists he knew back home in the States. Not long afterward, Walker and his Lost Gonzo Band recorded "London Homesick Blues" as a breakout hit on their *¡Viva Terlingua!* album. Willie Nelson also recorded Nunn's "The Last Thing I Needed First Thing This Morning," and Roseanne Cash released his song "Couldn't Do Nothin' Right," which hit number 2 and 15, respectively, on the country music singles charts.

At the Broken Spoke, Nunn's band performs mostly well-known cover songs by famous artists, but occasionally he sings his original material. Over the years, hundreds of local musicians and internationally known stars have joined him onstage, including Eliza Gilkyson, Jerry Jeff Walker, and Joe Ely. Whenever Nunn plays the Broken Spoke, James joins him onstage about 10:30 p.m. to sing along on the song "Rollin' in My Sweet Baby's Arms." Nunn says he appreciates the friendship he and James share. "He's been very good to me. We've been good friends over the years. He's given me the opportunity to play there and to become one of the regulars." James and Annetta call Nunn "one of our favorites." Nunn also credits writer Townsend Miller with changing the public's perception about the local music scene back in the 1970s with the column he wrote for the *Austin American-Statesman*. "Until then, if you didn't have a major record deal, nobody in the media would mention your name. Certainly, no radio stations would play your record. Nobody made any records locally."

One patron, Carl Anderson, nicknamed "Crazy Too Cool Carl," started coming out to the Broken Spoke whenever Alvin Crow performed, and he began the tradition of rolling the Broken Spoke's wagon wheel up to the stage one night as James White took the stage to sing. Anderson still occasionally rolls the iconic wagon wheel around the dance floor in front of the stage. James also calls Anderson his "ten to two singer," affectionately. "He can clear out a crowd real quick. He likes to sing that George Jones song 'He Stopped Lovin' Her Today.' Carl always sings a little flat, a little off key. So ten minutes to two a.m. I get Carl up there onstage to sing and everyone always runs out the door," James says. At one time, Anderson approached James about taking a job as a dishwasher at the Broken Spoke. "I told him,

'I'm gonna' give you ten dollars for washin' all these dishes.' He said, 'Oh, that's a good deal,' and then I said, 'But I'm gonna' charge you ten dollars because I'm gonna' teach you how to cook.' He scratched his head and said, 'Well, I ain't gonna' make no money.'" Eventually, Carl found work elsewhere.

In the 1980s, the roof over the dance hall extension began to leak. James designed the original pitched roof covering the dining room portion of the building, but he built a flat roof over the dance floor extension. Whenever it rained, water ran off the pitched roof onto the flat roof, where it pooled and leaked inside. The Whites always placed various containers around the dance floor to catch the water. "Alvin Crow used to say, 'Where else for a dollar or more could you get a waterfall on the bandstand?'" James says. Annetta, who in her younger years weighed about one hundred pounds, often climbed onto the flat roof to sweep the water off with a broom. Afterward she used tar to seal the holes. Her daughter Ginny recalls, "That [roof] was so horrible and an example of my stepgrandfather's engineering. When it would rain, the water would pool up on the roof and we would have a leaky roof—I mean leaky like waterfalls coming down. My dad used to say, 'That just adds to the ambiance. It's real romantic sitting next to a little waterfall on the dance floor.'" Ginny also marvels at her mother's flexibility to accept the challenges daily at the Broken Spoke without complaint. "She'd say, 'I have to go up on the roof and seal up all the holes,' and then she'd cuss my grandfather out quite a bit about the old flat roof," Ginny says. Finally, one day Annetta said she had had enough. That's when James enlisted the help of a bar patron and contractor, Rick Holloway, who built a pitched metal roof over the top of both the original building and its extension. It completely covers the old roof and the air conditioners. "The inside still looks the same with all my dad's tin roof and plywood drainage system," Ginny says.

Rick Holloway and former jack-of-all-trades Malcolm Cleveland began spending their days working as hired hands for the Whites and their nights drinking beer and dancing at the Broken Spoke. The retired wranglers, now both in their sixties, remember when they each paid a two-dollar cover charge to see a young Willie Nelson play his guitar with his father, Ira Doyle "Pop" Nelson, at the Broken Spoke. "I'm sittin' there, and I was just about to leave when some guy walks through the front door carrying a guitar case

Left to right: Ashley Carey, Alvin Crow, Stephanie Crow, Carl Anderson, Cathy Green, Don Green, James White, and Annetta White at a round table in the dining room, 1988. Courtesy of Rick Henson.

and it's Willie Nelson," Cleveland says. Pop Nelson's band included fiddle player Jesse Ashlock, a former Texas Playboy. "There I am, on a Tuesday night, just two dollars short and watching Willie Nelson playing at the Broken Spoke and it's less than half full." Cleveland would visit the Broken Spoke again to watch Willie Nelson perform songs from his 1975 *Red Headed Stranger* album. Holloway discovered that James White appreciated his friendships regardless of a person's fame. Over the years, he has helped James repair all kinds of things at the Broken Spoke. Holloway also built the bar that separates the dining room from the dance hall and remodeled the restrooms in the dance hall at least three times.

When Texas legislators raised the drinking age to twenty-one, James and his friends thought up new ways to round up business at the Broken Spoke. James held boxing matches after Phil Finazio, a former fighter, talked to him about his days as a boxer. He worked at the Pan Am Gym with Ed Cantu. "He said, 'All we gotta do is build us a boxing ring and put it on your dance floor.'" So James and Finazio built a boxing ring that opened on Tuesday nights when the Broken Spoke did not have a band. They tore down the ring and packed it away Wednesday through Saturday nights so that dancers could use the dance floor. Young fighters, from lightweight to heavyweight, rode buses from East Austin to the Broken Spoke and arrived by early afternoon. James often rang a bell and spoke into a microphone at the start and end of each match. Finazio served as the referee. "One time, they gave me a little ol' trophy for having the fights here at the Broken Spoke. I should have been worried about somebody getting hurt out there, but I never did," he says. After a few events, James stopped holding the boxing matches because the numbers of fighters dwindled and setting up and tearing down the ring took too much work.

James also held a belly dancers' convention at the Broken Spoke thanks to the People's Choice band. One of the band members told James that his aunt was a member of the Belly Dancer's Association and they were looking for a place to hold their convention. A Broken Spoke bumper sticker inside the Tourist Trap still serves as reminder: "I Belly Danced at the Broken Spoke." James recalls that the biggest attraction at the event was not the event itself but its preshow. The belly dancers did not have a dressing room in which to change, so the staff set up makeshift walls created from bed sheets. "They were thin sheets and then they put a light back there. Therefore, when they were changing clothes, they were silhouetting their bodies against the sheets. That really probably put on a better show than the belly dancing," James says. "Some of our customers enjoyed that show very much."

Small groups of the Texas Playboys occasionally performed in Austin at various venues throughout the late 1980s and also at the Broken Spoke. As many as six hundred musicians over the past five decades have claimed to have performed with the Texas Playboys since their inception in the late 1930s. In 1988 Al Dressen started the Texas Western Swing Hall of Fame and invited some of the most recent members of the Texas Playboys to perform during an induction ceremony. "We heard things we had never heard before, or if we had heard it, we didn't know what it was. One thing we learned was 'padding.' Back then they didn't always call it that," Dressen says. Padding essentially occurs by creating a sustained background mix of music that accentuates or supports a certain lead instrument on a song. "It could occur during part of a solo instrumental section or during a vocal part. It's a way to build up the song—to have a little crescendo." Dressen regrets that he never recorded the Playboys' get-togethers before the band members headed home.

Several musicians who performed at the Broken Spoke in the late 1980s have passed on, including the legendary yodeler Don Walser from La Mesa, Texas.[2] James recalls the well-liked performer. "Don Walser was probably one of the nicest, politest, and greatest singer-musician combination guys that ever came through here. Everybody liked him. He was a big tall guy, and he had a lot of weight on him too—he weighed over three hundred pounds. When he got up there and started yodeling and singing all those wonderful songs, I thought, 'I'm gonna get that guy back here again if he can sing that good.' So I did." Anytime James held a special event at the Broken Spoke, all he had to do was call Walser, who would show up to play. In 1994 Walser recorded a music video for the country song "Cowpoke" at the Whites' ranch. The video included Grammy Award–winning steel guitar player Cindy Cashdollar, Alvin Crow, and James, who pretended to play the concertina. "After it was over with, the director told me, 'You were the best one.' I thought that was kind of funny, because I was just going back and forth with the squeeze box and kind of singin' along with Don," James says. A 1996 *Texas Top Hand* DVD features photos of Walser sitting on the cabin's porch at the Whites' ranch or standing in front of the Whites' log smokehouse. Walser used to autograph his photos for fans at every Broken Spoke show. Guests attending his tribute shows at the Broken Spoke still receive the same photos of Walser every January.

In the 1980s Don Green and the Whites began the tradition of playing dominoes in the dining room at the Broken Spoke hours before the band started in the dance hall. "There was this one couple, Red and Marie Gregg, who also played dominoes. They always dressed alike and wore matching shirts and pants," Green says. Green, like other regulars at the Broken Spoke, had his own designated table in the back of the dance hall located to the left of the bandstand. At home, Green still possesses his very own authentic Broken Spoke plywood table that still bears his lucky number, "33." He retained custody of the table following a divorce. "The Don Green table has gum and writing all over it. It has one leg that can be folded up and hung up on the wall so that people can sweep under it," Green says.

In 1983 when Speaker of the House Gib Lewis succeeded former House

Speaker Billy Clayton, he continued the tradition of celebrating Speakers' Nights on Tuesdays at the Broken Spoke. James recalls, "Lobbyists would throw big parties—back when it was legal for them to spend more money than they do today." The parties ranged from barbecues to shrimp boils. "The best parties had a theme like 'El Paso Days.' Those parties always involved a lot of food, a lot of beer, and a lot of pretty girls." That's when Don Green and James developed the familiar saying: "What happened at the Spoke stayed at the Spoke," especially when the parking lot was filled with cars belonging to state officials. "Those good ol' boys liked to party," James says.

Country singer and songwriter Cornell Hurd tells anyone who will listen that he moved to Austin from California nearly thirty-five years ago for the sole purpose of performing at the Broken Spoke. Hurd recalls that he first discovered the Broken Spoke coincidentally after performing at the Armadillo World Headquarters in 1980, when someone referred to it as "the best place in town to buy a chicken-fried steak." During those early years, Hurd played in a country rock band that started a tradition of eating at the Broken Spoke before other gigs in town. These days, Hurd performs at the Broken Spoke regularly. "I get to play at the Broken Spoke. I feel sorry for musicians that do not get to do what we do in here."

During the late 1980s newcomers to the Broken Spoke included Chris Wall, Don Walser, the Derailers, Rosie Flores, Bruce and Charlie Robison, Dale Watson, and Junior Brown. Chris Wall's love affair with words and his ability to turn a phrase paid off for the first time during the summer of 1986 when he took a leap of faith, left a Montana cowboy lifestyle, and moved to Texas. Nothing prepared Wall for his overnight success as a country songwriter. Jerry Jeff Walker's wife, Susan, first booked Wall at the Broken Spoke about thirty-five years ago. He began his solo career as a country singer at the Broken Spoke not long after writing the song "Trashy Women," and Jerry Jeff Walker recorded it on his 1989 *Live at Gruene Hall* album. Since those days he has considered James White his friend. "It's not important necessarily who the act is, but if you consistently have really good music all the time, then people will come. I've seen it work in club after club, but James is the king of just treating musicians really really well. I love him," Wall says. Over the years, rain or shine, James has remained remarkably consistent, Wall recalls. "There are no moods. He's always James. Whether he picks up the phone or you see him in person, he's always the same. There are no surprises there. I remember one time he called, and he was just so apologetic. He was calling to ask me to give up a night so that he could get Ray Price in there. He'd been trying to get Ray Price in there for years, and they'd finally come to an agreement. It was about eight or ten years ago. I understood. I think I asked him if he could get me in the show free."

In 1989 when Dale Watson first performed at the Broken Spoke, his pompadour was black. Though Watson's hair may be solid white today, the youthful fifty-something-year-old still performs nearly seven days a week throughout Central Texas. He played his first gigs at the Broken Spoke as a band member first with Monte Warden, then Brent Wilson, Craig Allan Pettigrew, and Chris Wall. Later those contacts helped him create his own band, which would perform at the Broken Spoke in 1992. "It felt good to be playing in such a historical place," Watson says. "It's kind of like *Austin City Limits*; it's a place you aspire to play if you grew up in Texas and you want to play real dance halls in Austin—it's the only one left." Since then Watson has recorded twenty-two albums and at least once a year spearheads a nationwide awards show that recognizes musicians who play the roots of Americana and classic country music, including rockabilly and outlaw music. Onstage at the Broken Spoke, Watson drinks a lot of Lone Star beer, a magical elixir that he claims promotes good health and a long happy life. "It's the best beer in the world," he says. "It whitens your teeth, increases your brain cells, eats calories. If you drink one every day of your life, you'll never die—that's a money-back guarantee, though you must collect in person." Whenever he performs, he sings the same set, including his original tunes and a lot of Ray Price and Johnny Cash. "I've been lucky. The way it usually goes here at the Spoke is you play for a while on Tuesday night, and if you do good on that, you move to Wednesdays, and then Thursdays. Each one was a long while of performing on those nights. Once you proved yourself, you moved to a Friday or a Saturday," Watson says.

He calls the Broken Spoke "an original" Texas dance hall. "It's still got that down-home vibe. We've had over six hundred people in here and we were still able to talk to people. It's great," Watson says. He pays attention to requests made by dancers who want to waltz, polka, or two-step to his music. "They want to hear something to dance to for a dance they just learned during the dance lessons provided by [Terri White at] the Broken Spoke before the show," Watson says. Watson said his fans in Europe plan their trips to the States around his gigs at the Broken Spoke. Halfway through the night James joins Watson onstage to sing a medley of songs made famous by Buck Owens, "Act Naturally" and "Sam's Place." Watson attributes his success in the country music business to the help he has received from others, including the Whites. Watson recalls, "Having this place as a bimonthly or monthly gig—whether I'm touring or whatnot—has helped through the years, for me to support my family. It's helped me to meet other people that have furthered my career. I've gotten movie deals, commercials, and record deals through playing here."

Former two-term Austin mayor Will Wynn first visited the Broken Spoke in 1982 as a twenty-year-old Aggie student architect intern. "I started heading down there a couple of times a month if I had beer money," Wynn says. "The first time you go in there, you're just—you know, amazed that the place is standing physically, but then you realize just how authentic it is. James famously says, 'I ain't changin' nothin.' He obviously hasn't and I hope he doesn't." He calls the Broken Spoke "iconic" and vital to this city's cultural identity as the "Live Music Capital of the World." An undated photograph in the dining room at the Broken Spoke shows Wynn standing beside Clifford Antone with James White. Wynn sang "Hey Good Lookin'" with both White and Antone in the parking lot at the Broken Spoke to celebrate the historic honky-tonk's fortieth anniversary in 2004.

Wynn says he understands the struggles bar owners face to stay afloat: paying their utility bills and taxes; complying with city inspections that regulate fire safety, electrical wiring, and building construction; dealing with various code enforcement agencies that oversee food and alcohol sales; and federal laws that regulate employee insurance, liabilities, and Social Security. "As mayor I actually spent a lot of time thinking about how I could help these venues stay in business. They are an equally critical part of that proverbial three-legged stool of musicians, fans, and venues," he says. James always provides Wynn with his own reserved table. After he served the first of his two terms as Austin's mayor, he put together his 2006 reelection campaign party at the Broken Spoke. His parents and several other family members and friends attended the event that Wynn still refers to as "a gift." Benson sang some legendary western swing classics. "Ray and the Wheel got back up and started to play 'Faded Love.' My parents got up to dance, which I didn't remember having ever seen before. My folks are eighty-nine now, so I know that that will prove to have been the last time," he says. James and Wynn still share a special bond of friendship. "He's just one of the happiest guys; he's one of a kind," Wynn says. "He's just this great guy."

Dancing at the Broken Spoke over the last thirty-four years has kept eighty-something-year-olds Jim and Birdie Nachtigal young. They have been married for fifty-nine years, but they still enjoy "date nights" at the Broken Spoke twice a week. Jim offers the advice, "It's exercise for one thing. That's what the doctors say—'you have to exercise, eat well, and drink a lot of water'—only I substitute water with Lone Star beer. It's good." Recently, on a night out at the Broken Spoke, Jim led Birdie in a two-step. Birdie wore fresh makeup, a glittery headband, and a silk flower in her hair. She dressed in a feminine light lacy blouse, a long flowing and colorful tiered western skirt, and cowgirl boots. Jim wore Wranglers, a starched western shirt with mother-of-pearl buttons, and a Stetson hat along with his boots. Dressing up makes them feel good and keeps their romance alive, they say.

When the Nachtigals first visited the Broken Spoke in 1980, "Gary P. Nunn was playing. I'll never forget that," Jim says. "So by the time we walked out, we said, 'Man, this is the place for us.' We just kept going back there ever since." Jim enjoys drinking draft beer while reminiscing about the 1940s, before television, when he first began listening to country music on the radio, including the *Grand Ole Opry* and *Louisiana Hayride*. The Nachtigals wax nostalgic whenever a band plays their favorite songs at the Broken Spoke. "That's what we like about it. The bands play music from the forties, fifties, and sixties," Jim says. "It's traditional country music." When they dance, "we're just listening to the music," Birdie says. They estimate they must have seen at least one hundred bands perform at the Broken Spoke over the past thirty-four years. Their favorites are Gary P. Nunn, Dale Watson, and Chris Wall, Jim says. The Nachtigals enjoy seeing other seventy-something-year-olds and younger couples step out onto the dance floor beside them weekend nights at the Broken Spoke. Their favorite memory at the Broken Spoke concerns the night when they celebrated their fiftieth wedding anniversary. Their daughter visited from Alaska, and all Birdie's brothers and sisters attended their party. Dale Watson performed and brought them up onstage with him. About ten or fifteen years ago, the Nachtigals used to sit near the dance floor up at the front where their friends gathered regularly to dance and to socialize. "Eventually, they all disappeared, you know? Illness or different things," Jim says. "So, I guess we're the only ones left."

One regular customer, Donald "Winker" Emmons, a New York photographer, for the past thirty years has spent the coldest months of the year living in Austin while taking photographs of celebrities at the Broken Spoke. Emmons identifies himself as "Winker Withaneye" on his Facebook page and calls himself "a drinkin' photographer." Since the beginning of the 1980s he has photographed nearly every significant event at the Broken Spoke together with Allan Sanders. Nearly everyone who meets Winker identifies him as a Santa look-a-like. They also recognize his name because it graces one of the Broken Spoke's unofficial toy mascots provided by Ginny White-Peacock. She recalls, "One Christmas, I noticed this small fabric Santa looked a lot like Winker, so I named him 'Li'l Winker.' Now that Santa stays out all year long at the bar." James has regularly sent Emmons photographs of Li'l Winker seated beside a mug of beer or a Bud Light. "Working with folks in Austin, I used to come here on business," Emmons says. "One of the first places that somebody told me that I had to go see was the Broken Spoke. I fell in love with it the first time I walked in the place." At the Broken Spoke he has photographed actor Robert Duvall dancing with one of James White's granddaughters, Mollee Jo Montague; actor Peter Billingsley; Willie Nelson performing; Willie and his sister, Bobbie Nelson, together with James over the years standing beside other members of the White family; former Longhorn football Coach Darrell Royal; and Ray Benson.

In the 1980s Joel Gammage first visited the Broken Spoke as a boy when his late grandfather, Manny Gammage, founder of Texas Hatters and Texas Custom Boots, lived just down the street from the dance hall. Since then the Gammage family has remained close personal friends with the Whites. For eighty-eight years the family-owned business operated on South Lamar until it moved to Buda and then Lockhart, where the business continues to flourish. Manny Gammage passed away in 1995 when Joel was just eight years old. The family has provided hats for some musicians who have performed at the Broken Spoke. "From Texas to Nashville, they've all at one point worn a hat made by my grandfather and my family," Joel says.

Actor Robert Duvall dances with Mollee Jo Montague, James White's granddaughter, when she was nine years old. Courtesy of Don "Winker" Emmons.

Texans judge one another by their hats and their boots, he says. Joel has been a faithful Broken Spoke patron for the past ten years. Dancing at the Broken Spoke has been a family legacy. James represents a grandfather figure for the youngest Gammage. "James White took me under his wing a little bit. Not having my grandfather and kind of growing up without a father in the picture, Mr. White filled the role model spot. He introduced me to people, more people than I've met in my life."

John Dromgoole, founder of the Natural Gardener organic gardening store, has been friends with James and Annetta White and a Broken Spoke fan since he leased his first business location from them in Oak Hill twenty-five years ago. Dromgoole moved his business to his current location on Old Bee Caves Road. He still sees the Whites whenever he visits the Broken Spoke to dance and to hear good country music. Dromgoole has been widely known as an organic trailblazer for the past twenty years in Oak Hill and throughout Central Texas.

PART V

The 1990s

CHAPTER 13

Austin Becomes the "Live Music Capital of the World"

Austin became known as "the live music capital of the world" after *Austin American-Statesman* music writer Donald McLeese together with Nancy Coplin who served as a volunteer chairperson on the city's first music commission, coined the phrase in the early 1990s. Former mayor pro tem Max Nofziger pushed to have the Austin City Council adopt the slogan about the same time,[1] and it soon appeared inside Austin Bergstrom International Airport, which replaced Robert Mueller Municipal Airport. The phrase generated interest among visitors, who began to see Austin as not just a vacation destination but also as a musical entertainment nirvana. Some four hundred manufacturers of high-tech equipment also moved into the Austin Metropolitan area during the early 1990s. City developers built a new convention center, as well as a proliferation of apartment complexes and new homes and vast stretches of commercial real estate properties. As a result, more than 150 neighborhood groups and environmentalists sought to find an economic balance between old and new Austin.[2] Meanwhile, old and new patrons of the Broken Spoke regularly filled its dance hall to capacity several nights a week, and at the University of Texas the "Broken Spoke Series" began seasonal performances inside its Performing Arts Center.

CHAPTER 14

"If There's a Willie, There's a Way" Fund-Raiser and the "Broken Spoke Series"

The 1990s marked the heydays of the Broken Spoke. The historic honky-tonk became a household name in Austin. Images of the Broken Spoke graced the covers of three national magazines and one state publication featuring either James White or patrons of the dance hall. All of that free publicity began with the Whites' single gesture of friendship extended to an Austin icon and friend.

The Internal Revenue Service in 1990 attempted to collect a bill for Willie Nelson's unpaid taxes to the tune of about $16.7 million, the same year that he released his *Born for Trouble* album. Nelson's lawyers proved successful in lowering the liens on his Texas property by about $10 million, but he lost nearly everything he owned except his guitar, Trigger, after he paid the remaining $6.7 million. When the IRS placed liens on Willie Nelson's Texas property, James and Annetta White decided to step in to help. They held a "If There's a Willie, There's a Way" fund-raiser at the Broken Spoke that raised ten thousand dollars in local donations. Legendary guitarist Doug Sahm came out to play for the fund-raiser, along with Marcia Ball, Alvin Crow, Jimmie Dale Gilmore, and Gary P. Nunn.[1]

The Associated Press ran a story nationwide about the Whites helping Nelson with his tax troubles by collecting donations in a pickle jar that sat on the bar at the Broken Spoke, as James recalls. "The IRS took all Willie's property and all his money. They even took his pictures off the walls and his gold records. We just didn't think he should lose his family pictures or the gold records that he earned. I thought, 'Aw hell, I'll just get a gallon dill pickle jar, and I'll set it on the bar and write 'Where there's a Willie, there's a Way,' and people could put their dollars in there, and we'd give it to Willie to help pay off his tax bill." Meanwhile, Nelson, who had escaped to Hawaii, did not have enough money to come back home to

Austin for Christmas. "Willie was one of the good ol' boys, and we thought they should cut him a little slack," James says. "All he ever wanted to do was entertain people and travel all around the world doin' it. They should have just left him alone. His accountants were the ones who got him into trouble."

Both the *Austin American-Statesman* and *Texas Monthly* published articles about Willie's financial troubles with the IRS.[2] Soon James became something of a celebrity too. "I started getting phone calls from people all around the world—people were sending me money to give to Willie, and I gave him every nickel of it and every note that people wrote to brag about him," James says. "There were people who didn't have nothin' and they'd write a note: 'Well, Willie, we ain't got much, but you're welcome to drive our old truck or to stay here at the house.' There was some Indian reservation folks that called up to say, 'Man, you're welcome to stay right here on this Indian reservation as long as you want to,' and they sent money." Reporters from national networks such as CNN and FOX News began to call James, and radio talk-show hosts across the United States interviewed him.

When the IRS placed liens on Willie Nelson's Texas property on September 21, 1990, James and Annetta White held a fundraiser for him at the Broken Spoke and collected ten thousand dollars in a pickle jar on the bar.

"We helped to raise funds for Willie Nelson because we needed him in Austin, Texas," James says. "He didn't need to be stuck over there in Hawaii with no money to get back. So we helped get him back." Lana Nelson stopped by the Broken Spoke to pick up the ten thousand dollars. As James recalls, "Willie called me up, and he said, 'I got the package today.' Then Willie said, 'I want to thank you from the bottom of my heart, and I appreciate what you did.' I said, 'You didn't tell me to do it, but my heart told me to do it. I was trying to put my heart in the right place.' Then he said, 'I tell you what; I'm gonna come back to Austin for Christmas and I'm gonna do a little pickin' and eat a chicken-fried steak and drink a cold beer, and I'm gonna bring some of my friends with me up to the Broken Spoke to see you.'"

When Nelson returned home to Austin that December, he visited the Broken Spoke and brought his good friend Kris Kristofferson with him. The two performed a medley of songs onstage with White. A photo from that night hangs on the wall across from the bar.

Nelson still has a soft spot in his heart for the Whites and the Broken Spoke. As Nelson stated in an exclusive prepared statement, "My friends James and Annetta White have one of the best honky-tonks in the world called the Broken Spoke."[3] Nelson applauds James and Annetta's commitment to helping to keep country music alive. "The Spoke has supported hundreds of musicians like myself by providing a fun place for the pickers to pick and the dancers to come out and dance. 'I DANCE COUNTRY AT THE BROKEN SPOKE' isn't just a bumper sticker'; it's a way of life—a way of life that I hope sticks around for generations to come," Nelson wrote. Throughout the last five decades, Nelson has remained a loyal friend to the Whites. These days Nelson's long gray hair, usually worn in pigtail braids, together with his wry smile and blue eyes define him as much as his music has over the past half century. That totem twang of his, the southern slang, and his understated delivery of country lyrics have become iconic. His music has resonated for country music fans since the 1970s, but he also cofounded Farm Aid in 1985 with fellow musicians John "Cougar" Mellencamp and Neil Young, beginning with a concert in Champaign, Illinois, that helped raise nine million dollars in relief aid for American farmers.[4] The Country Music Hall of Fame inducted Nelson in 1993, and the National Agricultural Hall of Fame honored him in 2011 for his support of family farms.[5]

A photo of James White and Alvin Crow standing in front of the Broken

Willie Nelson gave a special performance when James and Annetta White raised ten thousand dollars to bring him home to Austin for Christmas in 1991. Courtesy of Rick Henson.

Willie Nelson and Kris Kristofferson sing harmony with James White and Joe Ely, 1991. Courtesy of Rick Henson.

Willie Nelson performs with his friends Kris Kristofferson, Doug Sahm, and Alvin Crow, 1991. Courtesy of Rick Henson.

Spoke made the cover of *Texas Highways* magazine in 1990. As James recalls, "We were voted 'the best honky-tonk in Texas.' That's really the best braggin' rights I had at the time—basically my whole life had revolved around honky-tonks, or at least the last fifty years and even all the way back to my childhood. It's something I can darn sure relate to for sure. Up until that time in 1990, I had taken a few pictures, but not an abundance. This one kind of put us over the top. So many people who had saved that issue of *Texas Highways* would want me to autograph the back cover and put it on the wall at their house," James says.

Not long afterward, *Entertainment Weekly* editors scheduled a photo shoot and an interview with James at the Broken Spoke. Benson came out and stood on the porch and acted like he was giving out autographs. James brought several of his horses down and had some female patrons pretend to ride them. The girls on the horses looked like they wanted Benson's autograph, and they lifted their boots up for him to autograph. *Entertainment Weekly* also voted the Broken Spoke "the best dance hall in the country" in 1990.[6] That same year one of *National Geographic*'s editors named the Broken Spoke her "favorite" Austin night spot.[7] A couple photographed for the magazine's cover, who were Broken Spoke regulars, dressed in a cowboy tuxedo and prom dress, Texas style.

During the 1990s James began to emcee the "Broken Spoke Series" in the Performing Arts Center (PAC) on the campus of the University of Texas at Austin at the invitation of its director, Pebbles Wadsworth. For the first show, White introduced performances by Nelson, Crow, Kimmie Rhodes, Johnny Gimble, and the Geezinslaw Brothers. PAC staff decorated the stage with bales of hay, a jukebox, and saddles. "We began each night with me standin' in the middle of the stage singin' 'The Broken Spoke Legend.' Then after the music, I'd say, 'Bring up the curtain.'" When the curtains went up and the lights came on, the symphony crowd loved him. For the second show White invited Chris Wall, Gary P. Nunn, Jimmie Dale Gilmore, Joe Ely, and Alvin Crow. A third show featured Ray Benson and Asleep at the Wheel along with Jerry Jeff Walker.

Before every show in the series, James parked his 1954 Cadillac Coupe de Ville in the parking lot in front of the PAC and provided barbecue and beer in the courtyard. Each night, he spoke to crowds as large as thirty-two hundred people. Willie Nelson and others also served as emcees. Before each

CHAPTER 14

Joe Ely, Jimmie Dale Gilmore, Chris Wall, and Gary P. Nunn stand on the stage at Bass Concert Hall on the University of Texas at Austin campus before a performance of the "Broken Spoke Series" concert, 1990. Courtesy of Rick Henson.

performance, James often enjoyed a few shots of peppermint schnapps to summon the courage to get out onstage. Not long after the first show, he discovered a storage room filled with props backstage and quickly turned it into his makeshift dressing room complete with a star on the door. The series boosted the PAC season's ticket sales. Wadsworth introduced James to everyone she knew within the high social circles of Austin's theater culture. "She called me 'Mr. Country.' She would introduce me to 'Mr. Ballet,' or 'Mr. Orchestra,' or 'Mr. Theater,'" James says.

One night Governor Ann Richards brought journalist, novelist, and screenwriter Edwin A. "Bud" Shrake with her to see the show. Together Wadsworth, Richards, and Shrake joined Coach Royal and James onstage to present Willie Nelson with a lifetime achievement award.[8] Wadsworth and James educated the entire UT academic community about country music.

Wadsworth recalls that although UT represented the state of Texas in Austin, it had not incorporated country music into its concert program. "I was also told that the 'God of the country world' lived in Austin and ran the most famous country place in the USA—the Broken Spoke." Later when Wadsworth made plans for the PAC to operate its own bars, James invited her to come up to the Broken Spoke to learn how to bartend. "That evening I did learn that I did not want the PAC to take over its bars, but I sure had fun," Wadsworth says. Her extracurricular work drew the negative attention of UT's president at the time, Bob Gibbons. Gibbons "called me and asked me, 'Are you bartending at the Broken Spoke?' and I said, 'Yes Bob, I am. You said to provide community outreach,'" Wadsworth says. Wadsworth broke all the rules by having the best country music performers at UT.

James recalls Wadsworth telling him he could do whatever he wanted with the "Broken Spoke Series." "My wife said to Pebbles, 'Don't tell him that—there's no tellin' what the hell he might come up with.'" James and his cast of country stars never rehearsed. Wadsworth says the UT crowd initially expressed astonishment about her plans. "People would say, 'You can't do something like that on the plaza in front of Bass Concert Hall.' Because somebody says 'you can't do it,' it just made me respond, 'Oh yeah? Want to make a bet?'" Wadsworth recalls that once she established credibility with her superiors, Bass ticket sales boomed and the criticism stopped. Wadsworth often gave White family members and friends the best seats in the house, dead center in the front row. James says Wadsworth's graciousness earned his respect. "There were always people waiting in line out there to see her. I didn't know who those people were," James says. "I used to say, 'Well, I better go and let those other people see you.' She always said, 'Oh hell, I'd rather talk to you.'"

Former fine arts dean Jon Whitmore supported Wadsworth's "Broken Spoke Series." Today Whitmore remains a loyal fan of the Broken Spoke, though he lives in Iowa City, Iowa. Whitmore and his wife, Jennifer, first visited the Broken Spoke at Wadsworth's suggestion in the 1990s. He fell in love with the place because he grew up in farming and ranching country in North Dakota and had worn cowboy boots all of his life; more important, he likes country music. Whitmore says that as the Broken Spoke became important to him, it also became important to the university. On campus, the music attracted people who might not have otherwise ever visited the

Bud Shrake and Governor Ann Richards with James White backstage at Bass Concert Hall on the University of Texas at Austin campus before a performance of the "Broken Spoke Series" of concerts held throughout the 1990s. Courtesy of Rick Henson.

Broken Spoke. Before he left UT, Whitmore befriended James White. "He didn't call me by my name but called me 'the Dean,' and I liked that, actually," Whitmore says. "If somebody asks 'what's the one bar or restaurant that exemplifies Austin?,' I'd say that's the Broken Spoke. There's no doubt about it," he says.

In September 1994 Ginny began working at the Broken Spoke full-time bartending, running the front register, and waiting tables in the dining room. She quickly learned to fill the job herself when an employee didn't show up to work. Annetta also taught Ginny her favorite multigenerational family recipes. "I've learned how to make all the gravy. The first time, I called my mom and I said, 'I haven't made gravy at the Spoke—ever.' So she had to walk me through it over the phone," Ginny says. "If you know everybody's job, you learn more and then you know how to train your employees better. You know how everything runs."

The Whites' second grandchild and Terri White's youngest daughter, Mollee Jo Montague, was born July 30, 1995. Mollee Jo's earliest memories include rollerblading at the Broken Spoke with her friends on weekends as a youngster. "When I was growing up, my mom wasn't really working there a lot. We just went up there once in a while," Mollee Jo says. "Once she started working there, me and two of my friends would go up there and rollerblade and meet people. It was the place to be." She remembers two groups of people—those who regularly visited the Broken Spoke and others who became surrogate members of the White "family," usually celebrities who performed. "We didn't really sit down much. We hung out. We made friends with everyone, like the regulars who used to come in," she says. "We did the same thing every weekend. We didn't really do much else. Sometimes we would go bother the cook and we wasted a lot of food." The Broken Spoke, because it is a family business, has required all of the Whites working to keep things running smoothly for more than fifty years. Mollee Jo says her grandparents "keep the family going."

The Whites in the 1990s began providing an open bar for all of their employees each December on the Sunday before Christmas. A "bad Santa" delivered gifts for a few years. However, the gift exchange did not last long because some of the gag gifts at times offended their recipients. "We had a lot of kids coming in. We didn't want them to see a bunch of naked (plastic) body parts that some people would give as gifts." The Whites also soon tired of providing an open bar to employees. "They'd get so dang loaded that it wasn't worth doing it because nobody wanted to clean up the place afterward," James says. Bartender Ed Cook served as the Broken Spoke Santa Claus for a long time. Another hefty bartender, Jack Norman, sat on Santa's lap, and pretty soon both would fall out of the chair. "Pretty soon Santa Claus would want to sit on Jack Norman's lap," James says.

CHAPTER 15

Making Movies and Introducing New Talent

Two feature-length movies and two music videos highlighted the 1990s at the Broken Spoke, but Dolly Parton, Willie Nelson, and presidential candidate and former Texas governor George W. Bush thrust the honky-tonk into the spotlight.

In 1991, Dolly Parton and Gary Busey starred in the movie *Wild Texas Wind*, with scenes filmed at the Broken Spoke; it also featured a performance by Ray Benson and Asleep at the Wheel. Benson recalls, "When Dolly asked me to do this movie, she asked, 'Well, where's the place where you're playing?' and I told her the Broken Spoke. She said, "Well, let's film it there.' That was really neat for the Broken Spoke to have Dolly in there." The night that Parton entered the back door of the Broken Spoke, the extras in the film began shouting "Big T, Big T, Big T." The term referred to Parton's character, the struggling country performer, Thiola "Big T" Rayfield, who spends her life on the road playing bars like the Broken Spoke. Benson and others saw a double entendre in the star's nickname. "Dolly didn't understand the joke there. We kept asking her, 'Dolly, do you really want to be called 'Big T?' and she did," Benson says. Benson stands so much taller than Parton that it challenged the film crew to shoot scenes of the two stars together onstage. "They used to have to stand Dolly on a box and put me in a hole to shoot the scenes," Benson says.

In a prepared statement, Parton provided some insight about the significant place that the Broken Spoke and James White still hold in her heart. Parton wrote, "There are a few places in the world that are legendary. All entertainers know them and love to perform at those places. The Broken Spoke is one of them. James M. White is to be commended for caring for this legend. He's pretty legendary himself. It was a great thrill to work with Ray Benson and Asleep at the Wheel at the Broken Spoke while filming *Wild Texas Wind*, a TV movie I did back in 1991. We had a great time and made

Introducing New Talent 143

Dolly Parton and James White during filming of the movie Wild Texas Wind at the Broken Spoke, 1991. James White had a small speaking role. Courtesy of Rick Henson.

some wonderful memories. So thank you Broken Spoke."[1] James recalls what a thrill he felt to have Parton sing on the Broken Spoke stage. The production company hired more than two hundred extras to film the opening scenes, he says. "My little ol' speakin' part was when I came up to Ray Benson and said, 'Where's "T" at? Let's get this show on the road,' and that's about all I got to say. It was a small part, but it was exciting to do it." He had his own dressing room with a star on it that read "James White's dressing room." James recalls, "Dolly couldn't have been nicer and I got my picture taken with her. She was kind of bouncing all over and huggin' me and laughin,' smilin' so I told the photographer [Rick Henson] to take all the time he wanted to, James says." It was a great picture, and it's been on our walls for a lot of years now. I'm proud to have it."

Newcomers who arrived on the local country music scene in Austin during the 1990s began performing regularly at the Broken Spoke, including the Derailers. The band, influenced by Buck Owens and the Buckaroos, found a home at least once a month onstage at the Broken Spoke in 1995, as a refuge from their peak touring of 320 days a year. Frontman Brian Hofeldt later cowrote a song about it, "Cold Beer, Hot Women and Cool Country Music." Hofeldt and guitarist and lead singer Tony Villanueva began the band that has since produced ten albums. "One of the many interesting and unique aspects of Texas is the dance hall scene. The Broken Spoke being one of the main and greatest ones in the state of Texas. To me, it's the greatest honky-tonk in the known universe," Hofeldt says. "People come together here. You'll have patrons from eight to eighty years old. Grandparents and the whole family come. That's something unique."

Moving to Austin from Portland as a twenty-six-year-old musician felt a lot like "going to trade school," he says. The band took Austin by storm. "We were fortunate. We had a magical partnership and the timing was perfect. Country music had gotten bigger than it ever was before," he says. "That's when Ann Richards was governor. She was popular and good to musicians too. Folks at the capitol started to focus more on Texas music." Hofeldt says that he realized at the time that his and Villanueva's fortunes depended on securing a future performing at the Broken Spoke. "[James White] already knew of us; we had come in and had talked to him before and had asked him for gigs. I think Ginny White had been out to our 'Train Wreck Wednesdays' at the Continental Club and had told her daddy about that. She helped us to get in," he says. "Our once-a-month gig at the Spoke ensured that we'd be home at least once a month. So it was our saving grace really; it always has been," he says. Hofeldt recalls playing in Austin meant that "at least we got to be in our own homes one night though, two maybe, and always back here at the Broken Spoke. We were door-to-door honky-tonk salesmen."

"There's a line in our song 'Cold Beer, Hot Women and Cool Country Music' that goes, 'Got me a table with my name right on it,' and it includes a bit of James's nightly spiel: 'We've got cold beer, good music, good whiskey, home of the best chicken-fried steak in town.' So we were kind of thinkin' about that when I wrote that song with my pal, Buzz Cason," Hofeldt says. "When you're first impressed by the Broken Spoke, it hits you pretty strong." Today when the Derailers perform, James joins them onstage halfway through the night to sing a medley of Buck Owens's songs. Hofeldt says that he feels a sense of fraternity among all the stars who have performed at the Broken Spoke. "It's interesting and really cool to be part of the legendary aspect of this dance hall," he says. At the end of every Saturday night when they perform there, the Derailers sing the old Hank Williams song "I Saw the Light." "I'll say, 'It's technically Sunday morning now everyone. It's after midnight; it's technically Sunday so we'll send you out with a little gospel number.'" Hofeldt says, "My life is great, and it's due in no small part to my relationship with James and Annetta White and the Broken Spoke. It's no small part, and that's somethin' that I'm grateful for and will always keep me deeply connected to this place."

Charlie and Bruce Robison both performed at the Broken Spoke throughout the 1990s together and separately with each of their own bands from Bandera. Once, James booked all three—Charlie Robison, Bruce Robison and his wife, Kelly Willis, on the same night. "Then they started getting popular, and I would have one of them one night and then have the next one another week. They played here a long time. I have good fond memories of them," James says. Singer-songwriter Bruce Robison spent more than ten years performing weekend nights in Austin's bars, including the Broken Spoke, before he released his self-titled solo album in 1996. He and Kelly Willis have four kids and two albums that they have created together. He continues to play regularly at the Broken Spoke and finds joy in performing there. "This whole dance hall thing is kind of a dying deal. There aren't a lot of these dance halls," Bruce says. "We do some of my songs and some dance songs. It's immediate. You're playing for people to dance. It's a whole 'nother thing and part of my culture and what I grew up in. People in rural areas worked really hard and went out on the weekends and dancing. That's what they did to have fun."

Playing at the Broken Spoke reminds Robison how far he has come since leaving his roots behind twenty years ago in Bandera. "This is the only place I still play where they dance. It's a very different show than any of the other shows that I perform. We play my songs, but we also play dance songs. We play a long night. This is the way that country music used to be," Bruce says. "The Broken Spoke is just the real Texas thing." Robison says James White reminds him of the men he grew up with, including his own father, Gerald Robison, who still lives in Bandera. "In Austin, there are all kinds of hipsters. It's becoming a real metropolitan town and place. So sometimes, we feel like dinosaurs. I don't know how Mr. White feels about it, but he could

Bruce Robison, November 1, 2013.

have been a guy from Bandera, Texas," he says. "We pride ourselves on a certain kind of simplicity, and we are from the country and we're definitely proud of that." Performing in a dance hall refreshes his spirit, while the current music scene sometimes stifles him with "retail politics." As he recalls, "I kind of pulled back for a while with all the kids and family life. So now, playing music is just kind of a simple, pleasant thing—a little break between chasin' kids. It's just music for its own sake, and I don't worry about any of the problems. We've been real lucky." A prolific songwriter, Bruce Robison became well known after writing massive hits for country music stars, including George Strait, "Wrapped"; Tim McGraw, "Angry All the Time"; the Dixie Chicks, "Travelin' Soldier"; and Kelly Willis, "Not Forgotten You." He and Kelly Willis have also performed duets on two albums and continue to headline events in Austin dubbed "The Bruce and Kelly Show."

In the 1990s singer, songwriter, guitar player, actor, screenwriter, and movie producer Jesse Dayton began performing with his band at the Broken Spoke on Thursday nights. Dayton claims James represents the roots of core country music in Austin. "He's so 'old school' in terms of how he approaches everything," he says. "There'll never be another James White." Dayton often performs both public and private shows at the Broken Spoke. "There's no tellin' who's going to come in. I've had so many people from Vince Vaughn, to Luke and Owen Wilson, to the rock-and-roll band the Black Crows, to Robert Plant come in," Dayton says. Forty-seven-year-old Dayton, a Beaumont native, credits the Broken Spoke with some of the connections he has made over the years in the music business. At an early age the Beaumont native began playing guitar with some of the biggest names in country music, including Waylon Jennings, Ray Price, Johnny Bush, Willie Nelson, and Glen Campbell. He formed his own record label in 2002 and has recorded five solo albums and produced records for other artists.

Country singer, songwriter, and television personality Kevin Fowler says he thought he had found his promised land at the Broken Spoke in 1991 after moving to Austin from Amarillo. Fowler began performing at the Broken Spoke on Wednesday nights when he really was a "Panhandle Poor Boy," also the title of his hit song on his seventh album, *How Country Are Ya?* Fowler sings about growing up amid tumbleweeds, dust, and barbed wire in a merciless habitat where its residents steadfastly flourish. Since becoming famous after writing "Beer, Bait and Ammo," Fowler still sits in with other performers on special occasions at the Broken Spoke. His CD covers also feature photos taken at the Broken Spoke. Fowler joined and quit several bands before landing a gig at the Broken Spoke in 1999 and enjoys a special relationship with James and Annetta White. "From all my experiences with them they have just been huge supporters of mine and other singers and songwriters of country music," Fowler says. The Whites helped Fowler build a fan base in Austin before he ventured out into other Central Texas cities. "The Broken Spoke definitely provided the foundation. All those Wednesdays playin' in Austin taught me a lot. [Younger country singers] never really learned how to entertain, to keep a crowd goin,'" Fowler says. "A place like the Broken Spoke is really instrumental to that. It's called 'cuttin' your teeth.'"

He attributes his showmanship, wit, and positive onstage energy to the years spent in training at the Broken Spoke and growing up in Austin, the "greatest place on earth. "You look at George Strait, Willie Nelson, Jerry Jeff Walker—you name it, they played the Broken Spoke while comin' up through the ranks. Everybody nearly, you name it—it's multigenerational, really," Fowler says. "It doesn't matter wherever I go—Nashville or New York, or wherever—if I tell somebody I'm from Austin, they say, 'Oh, the Broken Spoke.'" The recording artist has released seven albums with four singles that have appeared on Billboard's Hot Country Singles charts.

Sixty-eight-year-old singer, songwriter, and actor Jimmie Dale Gilmore remembers starting his solo career performing as a country roots artist at the Broken Spoke regularly in 1990. Earlier in his career during the 1970s he was a member of the Flatlanders, with Joe Ely and Butch Handcock. Gilmore's musical history stretches to Austin's glory days, shared with other legendary folk, country, blues, and rock-and-roll bands. The first place he and his T. Nickel House Band ever played in Austin was Threadgill's. Gilmore also played in Angela Strehli's band, Sunnyland Special, in the late 1960s long before her name became associated with Marcia Ball, Lou Ann Barton, Sue Foley, and Stevie Ray Vaughan. He played for years at other equally legendary venues. Gilmore's band, the Hub City Movers, first opened the Dillo in 1970 and became the last house band to perform at the Vulcan Gas Company. Gilmore has always felt at home performing at the Broken Spoke. "I have a lot of good memories of the Broken Spoke and the great dancing there," Gilmore says. "James White early on was a great supporter of mine before I became known nationally."

Monte Warden began performing at the Broken Spoke in 1991. For thirty-five years he has written songs recorded by the Wagoneers and other country music Hall of Famers while performing solo occasionally at the Broken Spoke. George Strait, Kelly Willis, Patty Loveless, Travis Tritt, Emmylou Harris, and others have recorded his songs. The Wagoneers reunited briefly in 2011, the same year they were inducted in the Texas Music Hall of Fame.[2] They had been formed with the help of Buddy Holly's widow, María Elena Holly, whom Warden had met while attending a horse show. Warden became inspired to write songs at an early age after hearing his first Buddy Holly song and doing research on the legendary Lubbock songwriter. His father gave him his first guitar, a 1963 C. F. Martin & Company D-18, which Warden still plays to this day.

Warden treasures his memories performing at the Broken Spoke, but one night stands out in particular—the same night that former football all-star and actor O. J. Simpson rode as a passenger in a white Ford Bronco driven by friend, Al Cowlings. As the two led twenty police cars on a crawling chase along the interstate south of Los Angeles, at the Broken Spoke patrons crowded around a wide-screen TV in the dining room to watch the live newscast. "It was one of the weirdest, wildest gigs I ever played," Warden says. "The O. J. thing was still going on when we took the stage. Some people started to wander in a little bit." Dancers began filing into the dance hall only after Simpson finally surrendered. More than a thousand people came and went through the front door that night. "I even talked about it from the stage, saying, 'Was that weird?'" The Wagoneers never performed at the Broken Spoke, though throughout the 1990s some of its members performed in Dale Watson's band. White never required Warden to play in the Broken Spoke dining room before he performed in the dance hall, as most other singers and songwriters have done.

George W. Bush held one of his presidential election campaign parties at the Broken Spoke in 1999. A photo taken of Bush while he served as governor of Texas hangs in the dining room of the Broken Spoke near the front door. In June 1999, after Bush delivered his first campaign speech as a presidential candidate, he celebrated with his staff at the Broken Spoke, James recalls.

Former Longhorn Coach Mack Brown remembers visiting the Broken Spoke in 1999 when Chris Wall performed. "Took my mom and my wife, Sally, there. Chris was great and Mom two-stepped with everyone there. We had a blast," Brown stated in a prepared statement.[3] Brown says it is no secret why the Broken Spoke has remained an Austin landmark for nearly fifty years. "It's Texas. Warm, friendly and fun." Brown fondly remembers meeting James White. "He came over and reached out to us. He was very friendly. Took pictures and made us feel at home," Brown says. Whenever anyone visits Austin, Brown says he always recommends a trip to the Broken Spoke. "It is the grass roots of Austin, Texas country music. If you like country music, you must go to the Broken Spoke—should be a requirement," he says. "It is what a Texas Dance Hall is all about. Everyone needs to experience it. I loved meeting James and Chris. They are all Texas," Brown says.

Governor George W. Bush, Annetta and James White, and Alvin Crow celebrate at Bush's presidential campaign party held at the Broken Spoke, 1999. Courtesy of Rick Henson.

Governor George W. Bush with Annetta and James White at Bush's presidential campaign party held at the Broken Spoke, 1999. Courtesy of Rick Henson.

Introducing New Talent

James White and Chris Wall stand with former Longhorn football coach Mack Brown in an undated photo from 2001. Brown has remained a faithful patron of the Broken Spoke. Courtesy of Rick Henson.

Before Austinite Rick Trevino won a Grammy award for "Best Mexican-American Musical Performance" with Los Super Seven in 1999, he began performing at the Broken Spoke. Los Super Seven included the legendary Hispanic stars Freddie Fender, Flaco Jiménez, David Hidalgo, and Cesar Rosas. "Rick got his start right here at the Broken Spoke. I had him during the week before he started college down at Texas A&M. I used to call him 'Ricky,' before he shortened it to Rick," James says. "He would get up onstage, and his mother did the booking and sold T-shirts, and his daddy would run the sound system from a table out front by the bandstand. He would also harmonize with his son." James recalls that Trevino told him the first time he performed at the Broken Spoke he would bring a brand-new full band with him. The Whites took out a large advertisement in the local newspaper to advertise his show. "Ricky called me up at about three o'clock that afternoon, and he said, 'Mr. White, I'm sorry, but I haven't got my band together yet.' I told him, 'Aw, hell, you've got five hours; you ought to be able to put a band together by then in Austin, Texas.' So I put him to the test, and he passed it.

He's got a great voice, and he sang out here a lot. I'm glad he was a big star in Nashville. I'll never forget when he came home from A&M, he had himself a maroon-colored pickup truck and he was real proud of that." James recalls that Trevino also met his current tour manager at the Broken Spoke. "Ricky's manager-to-be told me, 'I met Rick Trevino right here at the Broken Spoke; I met him in the men's restroom back there. While we were doin' our business, I introduced myself. Now I'm bookin' Rick Trevino," James says. Trevino has recorded seven albums with 14 singles that have appeared on Billboard's Hot Country Singles charts. His single "Running out of Reasons to Run" spent a week at number 1 in 1997.[4]

Abilene native singer-songwriter Lee Roy Parnell performed his top-five hits from country music charts and some cover songs at the Broken Spoke at the end of the 1990s. James recalls, "I've got a picture of Lee Roy Parnell hanging above the TV with him and Sammy Allred, Jerry Jeff Walker, Junior Brown, and the Geezinslaws all sittin' around at a round table." Parnell married Kerry Pryor, the daughter of the late Austin broadcast personality Richard S. "Cactus" Pryor. Apparently, Parnell wanted to even an old score with Jerry Jeff Walker during a television interview recorded at the Broken Spoke. While Allred, Walker, and Brown sat at one of the round tables, Parnell raised an awkward question, as James recalls. "All of a sudden Parnell got out of his chair. He took off Jerry Jeff's hat. Then he asked Jerry Jeff, 'Do you remember that first time I met you and you took my hat off?' Jerry Jeff kind of just looked at him." Parnell set Walker's hat on top of the table and then stomped on it. "Then he said, 'This is what you did to my hat when I first met you.' Jerry Jeff didn't know what to say," James says. Walker did not respond with anger; the two remain friends to this day. Parnell spent more than ten years performing in Austin, Houston, Dallas, and Fort Worth before moving to Nashville in 1987 and landing a recording contract. His most famous hits include "What Kind of Fool Do You Think I Am?" and "Tender Moment."[5]

Onstage at the Broken Spoke in 1990, Republican gubernatorial nominee Clayton "Claytie" Williams announced his race against Democratic State Treasurer Ann Richards for the governorship of Texas.[6] Williams announced his candidacy on Speaker's Night while some of the best-known politicians and lobbyists in town gathered to party and to carouse, James recalls. "Claytie was there with his campaign manager, and they got to drinking," James says. "When finally, he said, 'Well, hell I'm gonna announce for governor tonight.'" Clayton took the stage to sing two songs with the Geezinslaws. In August 1990 Williams led the governor's race by a narrow margin with his "good old boy" campaign, but he eventually lost to Richards after a public gaffe regarding the subject of rape and for refusing to shake Richards's hand during a public debate.[7]

The "Queen of Country Music," Kitty Wells, once sang at the Broken Spoke in 1993 after receiving a Grammy Lifetime Achievement Award two years earlier. About that time, Dolly Parton, Loretta Lynn, and Tammy Wynette collaborated to record the album *Honky Tonk Angels*, which featured Wells as a guest vocalist. Wells had earned the nickname "the Neon Angel" after releasing the song "It Wasn't God Who Made Honky-Tonk Angels" in 1952. The lyrics raised controversy, and the song, banned in some places, became the first number-1 hit by a female artist on *Billboard*'s Hot Country Singles chart. Her husband, Johnnie Wright, and their son, Bobby, also sang onstage with Wells the night she headlined at the Broken Spoke. Before Bobby Wright became a singer, he played Willy Moss on the TV show *McHale's Navy* during its entire run from 1962 until 1966.[8]

West Texas oilman and politician Clayton Williams sings "El Rancho Grande" with the Geezinslaws, 1990. Courtesy of Annetta White.

The US first lady from 1963 until 1969, Claudia Alta "Lady Bird" Johnson, visited the Broken Spoke in the 1990s with her daughter Lynda Johnson-Robb and granddaughter Jennifer Robb, accompanied by a US Secret Service bodyguard. The three had arrived about 9:00 p.m., around the time that the band had finished performing a sound test on their equipment. "I was able to get a picture with me and Lady Bird," James says. "She just went over and told the Secret Service guy, 'I'm gonna be standin' right over there talkin' with the owner for a bit and we're gonna get our picture taken.' She was very nice." The two talked for a bit, but not for long because Lady Bird interrupted James's nostalgic storytelling to ask when the band would start playing. "She just kind of blurted it out, sayin', 'Well, when's the band gonna get started? When is the music starting?' It was kind of like she wanted to dance, she was tired of waitin,' and she wanted to hear the music," James says. "It was a fun night. They had a lot of the family members out here and it went over real well." She became a lifelong advocate of the beautification of Texas roadways and cofounded the National Wildflower Research Center in Austin, which was later renamed in her honor.[9]

Country music artist Jack Ingram first performed at the Broken Spoke during South by Southwest in March 1999. Nine years later he won the 2008 Academy of Country Music award for "Best New Male Vocalist," after releasing his *That's a Man* album. Ingram also performed at two of the Broken Spoke's anniversary celebrations, its fiftieth in 2014 and again on its fifty-first. He performed with both Pauline Reese and Jerry Jeff Walker. "This is one of my favorite spots—hanging out at the Broken Spoke," Ingram said during the latter celebrations. "This place is home to every musician in Texas, more importantly to everybody in Austin. It's been home for me on the nights I've played here. Every time I pass by here when I'm on the road, it feels like I'm passing my old haunts."

Jeff Hughes, frontman for the Chaparral band, has played with a who's who list of Broken Spoke veteran musicians over the past three decades. "It's changed over the years, and I've got some people now that I started out with." Hughes turns rock-and-roll songs, "Don't Go Back to Rockville" by R.E.M. or "Just Like Heaven" by the Cure, into country shuffles. "It ['Just Like Heaven'] gets them out on the dance floor probably faster than any other song that we play," Hughes says. A version of "Sweet Child o' Mine" by Guns N' Roses becomes a two-step when Hughes plays it. He also sings

"Fade into You" by Mazzy Star. Hughes feels grateful to the Whites and to Broken Spoke fans for remaining constant supporters throughout his music career. Hughes also sings a lot of 1960s country—everything from George Jones to Buck Owens. He sings some 1970s covers by Conway Twitty, and Canadian pop folk singer Gordon Lightfoot. He also performs some of the most obscure songs by Johnny Cash and others including local favorite Johnny Horton, who died in 1960 following a performance in Austin. Hughes remembers one special night in the 1990s when Johnny Rodriguez performed at the Broken Spoke. Rodriguez's 1973 debut hit single "Pass Me By (If You're Only Passing Through)" became the first of fourteen consecutive singles to make the top-ten country music charts.[10] "James came up to me and said, 'Man, Johnny Rodriguez is here,'" Hughes says. Rodriguez and Hughes traded verses onstage that night as James watched proudly.

PART VI

The 2000s

CHAPTER 16

Movie and Music Mecca

When the recession struck, the nation's economy took a nosedive during the early 2000s, and Austin's tech industry suffered greatly from layoffs and job reductions, but the city suddenly became attractive to filmmakers, who found enthusiastic followers and tax incentives to make their movies here. In 2000 Austin Studios began welcoming moviemakers to its twenty-acre site as a full-service, fully equipped production center.[1] Three annual events—South by Southwest, Austin Film Festival, and Austin Film Society's Texas Film Awards—also helped increase Austin's status worldwide as a mecca both for both filmmakers and musicians. TV production crews came to town regularly to film, including the 2006 pilot team for the NBC TV series *Friday Night Lights*.[2] Mayor Will Wynn also generated interest in the city as a movie hub while serving in a leadership position for the US Conference of Mayors. When the PBS show *This Old House* filmed near Austin as part of a 2007 episode, he invited the cast to visit the Broken Spoke.[3] "As they pulled into the parking lot, James White is standing at the front door, and he says, 'I ain't changin' nothin.'" It was so perfect. They just wanted to go in and drink beer and listen to Dale Watson or somebody, but James thought I had sent the crew down there to finally insulate the Broken Spoke," Wynn says. Musicians also recorded two songs with the honky-tonk named in the lyrics and created a CD about the Broken Spoke while still others made several music videos inside its hallowed halls.

CHAPTER 17

Sale of the Land and a Rash of Health Issues

The Broken Spoke's landlord, former Austin city council member Jay Lynn Johnson Jr., died July 26, 2001. His children then began a nearly ten-year search to find just the right buyer for the family's land. The eldest child, Julie Johnson, remembers making the difficult decision to sell: "We decided to make a stipulation in the sale so that whoever bought it would keep the Broken Spoke and not bulldoze it." Meanwhile, a series of health issues plagued both James and Annetta and temporarily disrupted their roles at the Broken Spoke throughout the 2000s. First James suffered heart problems; then doctors diagnosed Annetta with breast cancer, and she underwent a mastectomy, chemotherapy, and radiation.

In August 2001 as James White lay in a bed at Austin Heart Hospital suffering from severe chest pains, he felt discouraged. He worried that he might lose everything he loved in the world: his family and friends, his ranch, and his beloved Broken Spoke. It did not soothe him to know that he had scheduled two of his favorite bands to play on the bandstand that weekend: the Derailers and Gary P. Nunn. He did not want to miss their performances. Feeling as vulnerable as he had ever felt before in his life, James began to pray that he would not miss any future weekends at the Broken Spoke. He prayed that he would feel well enough to walk his daughter Ginny down the aisle at her wedding and to someday see her future children enter school. He prayed that he would rise up out of his hospital bed, put on his western clothes, and finish what he had started at the Broken Spoke in 1964. He prayed that he would live long enough to see the Broken Spoke become the best dance hall in Austin, Texas, and world renowned for its live country music, the best dancing, and good food. He underwent a heart catheterization procedure to determine the specific problems with his heart, and doctors prescribed blood pressure medication.

After Austin Heart Hospital admitted James, Annetta received a phone call from an employee at the Broken Spoke who told her that Ginny also needed her help. As Ginny recalls, "My dad is everything to me, so it was a combination of probably being immature and not being able to grasp the magnitude of the situation, but it was really hard for me the first time he got sick—it's still hard for me." Ginny started drinking and did not stop that day until she fell asleep on the dance floor. When Annetta arrived, she threw a bucket of ice water on her daughter. Ginny realizes now that she used the wrong coping skills to deal with her father's poor health. "It really just came down to the fact that it was just hard for me to deal with the reality of the situation. When you're younger, you don't really know how to deal with those kinds of things, so you end up doing something incredibly stupid like that," she says.

Annetta underwent her first chemo treatment for breast cancer the day before the Broken Spoke's forty-first anniversary party on November 10, 2004. The Whites did not possess health insurance at the time. Annetta recalls a tense exchange with her oncologist, Dr. Dudley Youman. "I said, 'I'm not going to spend James's and my retirement money on me.'" Ever the nuts and bolts pragmatist, she continued, "I'm a big girl and I can deal with it. I can accept it if you can't save me." Youman had diagnosed Annetta with stage III inflammatory breast cancer and determined after surgery that it had not spread. Within months Annetta's cancer had gone into remission and has never returned. Youman to this day remains a family friend and faithful patron of the Broken Spoke. Terri helped out by preparing soup and soft foods and created velvet hats for Annetta to wear after she lost her hair. Ginny worried that she might lose her mom. "She's a tough lady. Like the band guys say, 'She kicked cancer's ass,'" Ginny says. She pitched in and learned how to book and to manage parties at the Broken Spoke for three hundred to four hundred people. Ginny also helped to make the barbecue and sometimes worked between twelve and eighteen hours a day. Terri and Ginny and her husband, Mike Peacock, all helped keep the Broken Spoke up and running smoothly during Annetta's absence. Annetta recalls, "I couldn't have made it through cancer without them; they really chipped in and took over."

Ginny had met Mike in 2005 one night while playing poker on the Internet while he still lived in England. He came to the United States for the sole purpose of courting Ginny, and they decided to marry after just two visits.

"I told him, 'I'm not moving—I see my parents every day. If that's okay with you, then we can keep seeing each other,'" she says. "He's thirteen years older than me, and he's a lot more mature, stable—and he lets me be the boss and he's made me a better person." The couple married on July 23, 2006. "After we married, we did all the legal paperwork so he could go for his citizenship. We 'Tex-ified' him," she says. These days Mike often wears a Resistol white straw hat, black T-shirt, Wranglers, and rawhide boots when he tends bar or collects the cover charges at the door to the dance hall, but he has retained his strong British accent. "We've got two great kids, and I married into a great family," Mike says. "My brother [Gary] followed me over here, and my mom lost both her sons to Texas. There must be something to be said about livin' in Texas."

Gary Peacock has worked on the Whites' ranch and occasionally subs at the door at the Broken Spoke taking cover charges. He seldom has time to explain his British accent to visitors. Gary says, "It can be quite tiring at times when you handle two hours of people nonstop like a production line. Once it slows down, you get to enjoy it and look around and watch people getting on and enjoying themselves." He's seen all kinds of things at the Broken Spoke. "I've seen some silly things and things that people have done that they shouldn't do," he says while pretending to zip his lips shut to avoid elaborating.

After recuperating from his hospital stay, James began dressing in more glamorous cowboy wear whenever he appeared at the Broken Spoke. Ginny embellished her father's floral western shirts with half-moon pockets in beads and natural stone settings at the yokes and collars, and added piping and fringe on the sleeves. The Whites took their inspiration from vintage western suits encased in glass within the dining room at the Broken Spoke. The handmade clothing had been created by two famous California tailors, Nathan Turk and Nudie Cohn, and had been handed down to James by his father, Bruce Lamar White, who had once been their customer. Turk's clientele also included famous country singers and actors Tom Mix, Gene Autry, Roy Rogers, John Wayne, Ernest Tubb, Hank Thompson, and Buck Owens.

Nudie Cohn, beginning in the 1940s, embellished clothing and automobiles for some of Hollywood's top celebrities and Nashville's western stars. During the 1950s, Cohn set up Nudie's Rodeo Tailors shop and became famous for his custom-made wardrobes not only for movie stars but also for country music stars like Hank Williams, Roy Rogers, and Gene Autry. Cohn also designed complete cars for his customers.[1] "[He put] western pistol door handles and silver dollars all over the dashboard, and he also put steer horns on the hood," James says. James still displays a Nudie Cohn suit and a Takamine acoustic guitar in a two-way glass case between the dining room and the game room at the Broken Spoke. Some of the stars over the years that have performed in the dance hall have signed the guitar include Ray Price, Don Walser, and Willie Nelson.

James White also cherishes the beautiful black leather saddle with silver-encrusted details that once belonged to his late father. More than twenty years ago, James placed the saddle inside its own protective glass display case and installed a security alarm. The saddle was custom-made by Hollywood Saddlery, once the maker of leather goods for Bob Wills, Gene Autry, and Roy Rogers and credited with helping to create the movie star cowboy image.[2]

In the early-morning hours of Thanksgiving 2000, thieves broke into the Broken Spoke to steal James's most cherished western possession.[3] "They broke out the front window, crawled through the ripped screen and jagged glass, and then they came over and busted out the glass inside the protective frame," he says. An officer later told James that he had mistaken Rowdy, the Broken Spoke's resident mannequin cowboy, for a burglar. After police left, the Whites sat down to celebrate Thanksgiving dinner at home. The next morning James called police again and radio station KVET, who reported the story. Then he called the *Austin American Statesman*. Pretty soon the town's media buzzed with details of the crime.

On the Monday following the burglary, James again called the police and then Mayor Will Wynn. Detective Dennis Clark told James that police had located a female witness to the crime. James volunteered to wear a wire while he and police interviewed the woman. The woman told police where the suspect had parked his car; however, by the time the detectives obtained a search warrant, the car had been towed. Detectives eventually were able to search the suspect's car and found James's saddle in the trunk. James said he was really glad to get his saddle back before Christmas.

In 2005 James recorded on his own record label, Broken Spoke Records, and released his own solo CD, *The Broken Spoke Legend*. Rick Henson took the photo for the CD's cover, which featured James standing against a vintage wagon wheel in the dirt parking lot of the Spoke. Musicians who performed on the album included Jason Crow on bass; Alvin Crow on fiddle, guitar, drums, rubboard, and background vocals; Neil Flanz and Herb Steiner on steel guitars; Earl Poole Ball on piano; John X. Reed, who goes by the nickname "Johnny X," on lead guitar; with Jon Chandler on drums, Micah Ater on bass, and Eric Hokkanen and Will Knack on guitar. Crow served as the master sound engineer. James wrote six of the album's ten songs, but he also sang four covers. James recalls, "That sound engineer [Alvin Crow] had me an iced-down half pint of peppermint schnapps that day in the recording studio." James nailed the song recordings on the first take. "Therefore, they started calling me 'one-take White,'" he says. That same year Crow recorded another album, *Honky-Tonk Trail*, on the Broken Spoke label featuring another of James's songs, "Dance with Who Brung You," inspired by UT Longhorn Coach Darrell Royal. Well into his retirement, Royal continued to visit the Broken Spoke. James recalls, "He loved the Broken Spoke. He had a saying when he got tired of people askin' him before a big game,

James White, the late Longhorn football coach Darrell Royal, Chris Wall, and UT baseball coach Augie Garrido following a performance by Kinky Friedman and Billy Joe Shaver, 2001. Courtesy of Rick Henson.

'Who you gonna start at quarterback?' He'd say, 'I'm gonna' dance with who brung me.'"

Mike and Ginny Peacock's first child, James Lamar, was born July 25, 2007. Ginny named him both after her grandfather, Bruce Lamar White Sr., and her father, James White. Willie Nelson held James Lamar at just six months old in 2007 at the Broken Spoke; the photo hangs near the doorway of the Tourist Trap. Today James Lamar attends Patton Elementary School, named after his great-great-great grandfather, James Andrew Patton.

CHAPTER 18

The Dixie Chicks, Kinky Friedman, Ray Price, and a Bus Crash

Mark Stuart, founder of the Bastard Sons of Johnny Cash (BSOJC) band (the late Johnny Cash actually gave his approval to use his name before he passed), performed for the first time at the Broken Spoke in 2000 during SXSW, along with Willie Nelson's daughter Paula. When his booking agent first arranged the gig, Stuart, a native of San Diego, worried that the Broken Spoke might be a bit out of their league. In those days, he and his band members changed clothes in the parking lot or in the Broken Spoke bathroom before their gigs. They had just recorded their first album, *Walk Alone*. However, fans in the audience immediately recognized their songs. "I have to say that we were pretty surprised by the reactions," Stuart says. Since then, the BSOJC has released five other albums.

Grammy-nominated hit maker Pat Green performed at the Broken Spoke with a band called Cooder Graw during SXSW in 2000. The band, formed in 1998, became an overnight sensation with the release of their hit single "Llano Estacado," which later also provided the sound track for several Dodge commercials. Green has since graced stages with the likes of country stars Keith Urban and Kenny Chesney. "That was probably one of the better bands that I booked, Cooder Graw and Pat Green along with Ray Benson and Asleep at the Wheel. They delivered real good for me," James says. "They all went on to be famous, and most of them were famous already." Green has recorded ten studio albums and has been nominated three times for a Grammy Award. Fifteen of his singles have appeared on *Billboard*'s Hot Country Singles charts, including "Wave on Wave," which reached number 3 in 2003.[1]

James began booking the San Antonio–based group Two Tons of Steel in 2000, and the band has continued to perform regularly at the Broken Spoke for the past sixteen years. Two Tons of Steel made the cover of Bill-

Ray Benson performs with the Asleep at the Wheel, June 27, 2014.

board magazine in 1996 and appeared in the IMAX film *Texas: The Big Picture*. Band members include Kevin Geil, lead vocalist and guitarist; Jake "Sidecar" Marchese on upright bass; Brian Duarte on lead guitar; and Paul Ward on drums. Geil calls the Broken Spoke "the Holy Grail to people of Europe when they want to come to the United States to see a real honky-tonk. It's a legendary place when you're talking about honky-tonks." One night Geil suffered a serious accident on the three-level wooden platform stage, which has less than a six-foot clearance below the low ceiling. Geil hit his head hard enough that he blacked out for a few minutes. "The most important thing to remember if you ever perform at the Broken Spoke is, if you're over six feet tall, don't stand up on the stage or the drum riser," he says. Minutes after Geil awoke from his injury, he performed. The band released the song Gail wrote "Hell Cat," in a 2011 music video featuring Terri White teaching dance lessons at the Broken Spoke. It quickly became an Internet sensation. Seventy-two-year-old Steel Hall of Famer Denny Mathis has sat in onstage with Two Tons of Steel.

Country/bluegrass singer and songwriter James "Slim" Hand first visited the Broken Spoke at age eighteen but performed there in 2003, when he sat onstage with Alvin Crow to launch a music career at age fifty-two. Hand sang "Fraulein," a 1957 song written by Lawton Williams and also recorded

Two Tons of Steel, fronted by Kevin Geil, August 30, 2014.

by Jerry Lee Lewis in 1969. He later held release parties at the Broken Spoke for his first nationally distributed 2006 CD, *The Truth Will Set You Free*, and his 2009 *Shadow on the Ground* album. Hand would promote *Stormclouds in Heaven* Sept. 9, 2014 at the Broken Spoke by performing all of the gospel-inspired songs he wrote for the CD. Hand says James White has never met a stranger; he treats everyone who visits or performs at the Broken Spoke like a celebrity. Hand feels indebted to James for all he has done for him over the years. "There were a couple of times that I didn't have enough money to really pay the band. Mr. White just put it in my hand. You can't beat that," Hand says. To paraphrase a James White analogy, Hand compared the Broken Spoke to America's favorite fast-food sandwich. "It's like a hamburger. A hamburger has got lettuce, tomato, pickles, and a hamburger patty and mayonnaise and mustard. The more you try to frill it up, or put somethin' on it, or add this or take somethin' away, it destroys the integrity of it," Hand says. "The gist of it is, people want to be part of something good. That's what they want to do. They want to go where they're happy and to be around happy people. If it wasn't that way, the Broken Spoke wouldn't be there. That's all there is to it." After touring the United States, the United Kingdom, and Europe and performing at the Grand Ole Opry, the Waco native has recently been recording his original songs for an album to be published by Hillgrass Bluebilly Records.

Actor Robert Duvall began visiting the Broken Spoke in 2003 during breaks in production for the movie *Secondhand Lions*, a comedy and drama written and directed by Tim McCanlies. The film starred Duvall and Michael Caine, who both portrayed bachelor uncles who live on a Texas farm in the 1960s and for the summer take in a nephew, played by actor Haley Joel Osment. All three actors visited the Broken Spoke during their off hours. Duvall continued to visit sporadically over the years. "I like the Broken Spoke. I've been coming here for years to eat food and dance. I even danced the tango over here and did the two-step and everything," Duvall said in a recorded statement. "This is a great place, the Broken Spoke. The Broken Spoke is the place."[2]

Renowned Southwest artist Amado Peña celebrated both his sixtieth and seventieth birthdays at the Broken Spoke in 2003 and in 2013, respectively. On his sixtieth birthday, his personal friend José María De León Hernández, better known as "Little Joe," and his band La Familia performed with actor

James Hand performs at the release party for his album Stormclouds in Heaven, *September 9, 2014.*

Lou Diamond Phillips. "When my family asked me, 'What do you want to do for your birthday?', the first thing that came to my mind was the Broken Spoke," Peña says. "I love country music—it's like my favorite music, but I very seldom venture out on my own to go to a honky-tonk at all. One day I just decided when I was a bachelor to come here. I had always heard about the Broken Spoke." Peña, a Mestizo of Mexican and Yaqui ancestry, lives among the descendants of the Anasazi near the small Nambé Oweenge Pueblo north of Santa Fe, New Mexico. However, Peña considers Texas his second home; he grew up in Laredo along the Texas-Mexico border and began his professional life as a painter nearly forty years ago in Austin. He first visited the Broken Spoke to see Alvin Crow and the Pleasant Valley Boys perform, and he soon became friends with James White. "He's one of those very special people. I feel so comfortable when I'm here," Peña says. "You read about historical places, but when you walk in here, you can tell that it hasn't changed much."

The Geezinslaws tour bus crashed through the back wall of the Broken Spoke on October 2, 2005, about 1:30 a.m., right after the band finished performing for the night.[3] "I had just stepped off the bus," their keyboard player Larry Telford says. "No one really knows what happened before the bus went through the wall." A pile of dirt located in front of the business created somewhat of a ramp that helped propel the bus through the wall, where it wedged up under the roof and remained stuck for four days, Telford says. "It's a wonder the driver wasn't decapitated. It was really serious." Austin firefighters had to lift the band members out through the safety hatch in the roof of the bus. Indoors, a mural and news clippings about the event still honor the spot where a construction crew eventually removed the bus and repaired the hole in the wall.

Several times throughout the 2000s, James also booked the biggest-selling female band of all time, the Dixie Chicks.[4] Sisters Martie and Emily Erwin, together with Natalie Maines, performed at the Broken Spoke both before and after the western-themed bluegrass band released their 1998 debut album, *Wide Open Spaces*. They continued to make appearances after winning a 2007 Grammy for *Taking the Long Way* and "Best Country Performance by a Group" for the song "Not Ready to Make Nice." Maines alone would also return to the Broken Spoke to film a music video in 2013 for her solo album, *Mother*. "They really got popular—big time," James says. "I was able to get Natalie out here also, and one time, they came out here

James White inspects the damage after the Geezinslaws' tour bus crashed through the south wall of the Broken Spoke within hours after the band finished their performance, October 2, 2005. Courtesy of Rick Henson.

with a crew to film a video. The crew filmed Natalie entering and exiting the Broken Spoke and also wanted her to drive James's 1954 Coupe de Ville Cadillac, but he did not like the idea. "I am very fond of my old Cadillac, and it's got a little bit of play in the wheel, and I can't afford to have anything bad happen to it. So when they first suggested Natalie drive, I kind of imagined that she might have kind of a lead foot and she might want to stomp the pedal to the metal. So I sort of changed the subject." James figures he was able to book the Dixie Chicks as often as he did because Natalie's father, Lloyd Maines, a Grammy Award–winning producer and multi-instrumentalist who hails from Lubbock, lives in Austin.

The Dixie Chicks soon outgrew James's price range for bookings at the Broken Spoke. The Chicks also became embroiled in a controversy when Natalie Maines told a London audience that she felt "ashamed" of fellow Texan and then-president George W. Bush. She made the statement the night before the US military invaded Iraq on March 19, 2003. Radio station producers retaliated by refusing to play the band's music,[5] and the women remained in seclusion for three years. Although the band earned the album and song of the year at the February 2007 Grammy Awards, some stations still shunned their music.[6]

Musician, actor, writer, and politician Kinky Friedman ran for Texas governor as an independent in 2006 and held his kickoff party at the Broken Spoke. "When you have a campaign party for Kinky Friedman, that's kind of going out there on a limb a little bit," Friedman says. "I like the feeling of the place. I always have. I'd like the Spoke to stay just like it is, but it probably won't be able to. It's been a fixed point in a changing world. As Joseph Heller says, 'Every change is for the worse.' It's really true of Austin. I call Austin 'Dallas with guitars.' That's pretty much what it seems to have become to me." Friedman says the Broken Spoke represents the very best of Austin's music and cultural history. "James White's place is a cathedral. The ceilings seem pretty low for a cathedral, but the people who have played there, it's staggering. It has a rich emotional history of country music; a parade of country musicians marched through there. James took a lot of chances. I think playing at the Spoke was always an interesting event for that reason. Not only has everybody that I love and admire in country music played there, but also he's tried a lot of different things. He's mixed it up pretty good."

James White, Billy Joe Shaver, Chris Wall, and Kinky Friedman during the "Two Moving Parts" tour, 2001. Courtesy of Rick Henson.

Billy Joe Shaver sings with Kinky Friedman during their "Two Moving Parts" tour, 2001. Courtesy of Rick Henson.

The latter statement could well be said about Friedman, who recorded fourteen albums from the 1970s to 2015. He also wrote several fiction and nonfiction books and finished fourth in the race for Texas governor in 2006.⁷ Like the Broken Spoke, Friedman remains immutable. "The Spoke really is a timeless kind of a place," Friedman says. "You can really walk in there and walk back in time, to a time—at least for country music, when the world was a better place. Country music is like a lost art. It's like letter writing; people don't do it anymore. It just disappeared like travel agents, like doctors driving Buicks. It doesn't happen anymore. The same thing has happened to Hollywood. James has held the line very well and still been open to new ideas. He's had people in there that didn't fit the mold, but the place is really established and it's an important part of what Austin used to be and hopefully what it will be again," he says. He says James "has real staying power. Maybe he should get into politics."

James paid legendary singer-songwriter and guitarist Ray Price $12,500 to perform at the Broken Spoke in 2001 during one of the lowest points in the country crooner's career, which spanned sixty-five years. "He had his piano player, Blondie [Moises Calderon], with him. Ray Price guaranteed two different forty-five-minute sets with an autograph session in between," James says. Unlike Price's early days with the Cherokee Cowboys, who all dressed western with fringe and rhinestones on their jackets, Price wore a tuxedo onstage at the Broken Spoke. James rented a piano and paid to have it tuned before and after the show. "So it cost me a lot of time and overhead. That was the last time I rented a piano; it's such a hassle, but I was very happy to book Ray Price," he says. "He sang a lot of good shuffles that folks liked to two-step to." Price's first hit, "Crazy Arms," in 1956 had created a sound that became known as the "Ray Price Shuffle."⁸

James says Price disliked singing drinking songs about cheating and fighting. Price, often called "the Frank Sinatra of country music," became famous for his smooth tenor voice and singing romantic and nostalgic songs such his definitive hit, penned by Kris Kristofferson, "For the Good Times." Price also discovered and added to his Cherokee Cowboys band in 1963 musicians who became stars in their own right: Buddy Emmons, Donald Lytle, aka: Donnie Young ("Johnny Paycheck"), Roger Miller, Willie Nelson, Johnny Bush, and Darrell McCall. In 2006, his *Last of the Breed* album rejuvenated his career, featuring friends Merle Haggard and Willie

Nelson.⁹ The Country Music Hall of Fame inducted Price in 1996, and the star continued to record well into his eighties before dying of cancer at the age of eighty-seven in 2013.

Country singer and songwriter Pauline Reese may have been the first person ever to ride her horse, Blue Diamond, through the back door of the Broken Spoke in 2008. "I had ridden her into a few bars over the years, but most of them had a big door," Reese says. "At the Spoke I had to get off of the horse, take her in, then get back on for the cameras." The plan worked, because afterward Reese earned a brief residency at the Broken Spoke. At sixteen she played at the Broken Spoke for the first time for the Texas Music Awards. The Whites welcomed Reese with open arms. "One of my goals was to get my picture on the wall with Dolly Parton, George Strait, and all of the others." She also performed at Amado Peña's fiftieth and sixtieth birthday parties. Reese has recorded seven albums to date and has built a repu-

Legendary singer-songwriter and guitarist Ray Price, who enjoyed a country music career that spanned sixty-five years, performed at the Broken Spoke in the late 1990s with his band, the Cherokee Cowboys. Courtesy of Rick Henson.

tation as a singer-songwriter among some of Austin's most elite celebrity performers and songwriters, including Willie Nelson.

James White appeared in a television commercial celebrating the hundredth anniversary of the HEB grocery chain in 2004. "All I had to do was to say real quick, 'Happy one-hundredth birthday, HEB.' Then Ray Benson of Asleep at the Wheel got in the commercial also." That night, James White also met Charles Butt, the CEO of HEB, one of Texas' largest grocery chains. His parents, Howard Edward and Florence Butt, founded the stores in Kerrville in 1905, and by 1995, the grocery chain owned 224 stores throughout Texas.[10] "Mr. Butt thanked me and said I was the best one in the commercial," James says with pride.

Also in 2004 little-known bands such as Roger Creager, Cowjazz, Big Iron Band, and Git Gone all played at the Broken Spoke.

Honky-tonk, rockabilly, and Elvis tribute singer Ted Roddy performed at the Broken Spoke under several names throughout the 2000s, such as Teddy & the Talltops, the Tearjoint Troubadours, and the Naughty Ones. Twice a year for the past decade Roddy has also performed his Graceland Revue tributes at the Continental Club on Elvis's birthday and on the anniversary of his death.[11] As a Corpus Christi high schooler, Roddy began his music career the day his grandmother bought him a snare drum and he began playing with the family band at social gatherings. Since the early 1980s, he has performed harmonica and drums on albums for Dale Watson and Chris Smither. Roddy released his 1995 solo debut, *Full Circle*, which breathed new life into thirteen dusty old country, R&B, and rockabilly songs.[12] Roddy's discography spans nearly forty years, and his credits appear on forty-five albums as composer, musician, and/or vocalist.[13]

Bass player Tee-Jay Hill and rhythm guitarist Jeremy Edens formed the Armadillo Road band and began performing in the dining room at the Broken Spoke in 2009. Lead guitar player Josh Jarratt, drummer Jessie Esquivel, and steel player Michael Small make up the rest of the band along with their dependable roadie, Jesse Trocino. They have also performed in the dance hall. Jarratt calls the Broken Spoke a "staple" of Americana or country roots music.

Since 2009 country singer and songwriter Weldon Henson has performed as part of Austin's own version of the reality TV show *Dancing with*

Weldon Henson performs on August 12, 2014, as part of his "Two-Stepping Tuesdays" residency gig at the Broken Spoke.

the Stars—a night that he calls "Two-Stepping Tuesdays." "This is *Dancing with the Stars* in South Austin. The best thing about 'Two-Stepping Tuesdays' at the Broken Spoke is we've got the best dancers in town. If it's danceable, it doesn't matter what kind of song we play, these dancers are good," Henson says. He has a great relationship with James White. "Mr. White always says, 'We ain't changin' nothin',' but that's Texas to me. Texas is all about doing things your way."

Mike Harmeier, lead singer for Mike and the Moonpies, first met James White while playing a private wedding reception held at the Broken Spoke fifteen years ago. The band includes bass player Preston Rhone, drummer Kyle Ponder, lead guitarist Catlin Rutherford, pedal steel player Zach Moulton, and keyboard player John Carbone. Mike and the Moonpies play a lot of Johnny Bush, Merle Haggard, and George Strait cover songs along with their own originals. Lead singer for the country rock band Eleven Hundred Springs, Matt Hillyer, has also often joined the Moonpies onstage at the Broken Spoke. Fiddler Doug Moreland, who has opened shows for Cory Morrow and Pat Green, sits in with the Moonpies occasionally.

PART VII

The 2010s

CHAPTER 19

The Whites' Small Family Business Thrives

In 2016 *Business News Daily* named Texas the best state in the nation for small businesses to thrive without the burden of corporate taxes or regulation.[1] The biggest challenge faced by the more than 2.4 million small business owners in Texas has been finding enough capital to open. Once small businesses open their doors, some proprietors struggle to stay afloat financially; for this reason their children do not generally accept the burden of keeping the family business running. *Forbes* magazine reported in 2013 that less than one-third of all family businesses survive beyond the first generation.[2] However, during this decade alone, families operated about 20 percent of the seven million businesses with one hundred or fewer employees located throughout the United States.[3] The Broken Spoke serves as one of Austin's greatest sustaining small businesses operated by two generations of a single family. Instinctively, the White family began forging the best small business practices fifty years before *Forbes* created its list: (1) keep money in the bank, (2) be punctual with customers and creditors, (3) respond quickly to problems, (4) answer questions before they are asked, (5) hire good full-time employees, and (6) train employees and reward them well.[4] The biggest problems that arise for small family business owners can be traced to interpersonal dynamics—personal disagreements, generational differences, and imbalances of power. Also, as the numbers of family business shareholders grow exponentially generation by generation, their founder cannot be taken for granted.[5] Three generations of the White family today provide testimony to these principles simply by sticking together and by working side by side in good times and in bad. A strong family work ethic has proved to be the Whites' greatest single strength, buoyed by collaborative thinking and the creation of joint financial resources.

CHAPTER 20

New Neighbors, Dance Lessons, and Celebrations

The first five years of the 2010s created challenges for the White family after their landlord died and his children decided to sell the land beneath and surrounding the Broken Spoke. The looming threat of the Broken Spoke's possible demolition combined with the constant stress of an unknown future likely contributed to a rash of health issues that followed for James, Annetta, and Ginny. The family also struggled to keep the Broken Spoke open and running for sixteen months during construction of the 704 apartments. Land movers and construction work created obstacles at the parking lot entrances for the Broken Spoke off South Lamar, keeping most customers away. Only a handful of customers walked to the Broken Spoke or parked in a nearby shopping center to have lunch daily. On weeknights the dining room filled to less than half its normal capacity. At times the dance hall drew as few as one hundred people on weeknights regardless of who performed; on weekends the family business did not fare much better. Still the White family persevered.

Troubles seemed nowhere in sight on May 12, 2010, when Al Dressen inducted James and Annetta into the Texas Western Swing Hall of Fame in San Marcos as part of the eighteenth Texas Natural and Western Swing Festival.[1] However, in July 2010, the Johnson family sold the nearly eight acres of land for an undisclosed price to Riverside Resources. As Julie Johnson recalls, "When we decided to sell the property, Riverside Resources wanted to buy it, and my family—all four of us—agreed that the Broken Spoke needed to stay intact and not get torn down, which a lot of developers would have done." The agreement was not in writing. "We asked the buyer to leave the Broken Spoke as it was as best they could. Riverside Resources agreed to do that," she says. The sale included other buildings that the Johnsons had leased to businesses but later demolished. "They just weren't making any money, and the economy was bad. We were struggling, and my family didn't want to be in business together," Julie says. "It took us a long time to find a buyer who wouldn't do that [demolish the Broken Spoke] because it's so much easier to just scrape the land off and to start over again." Today she has only good wishes for the future of the Broken Spoke. "I hope it stays here forever. To me, the Broken Spoke is James White, and he makes this place. I just hope he stays around for a long time, and he keeps coming here and getting up on the stage and talking to people," she says. The Johnson siblings also donated to the Broken Spoke their father's antique weight scale and a 1948 Wurlitzer wooden jukebox with stained-glass light fixtures. The vintage jukebox no longer plays 78 rpm records, but its brilliant multicolored lights still rotate within the pilasters, creating an impressive light show. People still load it with quarters occasionally, and over the years some inebriated customers have mistaken it for a slot machine, although a brass-engraved sign attached to its interior clearly reads "no gambling permitted."

After Riverside Resources became the Broken Spoke's new landlord, the company's manager, Jeremy Smitheal, said he felt "committed" to preserving it. Riverside's partners, John Needham and Don Reese, said that Needham's son, Joshua, had inspired the idea for the company's purchase of the land.

In November 2012, James again started feeling tired all the time and became less talkative, Ginny recalls. "He said when he lay down, it felt like he would or could suffocate, like he was drowning. So he started sleeping in his chair at home at night." A doctor prescribed diuretics and told James to exercise. James began taking short walks three times a week along the trails at Lady Bird Lake in downtown Austin. He walked slowly, often stopping to pick up pecans and then crack and eat them. Ginny recalls, "My mother would tell him, 'You're not walking fast enough if you're walking slow enough to stop to find and pick up pecans to eat.'"

The Whites enjoyed a brief reprieve from their troubles by attending a family wedding when Gary Peacock married his wife, Marcia, at the ranch on April 29, 2012. Weldon Henson performed at their reception and Marcia taught Gary to dance. Gary says that it felt like he had two left feet before he met Marcia. Marcia remembers being star-struck when she met Gary. "When you walk into the Broken Spoke and see that life-size Marlboro Man standing there and then you hear him speak, you have to ask, 'Are you from Australia?' He gets that all the time," Marcia says.

Riverside Resources sold the property to Transwestern developers on May 29, 2012. The sale price has never been disclosed. Transwestern immediately began building The 704, two four-story multiuse commercial and residential properties. Josh Delk, associate vice president of Transwestern, said that he never underestimated the Broken Spoke's appeal. "It is extremely valuable. It's part of the heritage and the city of Austin." In January 2013, Transwestern made improvements to the Broken Spoke's property by adding crushed granite to the parking lot to replace the caliche. Transwestern also paved the sidewalk that surrounds the building and added landscaping around its facade; eventually they added a driveway on the north side of the Broken Spoke that also shares an entrance to the apartment complex.

The Whites celebrated at the birth of their second grandson, Mike and Ginny's youngest son, Jackson Colt, on July 31, 2012. A photo in the dining room of the Broken Spoke shows Willie Nelson holding Jackson. Even the sale of the land beneath the Spoke could not diminish their joy.

Once again the Broken Spoke and the White family made national news headlines when Terri White's picture ran on the front page of the *Washington Post* on March 7, 2013, accompanied by a story about Texas dance halls.[2] Soon afterward, Terri began receiving invitations from across the country to teach private dance lessons at parties. Wednesday through Saturday at the Broken Spoke dance hall, she wears a halter top and a pair of fashionably ripped skinny jeans or cutoffs. She always wears cowboy boots, flashy earrings, and a necklace with a rhinestone initial "T." Her father proudly sings her praises: "She's probably the best country music teacher that there is. Her students come from all over, and they know about her because they've heard about her and read about her, so they come out. They not only get to listen to good country music; they get to get up and dance, and that's what it's all about—having fun," James says. Terri divides her dance classes up into two groups, "follows" and "leads," and lines couples up on opposite sides of the dance floor. She teaches all of her students the classic two-step, which Terri calls "the quick, quick, slow, slow." Country singer Dale Watson also wrote a song using the terms.

The old-timers like the two-step, and experienced dancers prefer to learn the western swing. Terri first demonstrates the dance alone, moving side to side. Next, she selects a volunteer from the audience to demonstrate. Toward the end of the lesson, couples try out dance moves on their own while Terri shifts around the dance floor adding support and redirection. She snaps her fingers to a steady beat. She starts the music on the jukebox—a song designed for a slow two-step. The dancers all stop and smile when the song ends. "Y'all are good dancers! I never would have believed it when you started, but you are!" Terri says. She claims that in country dancing the "follows" make all the mistakes on a dance floor. During the two-step, the only mistake that a "lead" dancer can make is to stop. "Every other mistake is made by 'the follows.' They're here to follow. No matter what," she says. "They've got to follow. They fight it and fight it." She said it is easy to tell the experienced lead dancers because they typically drive their partners with their left arm and lead with their right foot, and they always drag their feet on the two-step.

Terri teaches people from all over the world. The largest groups of foreigners have come from Asian countries or from Norway. She also teaches celebrities. "People like her because she B.S.'s them and makes it fun," James says. "After class she fusses at them if they haven't paid attention in her class." Terri has taught Led Zeppelin's frontman Robert Plant and Austin's singer Patty Griffin how to western swing dance. She charges eight dollars for dance lessons in addition to the Broken Spoke's cover charges: six dollars on Tuesdays, five dollars on Wednesdays, seven dollars on Thursdays, and twelve dollars on Fridays and Saturdays. The Broken Spoke closes for general business on Sundays and Mondays, when they book private parties. Terri says the toughest class she ever had to teach was a group of about forty male Koreans. "None of them spoke any English. I was able to teach them to dance the two-step by imitation. Those Koreans put their own spin on it at the end. They did this—'hi-yah,'" Terri says as she performed a kick with one leg lifted high up in the air.

Then in the early-morning hours of March 24, 2013, the Texas Top Hands tour bus that had been parked on Broken Spoke property more than fourteen years disappeared.[3] The Austin icon had been used until the late 1980s by one of the state's most beloved western swing groups. The Texas Western Swing Hall of Fame inducted the Texas Top Hands on May 9, 1992. William Wayne "Rusty" Locke, their last surviving band member, died in 2010 at the age of ninety. Three years later, Ray Sczepanik, former leader of the Texas Top Hands, moved the bus to Texas Pride Barbecue in Adkins, Texas.[4]

James White notified Austin police after he found an envelope with a note signed by Sczepanik attached to the front door of the Broken Spoke.

Transwestern developers had just spent about ten thousand dollars upgrading the tour bus before it disappeared. As Delk recalls, "We felt it was a terrific icon, not only for the Broken Spoke but for the project. That bus was relatively indicative of the spirit of the Broken Spoke in Austin and South Lamar." Transwestern had paid for modifications to the bus to make it more aesthetically pleasing and safer by reinforcing the frame and buying new tires, replacing the Plexiglas windows, and painting the exterior to remove some of the rust. "We woke up one Sunday morning to find the bus gone," Delk says. "The gentleman who had originally given the bus to Mr. White brought a flatbed trailer up from San Antonio and took it back. Unfortunately, we weren't able to recover it." Delk offered to create a propaganda campaign to have the bus returned to James. Ultimately Transwestern decided to "take the high road," he says.

James White, for the first time in twenty years, did not attend the Broken Spoke's annual "Fiddle Fest" performance on July 13, 2013. Instead, he rested at home after experiencing irregular heart rhythms. He had also suffered a stress fracture in one foot earlier in the week while walking along Lady Bird Lake. Afterward doctors instructed him to wear an orthopedic boot for more than a month. Fiddler Mary Hattersley and her Blazing Bows have performed for two decades at the Fiddle Fest as part of their summer camp's final performance at the Broken Spoke. About thirty elementary-age boys and girls and a half-dozen adults tuck their instruments under their chins to perform some good old-time string classics of folk and country music. The girls dress in their best embroidered ruffle skirts and lacy tops, and the boys wear plaid shirts and Wrangler jeans. Most all wear cowboy boots and Resistol straw hats. The Broken Spoke quickly turns into a romper room of G-rated fun. Mary's husband, Cleve, accompanies the group on guitar, and fiddler, Kay Mueller and Catherine Van Zanten join in. "Sweet Mary" Hattersley has earned a reputation as an accomplished fiddler player. Her musical career spans four decades performing with country, blues, jazz, and rock-and-roll Hall of Famers, including Jerry Jeff Walker, with whom she recorded under her former surname, Egan. Throughout the 1970s, the Hattersleys also performed around Austin, but never at the Broken Spoke, as part of the Greezy Wheels band.

In early January 2014, James was admitted again to Austin Heart Hospital to undergo another heart catheterization, and this time doctors implanted a cardioverter-defibrillator (ICD) in his chest. During his hospital stay he lost twenty pounds and later lost another ten pounds of fluid at home. He cut salt from his diet, cut back on his fluid intake, and continued taking diuretics. On July 3, 2014, doctors replaced the ICD in his chest after the one he had received six months earlier failed. The left side of his heart remains the most sluggish and has the most difficulty with arrhythmia. The ICD device continually monitors his heart rhythm and can send either low- or high-energy electrical pulses to his heart to correct any abnormal rhythms as needed. His cardiologist wants him to walk at least thirty minutes a day. "He has never exercised in his life, and he has a stress fracture on his foot, but he's doing it. He's still going," Ginny says. Within days after receiving his ICD, James visited the family ranch to inspect two water wells located on the land, and he worked outside for hours in the humidity and heat. Ginny recalls, "Nobody else knows what he knows. We don't even know where the water lines are at the ranch. He's particular about the way things get done."

On January 30, 2014, James also underwent sinus surgery to repair a deviated septum. The painful recovery kept him at home for a couple of weeks, but afterward he felt as good as new and returned to his weekend routine of introducing bands onstage at the Broken Spoke.

James's health appeared to be restored just in time to celebrate his seventy-fifth birthday with two parties—one at the Broken Spoke on Saturday April 12, 2014, and another at the Whites' ranch the next day. Dale Watson performed at both parties. The Broken Spoke filled to capacity with more than six hundred people the first night, and Watson and his band performed while more than one hundred invited guests feasted on barbecue at the ranch the next day. As a special gift from Annetta, James arrived at the party by way of a vintage stagecoach. Ben Rogers, who performs solo on guitar regularly at the Broken Spoke in the dining room and often demonstrates his extreme rope tricks in the dance hall, drove the stagecoach. Female dancers especially enjoy it when Rogers lassos them on the Broken Spoke's dance floor.

Attendees at James's birthday party included not only regular Broken Spoke performers but longtime dancers and friends as well, including New York transplant Denise Hosek and Washington, DC, native Mike Spillers, who became engaged on the Broken Spoke stage. Hosek and Spillers have graced the Broken Spoke's dance floor most weekend nights for the past five years. They refer to the Broken Spoke as "the cornerstone" of their relationship. They inspire others as they boot-scoot, tangle, and twirl in each other's arms. When Hosek first visited the Broken Spoke in 2010, the experience changed her life. "It looked, sounded, and smelled like what I imagined that a Texas honky-tonk dance hall should be. I just loved it and vowed I'd go back." Hosek soon moved to Austin, and Spillers entered her life five years ago when he spotted her dancing. "I was absolutely floored at her dancing. She just took my breath away." Spillers says he goes to the Broken Spoke as much for the dancing as the bands. "The people who are out there are as much a part of the performance as the performers," he says. Hosek notes the age differences between dance partners. "It's the only place I've ever been where you can see a twenty-five-year-old dancing with a seventy-five-year-old man, and he doesn't have any money; it's just dancing. She's just interested in his dancing; that's it," Hosek says.

Dance partners Elizabeth Reyes and Scott McHenry met in 2012 at the Broken Spoke when Dale Watson performed. "I love this Dean Martin song called 'Just in Time.' So when I went up there and got her to dance and when she turned the other way, I whispered to Dale to do 'Just in Time,'" McHenry says. Afterward, Watson asked McHenry if the song helped the romance. "I told him, 'Oh, yeah.'" Several of the couple's friends have married at the Broken Spoke during the breaks when Watson and his band have performed, Reyes says.

Dancers Olga Lozano-Hunter and Craig Hunter met and married at the Broken Spoke in 2014 when Dale Watson performed. "We went out, and we kept going out, and we kept going dancing," Olga says, giggling. Watson's music still keeps the passion alive for them at the Broken Spoke. Watson, also an ordained minister, married the couple at the Broken Spoke and also performed at their reception. They invited about thirty of their closest friends and family members. Meanwhile, another 570 people showed up. "There were six hundred people there," Hunter says. "The fire marshal showed up, but we just kept going on." When the Hunters brought their signed marriage certificate to the Travis County courthouse, the clerk recognized James White's name as their witness. During their honeymoon the

Dale Watson, February 8, 2014.

two visited Fredericksburg. As they visited boutiques in town, a few people stopped them to ask if they had recently wed at the Broken Spoke. "We were like, 'Uh, yeah.' Then they said, 'We were at your wedding,'" Olga says.

Philanthropist and recording artist Brad Moore first shared the Broken Spoke stage with Cornell Hurd in 2012. Moore calls it "the thrill of his life" performing in the place where legendary stars once performed. Hurd produced Moore's debut album, *That Old Texas Groove*, in 2012. Moore grew up in the Texas Panhandle. Brad and his wife, Michele, moved to Austin in 1985 and established an endowment that supports the Roots Music Series of books published by the University of Texas Press.

In late January 2013 country singer Jack Ingram sang "Mesquite Smoke and the Broken Spoke" in a commercial that ran during Super Bowl XLV. The lyrics included stereotypical notions of Texans. Paid for by Lone Star grocer HEB, Ingram's song detailed all of the things that he likes most about Texas, including the Broken Spoke, James recalls. "It was a great song and we were mentioned in the very first verse, so that's what they played in the commercial—so therefore we can say that we've been in the Super Bowl," James says.

Also in January 2013, Pitt Garrett, executive director of *Songwriters across Texas*, began filming his thirty-minute weekly variety show at the Broken Spoke. The program features emerging songwriters and singers of country, blues, and soft rock and airs on TV channel KNVA CW Austin. The show's producers often videotape a local band providing the background instrumentals for guest artists.

During October 2014 doctors admitted Ginny into Seton Hospital with a pulmonary embolism one night after she felt short of breath and fatigued. Afterward Ginny took a six-month sabbatical from the Broken Spoke at home on doctors' orders to rest. Meanwhile, Annetta, at seventy-two years old, took over her daughter's job managing parties and employees at the Broken Spoke. Annetta schedules as many as eight employees in the Broken Spoke restaurant and dance hall at least five days a week. "James always says he never promised me any rocking chair on the front porch," Annetta says.

The Whites' "mom-and-pop operation" supports several White family households, performing musicians, and eight employees. "I like to have a family member up here every night we're open; it just works better, plus they love the Broken Spoke as much as we do," Annetta says. "It's an 'all in the family thing.'" Together she and James have raised two daughters and have helped care for four grandchildren as well as three great-grandchildren. Their love affair has endured despite life's hardships.

The Whites' granddaughters, Ashley and Mollee Jo, have continued to fill in as bartenders whenever Annetta needs them. "The decisions we make every day affect our family and the families of our employees, as well as the incomes for hired musicians and singers. We've weathered a lot of life's storms together," Annetta says. "I try to remain unflappable as we travel life's ups and downs. Anything I need a little more backbone on, James is always at my back. We seem to have earned whatever we have made through hard work and perseverance." Annetta recalls that fifty-two years ago when the Broken Spoke opened, people told the Whites they would never stay

The extended White family at their ranch on April 12, 2014. Left to right: Ashley Carey holding Jackson Peacock, Annetta and James White, Terri White, Alex Espinoza, Ginny White-Peacock, Mollee Jo Montague, and Mike Peacock. In front are James Lamar Peacock and Brenn Espinoza, who holds Gretchen the Dachshund.

open. "All the know-it-alls used to tell James, 'Oh, you'll never make it in business because you're on the wrong side of the road. If you were on the right side of the road going home from work, you'd make it in business.' I'm glad they were wrong about us," she says.

James's stretch of good health continued through the Broken Spoke's fiftieth anniversary, celebrated in grand fashion during the entire week of November 4–8, 2014, with star performances, interviews, and news features. Highlights included a media blitz with interviews by representatives from every local television affiliate. *Texas Highways*, *Texas Monthly*, *Austin Monthly*, the *Austin American-Statesman*, and the *Austin Chronicle* each ran articles about the anniversary.[5] James's face became a familiar one to the media and he enjoyed celebrity status. Wells Fargo Bank officials on South Lamar commissioned the painting of a giant mural inside the bank's lobby located just above the front counter. The mural features an artistic collage of recognizable South Austin businesses, including the Broken Spoke with James White standing out front and center.

The hosts of the fiftieth anniversary celebrations held at the Broken Spoke included Alvin Crow, Jesse Dayton, Weldon Henson, and Dale Watson. Special guests included Brian Hofeldt, Cornell Hurd, Jack Ingram, Pau-

The Broken Spoke celebrated its fiftieth anniversary with a week of performances and accolades, November 4–8, 2014.

line Reese, Jerry Jeff Walker, and Chris Wall. Representative Elliott Naishtat bestowed James and Annetta White with the Texas Treasure Business Award on behalf of the Texas Historical Commission. When the celebrations ended, James called the event "the party of the century."

Then-mayor Lee Leffingwell proclaimed November 10, 2014, as "Broken Spoke Day" in Austin in part to recognize the fiftieth-anniversary opening date of the Broken Spoke. "James and Annetta White have been operating the Broken Spoke since 1964, and its reputation for good country music and good Texas cooking has spread worldwide," Leffingwell says. He called the Broken Spoke "Texas' most definitive dance hall." District 53 Representative Harvey "H." Hilderbran also delivered a Texas resolution to James and Annetta White, recognizing them as the founders of the Broken Spoke. Both documents hang in the Broken Spoke today.

"Cowgirl" Heidi Heinen nightly rolled the famous Broken Spoke wagon wheel during the anniversary. Inspired by *Grand Ole Opry* and regular *Hee Haw* cast member Minnie Pearl, Heidi wore a sun hat decorated with rattlesnake vertebrae, a raccoon's skull, a deer's jawbone, and some vintage television vacuum tubes, lit up and powered by low-voltage batteries. She topped off the look with a band of barbed wire around the brim. Heidi says, "Rolling that wagon wheel is just one of the high parts of my life. I couldn't be more

Gary P. Nunn performs with Alvin Crow and the Pleasant Valley Boys as part of the Spoke's fiftieth-anniversary party in November 2014.

Jerry Jeff Walker performs during the Spoke's fiftieth-anniversary party in November 2014.

Jack Ingram performs with the Pleasant Valley Boys as part of the Spoke's fiftieth-anniversary party in November 2014.

honored to do it." Heinen often appears at the Broken Spoke on weekend nights with her friend and sidekick, "The Jolly Rancher," the professional performer Jeff Eddins. He wears an eerie carnival-style Kewpie doll mask with a sinister grin. He also dons white work coveralls fitted with a vest decoration fashioned from television vacuum tubes that light up and flash. Together they make a startling impression.

San Antonio singer-songwriter Rich Minus attended the Broken Spoke's anniversary celebrations on November 8, 2014. The former Austin resident has been visiting the Broken Spoke for the past forty years. "A lot of my friends came here and played here, and that's why I kept coming," Minus says. Soon after moving to Austin, Minus befriended some of the city's finest musicians, including Doug Sahm and Augie Meyers, who formed the Sir Douglas Quintet. Sahm and Meyers then teamed up with famous Hispanic singer and recording artist Freddie Fender and accordion player Flaco Jiménez to form the Texas Tornados. The Tex-Mex group in the 1980s created a popular sound from blended country, rock and roll, and Mexican folk music. Minus's successful career as a songwriter began when the Texas Tornados recorded one of his songs, "Laredo Rose," on their first self-titled album in 1990.

As 2015 began, the Whites regularly welcomed their new neighbors, residents of The 704, into the Broken Spoke for happy hours and evening dance parties. Once Transwestern finished construction, attendance returned to normal. Life seemed good again for the Whites. However, in April 2015, Annetta began feeling short of breath and fatigued. She felt ill for a few days before Ginny finally convinced her to go to the emergency room at Austin Heart Hospital. Doctors admitted Annetta and operated and placed a stent in one of the valves of her heart to help increase blood flow. After being released, Annetta spent a couple of days resting at home, but soon she returned to working part-time at the Broken Spoke.

On February 4, 2016, about two hundred lucky country music fans enjoyed a private concert at the Broken Spoke by Willie Nelson, Ray Benson, and members of Asleep at the Wheel (fiddler Katie Shore, steel player Eddie Rivers, mandolin and fiddle player Dennis Ludicker, and drummer David Sanger). Bettie Girling, one of the founders of Girling Home Health Care and widow of Robert Girling, sponsored the event to celebrate her birthday. However, she was unable to attend due to illness, so she watched the party

Governor Greg Abbott stopped by the Broken Spoke on February 4, 2016, and met James White at a private party given by Bettie Girling. Willie Nelson and Ray Benson performed with Asleep at the Wheel.

via Skype from her home across town. Nelson and Benson, along with her guests, sang "Happy Birthday" to Bettie and then enjoyed a barbecue feast and spirited drinks. For about an hour and a half, Nelson sang a hit parade of songs that marked more than sixty years of his professional music career, including "Hello Walls," "Blue Eyes Crying in the Rain," and "On the Road Again." The eighty-two-year-old closed the night with an intimate crowd sing-along to "The Party's Over," a song Nelson wrote and Claude Gray first recorded in 1959. All evening Benson accompanied Willie on guitar and backup vocals together with keyboard player Emily Gimble, daughter of the late Texas Playboy Johnny Gimble. Governor Greg Abbott with his wife, Cecilia, made a brief appearance, flanked by several Texas State Troopers. Dozens of other local celebrities, such as writer/actor/filmmaker Turk Pipkin, sat on the dance floor to take photos up close and personal. Closing time came early at ten o'clock. James and Annetta White both waved goodbye from the porch as Nelson's tour bus left for a concert performance in Charlotte, North Carolina.

Reagan Outdoor Advertising erected two billboards in Austin during the spring of 2016 to recognize its own fiftieth anniversary. They featured photos of the Broken Spoke with the caption "celebrating Austin's originals."

CHAPTER 21

Documenting the Broken Spoke

James and Annetta White accepted the "Best Venue" award on behalf of the Broken Spoke at Austin's first Ameripolitan Music Awards held on February 18, 2014. The awards show, sponsored by Dale Watson, also recognized performers of roots music, including honky-tonk, rockabilly, outlaw, and western swing.[1]

Singer Paula Russell began performing classic country songs regularly in the dining room at the Broken Spoke twice a month in 2013. She and a variety of her band members have performed every other Saturday from 6:00 until 8:00 p.m. Russell draws a fan base from residents of the Continental Retirement Community in South Austin, who usually fill the dining room to capacity whenever she performs. She has also worked as an acting coach and actress for more than thirty years and teaches at the State Theater School of Acting.

The Sunset Valley Boys have drawn big crowds in the Broken Spoke's dining room since the spring of 2013. Steel player Mark Erlewine, who owns the custom guitar shop Erlewine Guitars, joined the band on New Year's Eve that year after taking over the spot previously held by Craig Park. Other original band members include attorney Polk Shelton, who plays rhythm guitar and sings lead vocals; semiretired businessman Ken Simpson on rhythm guitar and vocals; and professional artist Gordon Fowler on lead guitar. Other band members include bass player Charlie Irwin; drummer Sherman Lindsay, who works for Texas Parks and Wildlife Department; and the youngest member, fiddler Mark Seale, who works as a tech with Xerox. The band plays one Wednesday of the month in the dining room from 6:00 to 8:00 p.m. Fowler is also the husband of Marcia Ball and son of Wick Fowler, founder of Wick Fowler's Two-Alarm Chili. The band plays Merle Haggard and George Jones cover tunes and other country songs made popular before the 1960s, says Ken Simpson.

One of the biggest gatherings at the Broken Spoke every year, the Don

Walser Band Reunion and Tribute, usually takes place the second week of January. Called "The Pavarotti of the Plains," Walser did not become a Texas singing star until he was well into his fifties. Gigs performing in Austin's local bars earned him a record deal, a spot on the Grande Ole Opry, and a National Heritage Award. Walser's band played at the Broken Spoke regularly until Walser became too ill to perform in 2003. The Texas Swing Hall of Famer died in 2006 at the age of seventy-two. During the 1960s Walser called his band the Texas Plainsmen, and it became the Pure Texas Band in the 1980s.[2]

In 2014, 2015, and 2016, real estate agent Janie Quisenberry performed beneath the spotlights at the Broken Spoke onstage with Walser's former band members fiddler Howard Kalish and bass player "Skinny" Don Keeling. Quisenberry first met Walser in 1984 while she managed the BMI Music publishing company, Texas Crude. Dozens of musicians sit in onstage at the tributes to share stories or to sing Walser's hit songs like "John Deere Tractor" and "Waltz across Texas," says Howard Kalish. He and Keeling performed with Walser for more than fourteen years before landing a gig at the Broken Spoke with him in 1991. Kalish serves as the emcee and organizer of the Walser tributes. Keeling joined Walser's band in 1989 and gained a name for his style of "walking the bass," a chord progression that rises and falls in pitch over several bars in quarter-note movement by holding two, three, or four beats. This sound forms the heartbeat of many great country songs. Walser's former piano player, Floyd Domino, and former drummer, Phil Fajardo, often also perform as part of the Broken Spoke tributes and reunions to honor the late legendary yodeler. Guitarist and songwriter Slaid Cleaves usually performs a guest set of Walser's songs at the reunions, and he sings a song that he wrote about the man who later became his mentor:

> And every soul in that roadhouse
> felt the power of his song.
> Through life's joys and sorrows
> he brought us together as one.
> They called him "God's own yodeler,
> The Pavarotti of the plains."
> There's no bigger voice in Texas.
> Don Walser was his name.

Some say Cleaves may be the only person who can yodel with artistry anywhere near Walser's. Fiddler Wayne "Chojo" Jacques from Dripping Springs played a duet with Cleaves onstage as part of his tribute. Carl Hutchens often sits in to sing "Cattle Call" and "Don't Worry about Me," two songs that Walser liked to sing at the Broken Spoke.

Singer-songwriter and musician Shelley King performed for the first time at the Broken Spoke on March 31, 2014, together with Marcia Ball and singer-guitarist Carolyn Wonderland at a benefit for the Health Alliance for Austin Musicians (HAAM). "I loved it," King says. She released her album, Building a Fire, on August 26, 2014.

Jake Penrod, a former police officer, has been singing and playing both guitar and fiddle at the Broken Spoke since August 2014. He also happens to sing some of the songs once made famous by country music's "Singing Sheriff," the late Faron Young. Penrod has earned a reputation as a bit of a traditionalist for performing songs from the 1950s and 1960s once sung by Johnny Bush, Ray Price, and Hank Williams. Penrod says he has felt inspired to play at the historic honky-tonk since beginning his music career nearly ten years ago.

Fiddler Jason Roberts held his solo CD release party for That's My Home at the Broken Spoke on August 1, 2014. Roberts started playing fiddle at eleven years old, and his professional career took off seven years later when he joined Asleep at the Wheel and started performing between 150 and 200 shows a year. He left in 2013 to front his own band. Though not yet forty years old, Roberts has been inducted as an individual into three Western Swing Halls of Fame. "Even before I was probably allowed to be in here, I was coming here and playing music. The spirit in this place is intangible and lasting," Roberts says. "The Spoke is the real deal. It feels like home, and I'm humbled every time I get to play here." He called James a champion of country music. "He's as much a legend as the dance hall. I'll proudly play here as long as that old Broken Spoke wheel continues to roll across its dance floor."

Another British transplant, Tony Harrison, brings Swarovski crystal cool to the Broken Spoke's stage while wearing embellished western costumes and singing country classics with a big band reminiscent of Bob Wills and the Texas Playboys. Harrison and his band debuted August 29, 2014, in the dance hall following seven years of playing regularly every other Thursday

Jason Roberts performs at the release party for his album That's My Home, August 1, 2014.

night in its dining room. Band members include lead guitarist Rick McRae, who has played with Ace in the Hole and George Strait for more than twenty years; and piano player Jamie Hilboldt. Hilboldt tours with Gary Puckett and the Union Gap and formerly played with the Righteous Brothers. Terry Hale, one of the original members of Ace in the Hole, also sometimes performs with Harrison's band.

James White and Harrison share a love of bling when it comes to western wear. Harrison has added Swarovski crystals to three of James's shirts since 2014. "When you come into the Broken Spoke on any Saturday night, James is dressed up like in the old West—not like the movie cowboys, but like those that ride in the Rose Bowl parades. I think it's what people want when they come in here," Harrison says. Harrison, at seventy years old, has adopted the cowboy persona since moving to Texas forty-eight years ago from London. He considers himself a student of Texas culture and its rich musical history. James White fulfills Eric Hobsbawm's image of the mythical cowboy taken from American legends and described in the book *Fractured Times*, but James also represents the real thing with respect to his ranching skills.[3] Harrison testifies that "James is definitely a cowboy. He loves horses, and he has been breeding horses for quite some time and showing them. So yeah, he's the real McCoy."

Italian-born American and world champion racecar driver Mario Andretti visited the Broken Spoke on October 1, 2014, and enjoyed a taste of Lone Star beer, barbecue, and Texas country music. Andretti, a successful businessman and spokesperson for international auto racing around the world, retired from active driving in 1994 and currently lives in Pennsylvania. "I'm fortunate that I was able to come here. I had heard so much about it, and I had to experience it for myself. It's the place to go; it's the place to be and to learn and to experience all about Texas culture and the Texas two-step."

Eric Geadelmann, along with Kelly Magelsky and Ken Levitan, have filmed several scenes for a three-part documentary at the Broken Spoke from 2013 to 2015 for the Country Music Hall of Fame Museum in Nashville. The working title is *They Called Us Outlaws: Cosmic Cowboys, Honky-Tonk Heroes and the Rising of Redneck Rock*. The documentary includes interviews with James White as well as Kris Kristofferson, Ray Benson and Asleep at the Wheel, Jerry Jeff Walker, Guy Clark, Billy Joe Shaver, Bobby Bare, Rodney Crowell, Jessi Colter, Marcia Ball, Emmylou Harris, and the original members of the Flatlanders: Jimmie Dale Gilmore, Butch Hancock, and Joe Ely. Geadelmann grew up in rural Arkansas and became interested in this state's artistic history when his transplanted Texas high school football coach introduced him to progressive country music. After high school, he began visiting the Broken Spoke on weekends. As a professional documentary film producer, his other credits include *The Dance* (2003), *Dave* (2012), and *I Saw the Light* (2015).

Henry Horenstein created a twenty-one-minute documentary, *Spoke*, that screened at the Los Angeles Annenberg Space for Photography and at the Austin Film Festival in 2014. Austin cinematographer Lee Daniel worked on the film, and William "Bill" Anderson edited the film footage in Boston. The idea to make a documentary about the Broken Spoke began with Horenstein's general appreciation for Texas dance halls in the 1970s. Several of the Broken Spoke's bands also have performed regularly in the Boston area, he says. Since then, Horenstein has expressed his love of country music by keeping a focused camera lens on the Broken Spoke. He studied cultural history at the University of Chicago before becoming a professional photographer. Throughout the past four decades Horenstein has been a faithful patron of the Broken Spoke, despite the distance between Massachusetts and Texas. His book *Honky-Tonk: Portraits of Country Music*, published in 2003, includes photographs of country artists taken around the country and at the Broken Spoke since 1968.

In August 2015 a California-based real estate investment company, CWS Partners LLC, announced that it had purchased the Broken Spoke and The 704 from Transwestern developers for an undisclosed price. At the time of the purchase, CWS representative Mike Brittingham said that the company had "no immediate plans to change anything at the Broken Spoke." As James recalls, he signed a ten-year lease with an option to renew. "I can stay there as long as I want to. It's always been that way since I built it. I built it, and I've been paying the taxes on it since 1964," he said. "I don't have any worries about not having the Broken Spoke lease renewed. I worry more about Band-Aiding it together and trying to have it last fifty more years. I worry more about that than my lease agreement for sure."

During the week of March 11–19, 2016, the production company Wild Blue Yonder Films and its co-directors, Brenda Greene Mitchell and Sam Wainwright Douglas, screened their full-length documentary *Honky-Tonk Heaven: Legend of the Broken Spoke* at SXSW. John Parsons from radio station

KUTX interviewed Brenda and Sam on the air on the same day of the film's world premiere matinee, March 13, 2016, at the Alamo Drafthouse Cinema on South Lamar. Most of the country stars who had been interviewed for the documentary showed up at its premiere to celebrate, including Alvin Crow, Jesse Dayton, Weldon Henson, Billy Mata, Gary P. Nunn, Jerry Jeff Walker, and Dale Watson. After the screening, James White, along with Brian Hofeldt of the Derailers, sang a medley of Buck Owens songs, beginning with "Sam's Place" and ending with "Act Naturally." The film received the Audience Choice award in the SXSW "24 Beats per Second" category. The documentary screened several more times during the festival. Celebrations followed at C-Boy's Heart & Soul on South Congress. Guests stayed well into the evening as Dale Watson performed. The film screened three more times in Austin as part of SXSW: March 15 at the Marchesa Theatre, March 17 in the Topfer Theatre of the ZACH Theatre, and March 18 at the Alamo Drafthouse on South Lamar. Immediately following all of the screenings, James White and the documentary film crew answered questions from the audience. Besides the film's producers, 253 backers helped fund production by pledging an additional $62,668 to help bring the film project to life, and Tito's Handmade Vodka made a donation of $5,000.[4] As James recalls, "I enjoyed being in the spotlight and being in the movies. It's kind of hard to condense the story of fifty years of my being in business into a seventy-five-minute film."

Brenda Mitchell had been a fan of dance halls since her adolescent years growing up in East Texas when her Czech grandparents took her to La Grange and Kovar on the weekends. Brenda and her architect husband, Scott, also own Montesino Ranch, a 172-acre spread not far from Wimberley. The couple had previously bought and restored the Wunsche Bros. Cafe & Saloon in Spring, which has hosted countless folk musicians from Lyle Lovett to Jerry Jeff Walker. Brenda Mitchell first envisioned the documentary after celebrating her birthday at the Broken Spoke in 2011. Soon afterward her oldest son, Wade, and her youngest son, Cody, both became interested in filmmaking. In 2013 while her daughter, Shea, attended Austin High School, Brenda finally felt ready to begin work on the Broken Spoke documentary. She then met cinematographer Lee Daniel.

Now that two documentaries have been made about the Broken Spoke, James White looks forward to seeing the publication of this book. "I never

Brian Hofeldt and the Derailers, August 16, 2014.

thought the Broken Spoke would ever be this famous. I accepted it when we got famous in Austin, then in Texas, and then around the United States. You know, it still makes me feel good. All of a sudden, people come to visit from Belgium, from Russia, from China, Japan, Korea, Norway, and other places far away, and they all say, 'Yeah, we know about the Broken Spoke.' From every country, these people come because the Broken Spoke is on their bucket list. Before they kick the bucket, they want to come out to the Broken Spoke."

"The book is just going to be so good. It will be the icing on the cake. I want something that is everlasting. This book is great for that," James says. "It will be here when I'm no longer here. This book will be available somewhere for years to come. I'm kind of a dying breed. I'm the last of the true Texas dance hall owners. I've got the record of being in business for over fifty years. I don't know anybody else who's lasted that long in this business. Good God, I'm lucky that I started when I was twenty-five; I'm fixing to be seventy-seven soon. It's kind of hard to believe. I can remember—what seems just like yesterday—getting out of my truck and seeing that 'land for lease' sign on the side of the road on that dirt lot beside that old oak tree.

That tree in front of the Broken Spoke is still here, and so am I. I'm just gonna keep on rollin' with the times. Let the good times roll. I looked out over that raw Texas land and I visualized a place like no other. When I got it built, I named it the Broken Spoke."

Notes

Introduction
1. "Marty Robbins' Biography."
2. Clark, "Almost Everyone Was Wrong about 'Hee Haw.'"
3. Fisher, "Long Shadow of the 'National Nightmare.'"
4. Townsend, *San Antonio Rose*.
5. Gundersen, "Ray Benson, Rosie Flores Win Big."
6. Bayme, "Presenting the Utmost Talent."
7. "Texas Treasure Business Award."
8. D. Miller, "Honky-Tonk Haven."

Chapter 1
1. Folkins, "Come Together."
2. Bleiburg, "10 Best Dance Halls."
3. "Saving Texas Dance Halls."
4. "Tin Pan Alley."
5. Kingsbury, McCall, and Rumble, *Country Music*, 130.
6. Ibid., 228.
7. Trew, "Trew: This Is Why We Dance Counter Clockwise."
8. Casey, *Dance across Texas*, 5.
9. "History of Swing Dancing."
10. Burnett, "Saving Texas Dance Halls."
11. Bleiburg, "10 Best Dance Halls."

Chapter 2
1. "Camp Wallace."
2. *Camp Wallace (Tex.) World War II Collection*.

Chapter 3
1. M. Miller, "The First Picture Shows."
2. Gándara, "Austin Remembers Humorist Cactus Pryor."
3. "Ritter, Woodward Maurice [Tex]."
4. A. Gray, "Dessau Dance Hall."

Chapter 4
1. Hartman, "Country Music."
2. "David Guion, Wrote 'Home on the Range.'"
3. Palmer, "Singing Cowboys Ride the Comeback Trail."
4. Townsend, "Light Crust Doughboys."
5. Townsend, *San Antonio Rose*.

Chapter 5

1. "B-52 Stratofortress."
2. Mitchell, "Monuments to Peace Reveal Island's Violent History."
3. Bender, "The Nike Missile System."
4. Allison, "The Cuban Missile Crisis at 50."
5. "Sukoshi."
6. "Takusan."
7. Allen, "Fort Sam's Quadrangle Has a Rich, Storied Past."
8. "Jay Lynn Johnson."
9. "Doris Gerald Burrow."
10. Colloff, "96 Minutes."
11. Gándara, "Houston McCoy."
12. Harris and Sadler, *Texas Rangers and the Mexican Revolution*, 182, 260, 312–313, 318, 403; Jenkins, "Hamer, Francis Augustus."
13. "James Campbell 'Doc' White."
14. Harris and Sadler, *Texas Rangers and the Mexican Revolution*, 182 260, 312–313, 318, 403.
15. Bankston, "An Informal Look at Oak Hill History."
16. Kremer, "Apollo 11 Moon Landing."

Chapter 6

1. Casey, *Dance across Texas*, 93.
2. Boles, *Orange Blossom Boys*.
3. Kingsbury, McCall, and Rumble, *Country Music*.
4. Leggett, "Long, Enduring Journey of Cotton-Eyed Joe."
5. Boboltz, "Cotton-Eyed Joe."
6. Talley, *Negro Folk Rhymes*.
7. Scarborough, *On the Trail of Negro Folk Songs*.
8. Powell, "1950s Bunny Hop Dance."
9. Pugh, "Country Music Hall of Famer Member Hank Thompson Dies."
10. Martin, "Hank Thompson Is Dead."
11. Ruf, "Bert Rivera."
12. Adams, "The Geezinslaws."
13. Clanton, "One of the Last Oil Wildcatters."
14. Williams, "Racism on the Radio toward Barack Obama."
15. Nelson, *It's a Long Story*.
16. Fry, "Tubb, Ernest Dale."
17. "Ernest Tubb Biography."
18. Dauphin, "Country Star Jack Greene Dead at 83."
19. Mansfield, "Country Singer Jack Greene Dies."
20. Betts, "Grand Ole Opry Legend Little Jimmy Dickens Dead at 94."
21. Brown, "Oak Hill Yesteryear."
22. Betts, "Country Music Hall of Famer Jim Ed Brown Dead."
23. B. Mansfield, "Country Music Bids Farewell to Jim Ed Brown."

24. Dauphin, "'Wolverton Mountain' Singer Claude King Dies."
25. Kohout, "Hofner, Adolph."
26. Morthland, "Adolph Hofner and the Pearl Wranglers."
27. Pareles, "Roy Acuff, 89, Singer, Dies."
28. Schlappi, *Roy Acuff: The Smoky Mountain Boy*, 133.
29. "Opry's Bashful Brother Oswald Dies."
30. Hight, "Bobby Bare Sr. Continues to Do the Opposite."
31. "About David Houston."
32. Frazee, "Entertainer Shoji Tabuchi Is in Harmony with Ozarks."
33. Cubarrubia, "Slim Whitman Dead at 90."
34. Cobb, "Walker, Charles Levi, Jr. [Charlie]."
35. McDaniel, "What Ever Happened to Classic Country Great Charlie Walker?"
36. Bohls, "Legendary Coach Darrell Royal Dies at 88."
37. Northcott, "Night Moves."
38. "Peyton McKnight."
39. Burka, Northcott, and Loe, "The Ten Best and the Ten Worst Legislators."
40. Hall, "In Memory of Peyton McKnight."
41. Friskics-Warren, "Charlie Louvin."
42. Reid, "Millions Watched the Texas-Arkansas Game in 1969."
43. "Country Singer Henson Cargill Dies."
44. Branda, "Steinmark, Freddie Joe."
45. Curtis, "Freddie's Song."
46. "Happy Little Home in Arkansas."
47. "Buddy Alan Owens Headlines Llano Opry."
48. West, "Buddy Alan Owens."

Chapter 7

1. Rich, "Drinking through the Ages."
2. Bell, "Joe Grace."
3. Smith, "Austin's New © KOKE-FM Can't Beat the Real Thing."
4. Smith, "RIP Joe Gracey, Austin Media Giant."
5. "History of ACL."
6. Reid and Roth, "The Coming of Red Neck Hip."
7. Blackstock, Peter. "50 Years Later, the Broken Spoke Still Stands." *Associated Press*, November 9, 2014. http://www.washingtontimes.com/news/2014/nov/9/50-years-later-the-broken-spoke-still-stands/?page-=all.

Chapter 9

1. Wheat, "Armadillo World Headquarters."
2. Nemy, "Liz Carpenter"; Light, "Clifford Antone, 56, Is Dead"; Greene, "Legendary Delta Blues Pianist Pinetop Perkins Dies at 97."
3. Morthland, "Bill Kirchen—Tale of the Tele."
4. Forte, "Telemaster Offers a Word to the Wise."

5. Waddell, "George Strait."
6. George Strait, e-mailed statement, November 7, 2014.
7. "Tommy Hill and the Country Music Revue."
8. Wynn, "People's Choice Biography."
9. Curtin, "Last Man Standing: Ray Benson."
10. Cartwright, "Asleeping Beauty."
11. "Benson & Asleep at the Wheel Take 'A Ride with Bob.'"
12. Beal, "Bush Remembers Honky-Tonk Days."
13. Brennan, "Johnny Bush."
14. Bush, *Whiskey River*.
15. Robison, "Former House Speaker 'Country Slicker' Dies [Bill Clayton]."
16. Phillips, "Gibson D. 'Gib' Lewis."
17. Sapper, "Richards, Dorothy Ann Willis [Ann]."
18. Holly, "Former Texas Governor Ann Richards Dies."
19. Head and Jasinski, "Sahm, Douglas Wayne."
20. Davis, "Doug Sahm & West Side Horns."
21. Flippo, "Sir Douglas of the Quintet Is Back."
22. Levy, "Doug Sahm and the Sir Douglas Quintet."
23. Country Music Association of Texas website.
24. "About B. J. Thomas."
25. "Gene Watson [Bio]."
26. "Red Steagall: Great American Storyteller."
27. "CMA of Texas Announces 2015 Award Recipients."
28. Friedman, "The Wanderer [Jerry Jeff Walker]."
29. Corcoran, "Secret History of Austin Music."
30. "Frank Otto 'Dutch' Glauninger."
31. Hickinbotham, "Stevenson, Louis Charles [Buckwheat, B. W.]."
32. "Peyton McKnight."

Chapter 10
1. Waller and Spong, "*Urban Cowboy* Turns 35."
2. Dye, "Dale Watson."
3. Reese, "Remembering J. R. Ewing."
4. "SXSW History."

Chapter 11
1. Bankston, "An Informal Look at Oak Hill History."
2. Langer and Shapiro, "Former Rep. Charlie Wilson Dies."

Chapter 12
1. Rich, "Drinking through the Ages."
2. Rubin, "Song for My Father."

Chapter 13
1. Dearman, "The Evolution of Austin Music."
2. Humphrey, "Austin, TX (Travis County)."

Chapter 14
1. Head and Jasinski, "Sahm, Douglas Wayne."
2. Draper, "Poor Willie."
3. Willie Nelson, e-mailed statement, October 3, 2014.
4. Crapanzano, "A Brief History of Farm Aid."
5. Nelson, *It's a Long Story*.
6. Krause, "Broken Spoke."
7. Moize, "Austin: Deep in the Heart of Texans."
8. "UT Performing Arts Center Announces the Retirement of Director Pebbles Wadsworth."

Chapter 15
1. Dolly Parton, prepared statement, March 6, 2014.
2. Curtin, "Playback."
3. Mack Brown, statement, April 22, 2014.
4. Acosta, "Mi Son, Not-So-Little Rick Treviño."
5. Johnson, "Lee Roy Parnell."
6. Poole, "Whatever Happened to Clayton Williams?"
7. "Texas Candidate's Comment about Rape Causes a Furor."
8. Pugh, "Kitty Wells Dies at Age 92."
9. Nemy, "Lady Bird Johnson."
10. "About Johnny Rodriguez."

Chapter 16
1. Badt, "Studios off the Beaten Path."
2. Spong, "Big State, Small Screen."
3. "The Austin House."

Chapter 17
1. "Nudie: Hollywood Tailor to the Stars."
2. "Hollywood Saddlery."
3. Lieck, "Broken Spoke Is Broken Into."

Chapter 18
1. Wilson, "Pat Green."
2. Robert Duvall, recorded statement, March 11, 2014.
3. "Tour Bus Crashes into Country Bar in Austin."
4. Betts, "Dixie Chicks Announce Summer 2016 U.S. Tour."
5. Marbella, "Dixie Chicks Ruffle Feathers."
6. Leeds, "Grammy Sweep by Dixie Chicks Seen as Vindication."

7. Bernstein, "Kinky Friedman Talks Music."
8. Doyle, "Ray Price Dead at 87."
9. Ibid.
10. Ozmun, "Butt, Howard Edward."
11. C. Gray, "Sad Stories and Steel Guitars."
12. Beets, "Country-Soul Comes Full Circle."
13. "Ted Roddy."

Chapter 19
1. Uzialko, "State of Small Business: Texas."
2. "The Facts of Family Business."
3. Birnbaum, "Resilient in Hard Times."
4. Steimle, "Small Business Practices That Make a Big Difference."
5. Caspar, Dias, and Elstrodt, "Five Attributes of Enduring Family Businesses."

Chapter 20
1. H. Mansfield, "Western Swing Hall of Fame Swings This Weekend."
2. Kaplan, "Two-Stepping Her Way across Texas."
3. Kelso, "Broken Spoke Owner Says Bus Hauled Away."
4. Jordan, "Texas Top Hands."
5. Corcoran, "If It Ain't Broken"; Blackstock, "50 Years Later."

Chapter 21
1. Gundersen, "Ray Benson."
2. Block, "Don Walser, Yodeler Extraordinaire."
3. Hobsbawm, "The Myth of the Cowboy."
4. "*Honky Tonk Heaven.*"

Bibliography

General Sources

"About B. J. Thomas." CMT Artists Beta, 2015. http://www.cmt.com/artists/bj-thomas-1/biography/.

"About David Houston." CMT Artists Beta, 2015. http://www.cmt.com/artists/david-houston-2/biography/.

"About Johnny Rodriguez." CMT Artists Beta, 2015. http://www.cmt.com/artists/johnny-rodriguez/biography/.

Acosta, Belinda. "Mi Son, Not-So-Little Rick Treviño y Su Familia." *Austin Chronicle*, June 8, 2001. http://www.austinchronicle.com/music/2001-06-08/82004/.

Adams, Greg. "The Geezinslaws: The Kooky World of the Geezinslaw Brothers." *AllMusic*, 2015. http://www.allmusic.com/album/the-kooky-world-of-the-geezinlaw-brothers-mw0000957570.

Allen, Paula. "Fort Sam's Quadrangle Has a Rich, Storied Past." mySA, November 20, 2015. http://www.mysanantonio.com/150years/military-sports/article/Fort-Sam-s-Quadrangle-has-a-rich-storied-past-6083911.php.

Allison, Graham. "The Cuban Missile Crisis at 50: Lessons for US Foreign Policy Today." *Foreign Affairs*, July/August 2012. https://www.foreignaffairs.com/articles/cuba/2012-07-01/cuban-missile-crisis-50.

"The Austin House." *This Old House*, February 8, 2007. http://www.thisoldhouse.com/toh/tv/house-project/show-descriptions/0,,1546552,00.html.

Badt, Karen. "Studios off the Beaten Path." *MovieMaker*, June 23, 2011. http://www.moviemaker.com/archives/moviemaking/producing/articles-producing/studios-off-the-beaten-path-20110623/.

Bankston, James Scott. "An Informal Look at Oak Hill History." *Oak Hill Gazette*, December 6, 2011. http://oakhillgazette.com/history/2011/12/an-informal-look-at-oak-hill-history/.

Bayme, Molly. "Presenting the Utmost Talent . . . the Ameripolitan Music Awards." *Brilliant* magazine, February 10, 2015. http://www.brilliantmagazine.com/blog/presenting-the-utmost-talentthe-ameripolitan-music-awards.

Beal, Jim, Jr. "Bush Remembers Honky-Tonk Days, but He's Not Nostalgic." *San Antonio Express-News*, reprinted by *Chicago Tribute*, March 14, 2007. http://articles.chicagotribune.com/2007-03-14/features/0703120280_1_texas-honky-tonk-johnny-bush-forgiven.

Beets, Greg. "Country-Soul Comes Full Circle: Too Tall Ted Roddy." *Austin Chronicle*, November 24, 1995. http://www.austinchronicle.com/music/1995-11-24/530152/.

Bell, Brenda. "Joe Gracey, Seminal Figure in the History of Austin's Music Scene, Dies after Battling Cancer." *Austin American-Statesman*, November 20, 2011. http://www.statesman.com/news/news/local/joe-gracey-seminal-figure-in-the-history-of-aust-1/nRhJC/.

Bender, Donald E. "The Nike Missile System: A Concise Historical Overview." 1997, updated May 26, 2004. http://alpha.fdu.edu/~bender/N-view.html.

"Benson & Asleep at the Wheel Take 'A Ride with Bob.'" *Billboard*, March 2, 2005. http://www.billboard.com/articles/news/63899/benson-asleep-at-the-wheel-take-a-ride-with-bob.

Bernstein, Jonathan. "Kinky Friedman Talks Music, Texas and a Trump/Sanders Ticket." *Rolling Stone*, September 22, 2015. http://www.rollingstone.com/politics/news/kinky-friedman-talks-music-texas-and-a-trump-sanders-ticket-20150922.

Betts, Stephen L. "Country Music Hall of Famer Jim Ed Brown Dead at 81." *Rolling Stone Country*, June 11, 2015. http://www.rollingstone.com/music/news/jim-ed-brown-dead-dies-20150611.

———. "Dixie Chicks Announce Summer 2016 U.S. Tour." *Rolling Stone*, CNN.com, November 17, 2015. http://www.cnn.com/2015/11/17/entertainment/dixie-chicks-tour-rs-feat/.

———. "Grand Ole Opry Legend Little Jimmy Dickens Dead at 94." *Rolling Stone Country*, January 2, 2015. http://www.rollingstone.com/music/news/grand-ole-opry-legend-little-jimmy-dickens-dead-at-94-20150102.

"B-52 Stratofortress: Historical Snapshot." Boeing, 1995. http://www.boeing.com/history/products/b-52-stratofortress.page.

Birnbaum, Jane. "Resilient in Hard Times: The Family Business." *New York Times*, February 4, 2009. http://www.nytimes.com/2009/02/05/business/smallbusiness/05sbiz.html.

Blackstock, Peter. "50 Years Later, the Broken Spoke Still Stands." *Associated Press*, November 9, 2014. http://www.washingtontimes.com/news/2014/nov/9/50-years-later-the-broken-spoke-still-stands/?page=all.

Bleiburg, Larry. "10 Best Dance Halls Where Texas Country Still Swings." *USA Today*, March 28, 2014. http://www.usatoday.com/story/travel/destinations/10greatplaces/2014/03/27/texas-dance-halls/6957465/.

Block, Melissa. "Don Walser, Yodeler Extraordinaire." NPR, September 21, 2006. http://www.npr.org/templates/story/story.php?storyId=6119322.

Boboltz, Sara. "Cotton-Eyed Joe: Where Did He Come From, Where Did He Go?" *Huffington Post*, August 18, 2015. http://www.huffingtonpost.com/entry/cotton-eyed-joe-origins_us_55b8ffade4b0a13f9d1b1b15.

Bohls, Kirk. "Legendary Coach Darrell Royal Dies at 88." *Austin American-Statesman*, November 7, 2012. http://www.statesman.com/news/sports/college-football/legendary-coach-darrell-royal-dies-at-88/nSzM2/.

Boles, Randy. *Orange Blossom Boys: The Untold Story of Ervin Rouse, Chubby Wise, and the World's Most Famous Fiddle Tune*. Anaheim, CA: Centerstream Publications, 2002.

Branda, Eldon S. "Steinmark, Freddie Joe." *Handbook of Texas Online*, June 15, 2015. Modified July 25, 2016. Published by the Texas State Historical Association. http://www.tshaonline.org/handbook/online/articles/fst32.

Brennan, Sandra. "Johnny Bush." AllMusic, 2007. http://www.allmusic.com/artist/johnny-bush-mn0000242977.

Brown, Kevin. "Oak Hill Yesteryear: Honky-Tonks and Juke Joints." *Oak Hill Gazette*,

March 20, 2012. http://oakhillgazette.com/history/2012/03/oak-hill-yesteryear-honky-tonks-and-juke-joints/.

Burka, Paul, Kaye Northcott, and Victoria Loe. "The Ten Best and the Ten Worst Legislators." *Texas Monthly*, July 1981. http://www.texasmonthly.com/articles/the-ten-best-and-the-ten-worst-legislators-2/.

Burnett, John. "Saving Texas Dance Halls, One Two-Step at a Time." NPR, *Around the Nation*, January 4, 2010. http://www.npr.org/templates/story/story.php?storyId=122009049.

Bush, Johnny, with Rick Mitchell. *Whiskey River (Take My Mind): The True Story of Texas Honky-Tonk*. Austin: University of Texas Press, 2007.

"Camp Wallace." *Handbook of Texas Online*, June 12, 2010. Published by the Texas State Historical Association. http://www.tshaonline.org/handbook/online/articles/qbc30.

Camp Wallace (Tex.) World War II Collection, 1943. Dolph Briscoe Center for American History, University of Texas at Austin.

Cartwright, Gary. "Asleeping Beauty." *Texas Monthly*, November 1995. http://www.texasmonthly.com/articles/asleeping-beauty/.

Casey, Betty. *Dance across Texas*. Austin: University of Texas Press, 1985.

Caspar, Christian, Ana Karina Dias, and Heinz-Peter Elstrodt. "The Five Attributes of Enduring Family Businesses." *McKinsey & Company*, January 2010. http://www.mckinsey.com/business-functions/organization/our-insights/the-five-attributes-of-enduring-family-businesses.

Clanton, Brett. "One of the Last Oil Wildcatters Is Upbeat about the Energy Biz." *Houston Chronicle*, June 13, 2011. http://www.chron.com/business/energy/article/One-of-the-last-oil-wildcatters-is-upbeat-about-1692105.php.

Clark, Roy. "Almost Everyone Was Wrong about 'Hee Haw.'" *Huffington Post*, December 7, 2015. http://www.huffingtonpost.com/roy-clark/almost-everyone-was-wrong_b_8713996.html.

"CMA of Texas Announces 2016 Award Recipients [Bud Fisher Lifetime Achievement Award—James White]." *Country Music Association of Texas and Hall of Fame*, September 19, 2015. http://www.countrymusicassociationoftexas.com/ - !news/c1°u4.

Cobb, Jennifer. "Walker, Charles Levi, Jr. [Charlie]." *Handbook of Texas Online*. March 17, 2015. Modified November 1, 2015. Published by the Texas State Historical Association. http://www.tshaonline.org/handbook/online/articles/fwabm.

Colloff, Pamela. "96 Minutes." *Texas Monthly*, August 2006. http://www.texasmonthly.com/articles/96-minutes/.

"Congressman Lloyd Doggett." Accessed July 31, 2016. http://doggett.house.gov/index.php/about-lloyd/biography.

Corcoran, Michael. "If It Ain't Broken." *Texas Highways*, November 2014. http://texashighways.com/culture-lifestyle/item/7629-if-it-aint-broken-austin-broken-spoke-honky-tonk.

———. "Secret History of Austin Music, Part 3: Dolores and the Blue Bonnet Boys." *Austin 360*, July 24, 2010. http://www.austin360.com/news/entertainment/music/secret-history-of-austin-music-part-3-dolores-an-1/nRwWP/.

"Country Singer Henson Cargill Dies." *Billboard Biz*, March 7, 2007. http://www.billboard.com/biz/articles/country/1325512/country-singer-henson-cargill-dies.

Crapanzano, Christina. "A Brief History of Farm Aid." *Time*, October 1, 2010. http://content.time.com/time/arts/article/0,8599,2023006,00.html.

Cubarrubia, R. J. "Slim Whitman Dead at 90." *Rolling Stone*, June 19, 2013. http://www.rollingstone.com/music/news/slim-whitman-dead-at-90-20130619.

Curtin, Kevin. "Last Man Standing: Ray Benson." *Austin Chronicle*, September 6, 2013. http://www.austinchronicle.com/daily/music/2013-09-06/last-man-standing-ray-benson/.

———. "Playback: Golden Years Wagoneers." *Austin Chronicle*, April 12, 2013. http://www.austinchronicle.com/music/2013-04-12/playback-golden-years-wagoneers/.

Curtis, Bryan. "Freddie's Song." *Texas Monthly*, September 2011. http://www.texasmonthly.com/articles/freddies-song/.

Dauphin, Chuck. "Country Star Jack Greene Dead at 83." *Billboard*, March 15, 2013. http://www.billboard.com/articles/columns/the-615/1552303/country-star-jack-greene-dead-at-83.

———. "'Wolverton Mountain' Singer Claude King Dies." *Billboard*, March 7, 2013. http://www.billboard.com/articles/news/1551135/wolverton-mountain-singer-claude-king-dies.

"David Guion, Wrote 'Home on the Range'" [Obituary]. *New York Times*, October 21, 1981. http://www.nytimes.com/1981/10/21/obituaries/david-guion-wrote-home-on-the-range.html.

Davis, John T. "Doug Sahm & West Side Horns." In *The Austin Chronicle Music Anthology*, ed. Austin Powell and Doug Freeman, 85. Austin: University of Texas Press, 2011.

Dearman, Eleanor. "The Evolution of Austin Music." *Daily Texan*, April 20, 2014. http://www.dailytexanonline.com/2014/04/29/the-evolution-of-austin-music.

Deen, Amanda. "Miller, Townsend Clare." *Handbook of Texas Online*, June 4, 2015. Modified August 6, 2015. Published by the Texas State Historical Association. http://www.tshaonline.org/handbook/online/articles/fmiwc.

"Doris Gerald Burrow" [Obituary]. Riser Funeral Homes, November 10, 2009. https://www.meaningfulfunerals.net/fh/print.cfm?type=obituary&o_id=454453&fh_id=11543.

Doyle, Patrick. "Ray Price Dead at 87: Country Star Loses Cancer Battle." *Rolling Stone*, December 16, 2013. http://www.rollingstone.com/music/news/ray-price-dead-at-87-country-star-loses-cancer-battle-20131216.

Draper, Robert. "Poor Willie." *Texas Monthly*, May 1991. http://www.texasmonthly.com/the-culture/poor-willie/.

Dye, David. "Dale Watson: 'Ameripolitan' Music." NPR, December 12, 2007. http://www.npr.org/templates/story/story.php?storyId=17179732.

"Ernest Tubb Biography." Bio. Accessed July 25, 2016. http://www.biography.com/people/ernest-tubb-9511419.

"The Facts of Family Business." *Forbes*, July 31, 2013. http://www.forbes.com/sites/aileron/2013/07/31/the-facts-of-family-business/#7cbdc3d346e7.

Fisher, Marc. "The Long Shadow of the 'National Nightmare.'" *Washington Post*, June 14, 2012. https://www.washingtonpost.com/politics/watergate/.

Flippo, Chet. "Remembering the Cosmic Cowboy Years." In *The Austin Chronicle Music Anthology*, ed. Austin Powell and Doug Freeman, 131–33. Austin: University of Texas Press, 2011.

———. "Sir Douglas of the Quintet Is Back (in Texas.)." *Rolling Stone*, July 8, 1971. http://www.rollingstone.com/music/features/like-to-send-this-out-to-everybody-sir-douglas-of-the-quintet-is-back-in-texas-hed-like-to-thank-all-his-beautiful-friends-all-over-the-country-for-all-their-beautiful-vibrations-he-loves-you-19710708.

Folkins, Gail. "Come Together: A Cultural Tour of Texas Dance Halls." *Texas Highways*, August 2013. http://texashighways.com/culture-lifestyle/item/394-come-together-a-cultural-tour-of-texas-dance-halls.

Forte, Dan. "Telemaster Offers a Word to the Wise." *VintageGuitar*, July 2010. http://www.vintageguitar.com/7699/bill-kirchen-2/.

"Frank Otto 'Dutch' Glauninger." *Find a Grave*. Accessed July 25, 2016. http://www.findagrave.com/cgi-bin/fg.cgi?page=gr&GRid=48270049.

Frazee, Brent. "Entertainer Shoji Tabuchi Is in Harmony with Ozarks." *Kansas City Star*, September 19, 2015. http://www.kansascity.com/sports/outdoors/article35772909.html.

Friedman, Kinky. "The Wanderer [Jerry Jeff Walker]." *Texas Monthly*, January 2004. http://www.texasmonthly.com/articles/the-wanderer/.

Friskics-Warren, Bill. "Charlie Louvin, Country Singer, Dies at 83." *New York Times*, January 26, 2011. http://www.nytimes.com/2011/01/27/arts/music/27louvin.html.

Fry, Phillip L. "Tubb, Ernest Dale." *Handbook of Texas Online*, June 15, 2010. Modified November 1, 2015. Published by the Texas State Historical Association. http://www.tshaonline.org/handbook/online/articles/ftu16.

Gándara, Ricardo. "Austin Remembers Humorist Cactus Pryor." *Austin American-Statesman*, August 31, 2011. http://www.chron.com/news/houston-texas/article/Austin-remembers-humorist-Cactus-Pryor-2149334.php.

———. "Houston McCoy, Police Officer Who Shot UT Tower Sniper Charles Whitman, Dies." *Austin American-Statesman*, December 27, 2012. http://www.statesman.com/news/news/local-obituaries/houston-mccoy-the-police-officer-who-shot-ut-tower/nTgcC/.

Gray, Andrew. "Dessau Dance Hall." *Handbook of Texas Online*, June 26, 2014. Modified November 1, 2015. Published by the Texas State Historical Association. http://www.tshaonline.org/handbook/online/articles/xdd03.

Gray, Christopher. "Sad Stories and Steel Guitars: Tearjoint Troubador Ted Roddy's Country Soul." *Austin Chronicle*, November 10, 2000. http://www.austinchronicle.com/music/2000-11-10/79315/.

Greene, Andy. "Legendary Delta Blues Pianist Pinetop Perkins Dies at 97." *Rolling Stone*, March 22, 2011. http://www.rollingstone.com/music/news/legendary-delta-blues-pianist-pinetop-perkins-dies-at-97-20110322.

Gundersen, Edna. "Ray Benson, Rosie Flores Win Big at Ameripolitan Awards." *USA Today*, February 19, 2014. http://www.usatoday.com/story/life/music/2014/02/19/ray-benson-rosie-flores-win-big-at-ameripolitan-music-awards/5615747/.

Hall, Ralph M. "In Memory of Peyton McKnight." *Capitol Words* 142, no. 10 (January

25, 1996). http://capitolwords.org/date/1996/01/25/E101-2_in-memory-of-peyton-mcknight/.

"Happy Little Home in Arkansas Eases Sad Memories for Grandpa Jones." *Echoes of the Ozarks* (blog), June 22, 2010. https://echoesoftheozarks.wordpress.com/2010/06/22/happy-little-home-in-arkansas-eases-sad-memories-for-grandpa-jones/.

Harris, Charles H., and Louis R. Sadler. *Texas Rangers and the Mexican Revolution: The Bloodiest Decade, 1910–1920*. [John Dudley White.] Albuquerque: University of New Mexico Press.

Hartman, Gary. "Country Music." *Handbook of Texas Online*, June 12, 2010. Modified April 6, 2016. Published by the Texas State Historical Association. https://tshaonline.org/handbook/online/articles/xbc03.

Head, James, and Laurie E. Jasinski. "Sahm, Douglas Wayne." *Handbook of Texas Online*, June 15, 2010. Modified November 1, 2015. Published by the Texas State Historical Association. http://www.tshaonline.org/handbook/online/articles/fsa88.

Hickinbotham, Gary S. "Stevenson, Louis Charles [Buckwheat, B. W.]." *Handbook of Texas Online*, June 15, 2010. Modified October 10, 2015. Published by the Texas State Historical Association. http://www.tshaonline.org/handbook/online/articles/fstce.

Hight, Jewly. "Bobby Bare Sr. Continues to Do the Opposite of What Everyone Else Is Doing, and Continues to Do It Well." *Nashville Scene*, November 8, 2012. http://www.nashvillescene.com/nashville/bobby-bare-sr-continues-to-do-the-opposite-of-what-everyone-else-is-doing-and-continues-to-do-it-well/Content?oid=3072495.

"History of ACL." *Austin City Limits*. Accessed July 25, 2016. http://acltv.com/history-of-acl/.

"History of Swing Dancing." *EWIE ECHO* 3, no. 4 (August 1995). Reprinted by Centralhome.com, June 21, 1998. http://www.centralhome.com/ballroomcountry/swing.htm.

Hobsbawm, Eric. "The Myth of the Cowboy." *The Guardian*, March 20, 2013. http://www.theguardian.com/books/2013/mar/20/myth-of-the-cowboy.

Holly, Joe. "Former Texas Governor Ann Richards Dies." *Washington Post*, September 14, 2006. http://www.washingtonpost.com/wp-dyn/content/article/2006/09/14/AR2006091400591.html.

"Hollywood Saddlery." Highnoon.com, 2014. http://www.highnoon.com/bios/hollywoodbio.htm.

"Honky Tonk Heaven: The Story of the Broken Spoke." Kickstarter.com, May 2016. https://www.kickstarter.com/projects/brokenspokefilm/honky-tonk-heaven-the-story-of-the-broken-spoke.

Humphrey, David C. "Austin, TX (Travis County)." *Handbook of Texas Online*, June 9, 2010. Modified July 7, 2010. Published by the Texas State Historical Association. https://tshaonline.org/handbook/online/articles/hda03.

"James Campbell 'Doc' White." Find a Grave. Accessed July 25, 2016. http://www.findagrave.com/cgi-bin/fg.cgi?page=gr&GRid=42252929.

"Jay Lynn Johnson." *Texas State Cemetery*. Accessed July 25, 2016. http://www.cemetery.state.tx.us/pub/user_form.asp?pers_id=8150.

BIBLIOGRAPHY

Jenkins, John H. "Hamer, Francis Augustus." *Handbook of Texas Online*, June 15, 2010. Modified September 30, 2013. Published by the Texas State Historical Association. http://www.tshaonline.org/handbook/online/articles/fha32.

Johnson, Anne. "Lee Roy Parnell." Encyclopedia.com, 1996. http://www.encyclopedia.com/doc/1G2-3493300060.html.

Jordan, J. E. "Texas Top Hands." *Handbook of Texas Online*, June 15, 2010. Modified November 1, 2015. Published by the Texas State Historical Association. https://tshaonline.org/handbook/online/articles/xgt01.

Kaplan, Melanie D. G. "Two-Stepping Her Way across Texas." *Washington Post*, March 7, 2013. https://www.washingtonpost.com/lifestyle/travel/two-stepping-her-way-across-texas/2013/03/07/7064d72c-7d25-11e2-82e8-61a46c2cde3d_story.html.

Kelso, John. "Broken Spoke Owner Says Bus Hauled Away." *Austin American-Statesman*, April 4, 2014. http://www.mystatesman.com/news/news/local/kelso-broken-spoke-owner-says-bus-hauled-away/nXCkj/.

Kohout, Martin Donell. "Hofner, Adolph." *Handbook of Texas Online*, June 15, 2010. Modified May 11, 2016. Published by the Texas State Historical Association. http://www.tshaonline.org/handbook/online/articles/fhobv.

Krause, Tanya. "Broken Spoke." *Handbook of Texas Online*, June 12, 2010. Modified September 16, 2015. Published by the Texas State Historical Association. http://www.tshaonline.org/handbook/online/articles/xdb03.

Kremer, Ken. "Apollo 11 Moon Landing 45 Years Ago on July 20, 1969: Relive the Moment!" *Universe Today*, updated December 23, 2015. http://www.universetoday.com/113347/apollo-11-moon-landing-45-years-ago-on-july-20-1969-relive-the-moment-with-an-image-gallery-and-watch-the-restored-eva-here/.

Laddish, Kate. "Telecaster Master Bill Kirchen Finds Fellow Lost Planet Airmen." *Davis Enterprise*, October 8, 2014. http://www.davisenterprise.com/arts/telecaster-master-bill-kirchen-finds-fellow-lost-planet-airmen/.

Langer, Emily, and T. Rees Shapiro. "Former Rep. Charlie Wilson Dies: Led US Support of Afghans against Soviets." *Washington Post*, February 11, 2010. http://www.washingtonpost.com/wp-dyn/content/article/2010/02/10/AR2010021003848.html.

Leeds, Jeff. "Grammy Sweep by Dixie Chicks Seen as Vindication." *New York Times*, February 13, 2007. http://www.nytimes.com/2007/02/13/arts/music/13gram.html?_r=0.

Leggett, Steve. "The Long, Enduring Journey of Cotton-Eyed Joe." *AllMusic*, January 18, 2008. http://www.allmusic.com/blog/post/the-long-enduring-journey-of-cotton-eyed-joe.

Lieck, Ken. "Broken Spoke Is Broken into and Thieves Ride Away with Owner James White's Family Heirloom: A Saddle, Mister." *Austin Chronicle*, December 1, 2000. http://www.austinchronicle.com/music/2000-12-01/79619/.

Light, Alan. "Clifford Antone, 56, Is Dead; Started Texas Blues Club." *New York Times*, May 25, 2006. http://www.nytimes.com/2006/05/25/arts/25antone.html?_r=0.

"Mack Brown: College Football Studio & Game Analyst." *ESPN MediaZone*, July 14, 2016. http://espnmediazone.com/us/bios/mack-brown/.

Mansfield, Brian. "Country Music Bids Farewell to Jim Ed Brown." *USA Today*, June 15, 2015. http://www.usatoday.com/story/life/music/2015/06/15/jim-ed-brown-funeral-country-music/71260640/.

———. "Country Singer Jack Greene Dies." *USA Today*, March 15, 2013. http://www.usatoday.com/story/life/music/2013/03/15/jack-greene-dies-country-singer/1989819/.

Mansfield, Hap. "Western Swing Hall of Fame Swings This Weekend." *San Marcos Mercury*, May 12, 2010. http://smmercury.com/2010/05/13/western-swing-hall-of-fame-swings-this-weekend/.

Marbella, Jean. "Dixie Chicks Ruffle Feathers." *Baltimore Sun*, April 3, 2003. http://articles.baltimoresun.com/2003-04-03/news/0304030143_1_dixie-chicks-country-music-traditional-country.

———. "Hank Thompson Is Dead; Country Singer Was 82." *New York Times*, November 8, 2007. http://www.nytimes.com/2007/11/08/arts/08thompson.html.

"Marty Robbins' Biography." Accessed July 25, 2016. http://www.biography.com/people/marty-robbins-20651271#death-and-legacy.

McDaniel, Randy. "What Ever Happened to Classic Country Great Charlie Walker?" *Classic KXRB Country 1000*, January 7, 2016. http://kxrb.com/whatever-happened-to-classic-country-great-charlie-walker/.

Miller, Donna Marie. "Honky-Tonk Haven: 50 Years of the Iconic Broken Spoke." *Austin Monthly*, October 27, 2014. http://www.austinmonthly.com/AM/November-2014/Honky-Tonk-Haven/.

Miller, Mike. "The First Picture Shows: Historic Austin Movie Houses." *Austin History Center Association*, Spring 2012. http://austinhistory.net/wp-content/uploads/2015/08/spring-2012.pdf.

Mitchell, Jon. "Monuments to Peace Reveal Island's Violent History." *Japan Times*, August 9, 2014. http://www.japantimes.co.jp/life/2014/08/09/lifestyle/monuments-peace-reveal-islands-violent-history/#.Vls-yNBq5Fg.

Moize, Elizabeth A. "Austin: Deep in the Heart of Texans." *National Geographic* 177, no. 6 (June 1990): 61.

Morthland, John. "Adolph Hofner and the Pearl Wranglers." *Texas Monthly*, April 2000. http://www.texasmonthly.com/articles/adolph-hofner-and-the-pearl-wranglers/.

———. "Bill Kirchen—Tale of the Tele." *Journal of Roots Music: No Depression*, February 28, 2007. http://nodepression.com/article/bill-kirchen-tale-tele.

Mullins, Jesse, Jr. "Cowboy Goodwill Ambassador: Red Steagall." *American Cowboy*, September–October 1999, 46–50.

Nelson, Willie, with David Ritz. *It's a Long Story: My Life*. New York: Little, Brown, 2015.

Nemy, Enid. "Lady Bird Johnson, Former First Lady, Dies at 94." *New York Times*, July 11, 2007. http://www.nytimes.com/2007/07/11/washington/12cnd-johnson.html.

———. "Liz Carpenter, Journalist, Feminist, and Johnson Aide, Dies at 89." *New York Times*, March 20, 2010. http://www.nytimes.com/2010/03/21/us/politics/21carpenter.html?_r=0.

Northcott, Kaye. "Night Moves ['Legislators' Night' at the Broken Spoke]." *Texas Monthly*, June 1979, 96.

"Nudie: Hollywood Tailor to the Stars." *Museum of Western Film History*, 2010. http://www.lonepinefilmhistorymuseum.org/nudie-hollywood-tailor-to-the-stars.html.

"Opry's Bashful Brother Oswald Dies." *Billboard*, October 18, 2002. http://www.billboard.com/articles/news/73773/oprys-bashful-brother-oswald-dies.

Ozmun, Kristy. "Butt, Howard Edward." *Handbook of Texas Online*, June 12, 2010. Published by the Texas State Historical Association. http://www.tshaonline.org/handbook/online/articles/fbu85.

Palmer, Robert. "Singing Cowboys Ride the Comeback Trail." *New York Times*, April 18, 1982. http://www.nytimes.com/1982/04/18/arts/singing-cowboys-ride-the-comeback-trail.html?pagewanted=all.

Pareles, Jon. "His Life Was a Country Song [George Jones]." *New York Times*, April 26, 2013. http://www.nytimes.com/2013/04/27/arts/music/george-jones-country-singer-dies-at-81.html.

———. "Roy Acuff, 89, Singer, Dies; The King of Country Music." *New York Times*, November 24, 1992. http://www.nytimes.com/1992/11/24/arts/roy-acuff-89-singer-dies-the-king-of-country-music.html.

Patoski, Joe Nick. "The Cult of Ray." *Austin Chronicle*, July 18, 2003. http://www.austinchronicle.com/music/2003-07-18/169097/.

"Peyton McKnight." Texas State Cemetery online. Accessed July 25, 2016. http://www.cemetery.state.tx.us/pub/user_form.asp?pers_id=2867.

Phillips, Michael. "Gibson D. 'Gib' Lewis." *Briscoe Center for American History*, University of Texas at Austin. Accessed May 15, 2015. https://www.cah.utexas.edu/projects/speakers_lewis.php.

Poole, Claire. "Whatever Happened to Clayton Williams." *Texas Monthly*, June 1999. http://www.texasmonthly.com/articles/what-ever-happened-to-clayton-williams/.

Powell, Azizi. "1950s Bunny Hop Dance & 2000s Hip-Hop/Club Music Bunny Hop Dances." *Pancocojams (blog)*, April 19, 2014. http://pancocojams.blogspot.com/2014/04/1950s-bunny-hop-dance-2000s-hip-hopclub.html.

Pugh, Ronnie. "Country Music Hall of Famer Member Hank Thompson Dies." *CMT News*, November 7, 2007. http://www.cmt.com/news/1573692/country-music-hall-of-fame-member-hank-thompson-dies/.

———. "Kitty Wells Dies at Age 92." *CMT News*, July 16, 2012. http://www.cmt.com/news/1689742/kitty-wells-dies-at-age-92/.

"Ray Price." In *Country Music: The Encyclopedia*, ed. Paul Kingsbury, Michael McCall, and John W. Rumble, 2nd ed., 383–85 Oxford: Oxford University Press, 2012.

Reese, Diana. "Remembering J. R. Ewing: 'Dallas' Says Goodbye to Larry Hagman." *Washington Post*, March 11, 2013. https://www.washingtonpost.com/blogs/she-the-people/wp/2013/03/11/remembering-j-r-ewing-dallas-says-goodbye-to-larry-hagman.

Reid, Jan, and Don Roth. "The Coming of Redneck Hip." *Texas Monthly*, November 1973. http://www.texasmonthly.com/the-culture/the-coming-of-redneck-hip/.

Reid, Scott M. "Millions Watched the Texas-Arkansas Game in 1969." *Orange County Register*, December 23, 2005, updated August 21, 2013. http://www.ocregister.com/sports/-85343—.html.

Rich, Gerald. "Drinking through The Ages: Thirsty Thursday Investigates." *Daily Texan*, July 20, 2011. http://www.dailytexanonline.com/life-and-arts/2011/07/20/drinking-through-the-ages.

"Ritter, Woodward Maurice [Tex]." *Handbook of Texas Online*, June 15, 2010. Modified October 3, 2015. Published by the Texas State Historical Association. http://www.tshaonline.org/handbook/online/articles/fri25.

Robison, Clay. "Former House Speaker 'Country Slicker' Dies [Bill Clayton]." *Houston Chronicle*, January 8, 2007. http://www.chron.com/news/houston-deaths/article/Former-House-speaker-country-slicker-1821909.php.

Rubin, Mark. "Song for My Father: The House That Don Walser Built, 1934–2006." *Austin Chronicle*, September 29, 2006. http://www.austinchronicle.com/music/2006-09-29/406119/.

Ruf, Hank. "Bert Rivera." *Steel Guitar Network*, July 19, 2009. http://steelguitarnetwork.net/forums/topic/1413/bert-rivera-article.

Sapper, Neil. "Richards, Dorothy Ann Willis [Ann]." *Handbook of Texas Online*, June 15, 2010. Modified February 26, 2016. Published by Texas State Historical Association. http://www.tshaonline.org/handbook/online/articles/fri62.

"Saving Texas Dance Halls One Two-Step at a Time." *Texas Dance Hall Preservation Inc.*, 2014. http://texasdancehall.org/about-us/.

Scarborough, Dorothy, assisted by Olla Lee Gulledge. *On the Trail of Negro Folk Songs*. Cambridge, MA: Harvard University Press, 1925.

Schlappi, Elizabeth. *Roy Acuff: The Smoky Mountain Boy*. 2nd ed. Gretna, LA: Pelican Publishing, 1993.

Smith, William Michael. "Austin's New © KOKE-FM Can't Beat the Real Thing." *Houston Press*, August 31, 2012. http://www.houstonpress.com/music/austins-new-c-koke-fm-cant-beat-the-real-thing-6505671.

———. "RIP Joe Gracey, Austin Media Giant." *Houston Press*, November 17, 2011. http://www.houstonpress.com/music/rip-joe-gracey-austin-media-giant-6525443.

Spong, John. "Big State, Small Screen." *Texas Monthly*, October 2010. http://www.texasmonthly.com/articles/big-state-small-screen/.

Steimle, Josh. "Small Business Practices That Make a Big Difference." *Forbes*, February 4, 2014. http://www.forbes.com/sites/joshsteimle/2014/02/04/small-business-practices-that-make-a-big-difference/#7adccda811f4.

"Sukoshi." *Japanese-English Dictionary* online. Accessed July 25, 2016. http://www.kanjijapanese.com/en/dictionary-japanese-english/sukoshi.

"SXSW History." SXSW, 2015. http://www.sxsw.com/about/sxsw-history#1987.

"Takusan." *Japanese-English Dictionary* online. Accessed July 25, 2016. http://www.kanjijapanese.com/en/dictionary-japanese-english/TAKUSAN.

Talley, Thomas W. *Negro Folk Rhymes: Wise and Otherwise*. New York: Macmillan, 1922.

"Ted Roddy." Allen Hill Entertainment.com, 2007. http://www.allenhillentertainment.com/bands/50s60s/ted-roddy/.

"Texas Candidate's Comment about Rape Causes a Furor." *New York Times*, March 25, 1990. http://www.nytimes.com/1990/03/26/us/texas-candidate-s-comment-about-rape-causes-a-furor.html.

"Texas Treasure Business Award." *Texas Historical Commission*, 2015. http://www.thc.state.tx.us/preserve/projects-and-programs/texas-treasure-business-award.

"Tin Pan Alley." *Encyclopedia Britannica* online, February 27, 2016. http://www.britannica.com/art/Tin-Pan-Alley-musical-history.

"Tommy Hill and the Country Music Revue." *Sonobeat*, 2004. http://sonobeatrecords.com/tommy-hill-and-the-country-music-revue.html.

"Tour Bus Crashes into Country Bar in Austin." *CMT News*, October 4, 2005. http://

www.cmt.com/news/1510901/tour-bus-crashes-into-country-bar-in-austin/.
Townsend, Charles R. "Light Crust Doughboys." *Handbook of Texas Online*, June 15, 2010. Modified October 10, 2015. Published by the Texas State Historical Association. https://tshaonline.org/handbook/online/articles/xgi01.
———. *San Antonio Rose: The Life and Music of Bob Wills*. Urbana: University of Illinois Press, 1986.
Trew, Delbert. "Trew: This Is Why We Dance Counter Clockwise." *Amarillo Globe-News*, December 13, 2010. http://amarillo.com/news/news-columnist/2010-12-13/trew-why-we-dance-counter-clockwise.
"UT Performing Arts Center Announces the Retirement of Director Pebbles Wadsworth." *UT News*, March 27, 2007. http://news.utexas.edu/2007/03/27/fine_arts.
Uzialko, Adam C. "The State of Small Business: Texas." *Business News Daily*, January 27, 2016. http://www.businessnewsdaily.com/8743-doing-business-in-texas.html.
Vinopal, David. "Gene Watson Biography." *AllMusic*. Accessed July 31, 2016. http://www.allmusic.com/artist/gene-watson-mn0000803757/biography.
Waddell, Ray. "George Strait: The Billboard Cover Story Q&A." *Billboard*, August 16, 2013. http://www.billboard.com/articles/columns/the-615/5657700/george-strait-the-billboard-cover-story-qa.
———. "Ray Price, Country Music Legend, Dead at 87." *Billboard Biz*, December 16, 2013. http://www.billboard.com/biz/articles/country/5839794/ray-price-country-music-legend-dead-at-87.
Waller, Annette, and John Spong. "Urban Cowboy Turns 35." *Texas Monthly*, June 2015. http://www.texasmonthly.com/the-culture/urban-cowboy-turns-35/.
West, Jim. "Buddy Alan Owens." In *The Phoenix Sound: A History of Twang & Rockabilly Music in Arizona*, 103–4. Charleston, SC: History Press, 2015.
Wheat, John. "Armadillo World Headquarters." *Handbook of Texas Online*, June 9, 2010. Modified September 7, 2015. Published by the Texas State Historical Association. http://www.tshaonline.org/handbook/online/articles/xda01.
White, James, and Annetta White. *They Came to Texas: Patton-White-Campbell Families and Connecting Branches*. Self-published, 2000.
"William Gardner Tatsch." Geni.com, June 28, 2015. http://www.geni.com/people/William-Tatsch/6000000001791729318.
Williams, Jackson. "Racism on the Radio toward Barack Obama." *Huffington Post*, May 25, 2011. http://www.huffingtonpost.com/jackson-williams/racism-on-the-radio-towar_b_42545.html.
Wills, Rosetta. *The King of Western Swing: Bob Wills Remembered*. New York: Watson-Guptill, 2000.
Wilson, MacKenzie. "Pat Green." *AllMusic*. Accessed July 14, 2016. http://www.allmusic.com/artist/pat-green-mn0000134761/biography.
Wynn, Ron. "People's Choice Biography." *AllMusic*. Accessed May 15, 2015. http://www.allmusic.com/artist/peoples-choice-mn0000251438.

Interviews

Allred, Sammy (singer/songwriter/entertainer). Discussion with the author by phone, March 24, 2014.

Andretti, Mario (retired world champion racecar driver). Discussion with the author, Broken Spoke, October 23, 2014.

Ball, Marcia (singer/piano player). Discussion with the author by phone, March 29, 2014.

Baumann, Chris (longtime patron of the Broken Spoke). Discussion with the author, Whites' ranch, April 13, 2014.

Bear Eagle (Native American musician). Discussion with the author, Broken Spoke, November 11, 2014.

Benson, Ray (singer/guitar player). Discussion with the author by phone, February 6, 2014.

Brittingham, Mike (representative of CWS Capital Partners LLC). Discussion with the author by phone, July 1, 2015.

Brown, Mack (former Longhorn football coach). Statement forwarded from Elsa Hagameier, administrative assistant, Office of Intercollegiate Sports, University of Texas at Austin, April 22, 2014.

Carey, Ashley (granddaughter of James and Annetta White). Discussion with the author, Waterloo Ice House Southwest, April 15, 2014.

Cleaves, Slaid (singer/songwriter/guitar player). Discussion with the author by phone, February 15, 2014.

Cleveland, Malcolm (longtime patron of the Broken Spoke and its former handyman). Discussion with the author, Whites' ranch, April 13, 2014.

Crow, Alvin (singer/songwriter/fiddle player/entertainer). Discussion with the author, Broken Spoke, August 20, 2013.

Crow, Stephanie (wife of Alvin Crow). Discussion with the author, Central Market North café and by phone, September 12, 2014.

Dayton, Jesse (singer/songwriter/guitar player/actor/movie producer). Discussion with the author by phone, February 13, 2014.

Delk, Josh (representative for Transwestern developers). Discussion with the author by phone, November 10, 2014.

Dressen, Al (singer/songwriter/guitar player). Discussion with the author, Broken Spoke, May 5, 2014.

Dromgoole, John (owner of the Natural Gardener). Discussion with the author by phone, April 13, 2014.

Duvall, Robert (actor). Statement recorded in a message and sent by phone by James White, March 11, 2014.

Edens, Jeremy (singer/songwriter/guitar player/member of Armadillo Road). Discussion with the author, Broken Spoke, August 12, 2014.

Emmons, Don "Winker" (photographer). Discussion with the author, Broken Spoke, February 13, 2014.

Erlewine, Mark (steel player for Sunset Valley Boys/owner of Erlewine Guitars). Discussion with the author by phone, March 19, 2014.

Esquivel, Jessie (drummer for Armadillo Road). Discussion with the author, Broken Spoke, March 2014.

Foote, Tom (original drummer for George Strait and Ace in the Hole Band). Discussion with the author by phone, February 2, 2014.

Fowler, Gordon (singer/songwriter/artist). Discussion with the author, Broken Spoke and by phone, February 13, 2014.

BIBLIOGRAPHY

Fowler, Kevin (singer/songwriter/entertainer). Discussion with the author by phone, August 1, 2014.

Friedman, Richard Samet "Kinky" (singer/songwriter/humorist/novelist). Discussion with the author by phone, September 17, 2014.

Gammage, Joel (owner of Texas Hatter and Texas Custom Boots in Buda/longtime patron of the Broken Spoke). Discussion with the author, Broken Spoke, March 30, 2014.

Garrett, Pitt (executive director, *Songwriters across Texas*). Discussion with the author, Broken Spoke, August 1, 2013.

Geadelmann, Eric (filmmaker). Discussion with the author, Broken Spoke, June 23, 2014.

Geil, Kevin (singer/songwriter/frontman for Two Tons of Steel). Discussion with the author by phone, August 15, 2014.

Gilmore, Jimmie Dale (singer/songwriter/guitar player for the Flatlanders/solo artist/actor). Discussion with the author, El Mercado South and by phone, March 10, 2014.

Green, Don (chief financial officer for Teacher Retirement System of Texas). Discussion with the author, Broken Spoke, August 7, 2013.

Hand, James (singer/songwriter/guitar player). Discussion with the author, Sleep Inn & Suites, Austin, April, 10, 2014.

Harmeier, Mike (singer/songwriter/guitar player/frontman for Mike and the Moonpies). Discussion with the author by phone, August 2014.

Harrison, Tony (singer/songwriter/entertainer/guitar player). Discussion with the author by phone, August 2014.

Hattersley, Mary (fiddle teacher/member of Greezy Wheels). Discussion with the author at a private residence, August 1, 2013.

Heinen, "Cowgirl" Heidi (performance artist). Discussion with the author, Broken Spoke and by phone, November 10, 2014.

Henson, Rick (photographer). Discussion with the author at a private residence, December 19, 2014.

Henson, Weldon (singer/songwriter). Discussion with the author, Broken Spoke, August 12, 2014.

Hilderbran, Harvey "H." (former Republican member, Texas House of Representatives, District 53). Discussion with the author, Texas State Capitol, July 5, 2014.

Hill, Tee-Jay (singer/songwriter/bass player/frontman for Armadillo Road). Discussion with the author, Broken Spoke, August 12, 2014.

Hofeldt, Brian (singer/songwriter/frontman for the Derailers). Discussion with the author, Broken Spoke, July 4, 2014.

Holloway, Rick (builder/horse wrangler). Discussion with the author, Whites' ranch, April 13, 2014.

Horenstein, Henry (professional photographer/filmmaker). Discussion with the author by phone, November 9, 2014.

Hosek, Denise (country dancer/regular patron of the Broken Spoke). Discussion with the author, Whites' ranch, April 13, 2014.

Hughes, Jeff (singer/songwriter/guitar player/frontman for the Chaparral). Discussion with the author, Bouldin Creek Café, September 3, 2014.

Hunter, Craig (regular patron of Broken Spoke). Discussion with the author, Whites' ranch, April 13, 2014.

Hurd, Cornell (singer/songwriter/guitar player). Discussion with the author, Broken Spoke, February 20, 2014.

Ingram, Jack (singer/entertainer). Discussion with the author, Broken Spoke, November 10, 2014.

Jarratt, Josh (guitar player for Armadillo Road). Discussion with the author, Broken Spoke, March 9, 2014.

Johnson, Julie (daughter of the late Jay Johnson Jr.). Discussion with the author, Broken Spoke and by phone, May 9, 2014.

Kalish, Howard (fiddle player formerly with Don Walser's band). Discussion with the author, Kerbey Lane Cafe South, January 19, 2014.

Keeling, "Skinny" Don (bass player formerly with Don Walser's band). Discussion with the author, Kerbey Lane Cafe South, January 19, 2014.

Kelso, John (columnist for *Austin American-Statesman*). Discussion with the author by phone, March 2, 2015.

King, Shelley (singer/songwriter/guitar player). Discussion with the author, Threadgill's World Headquarters, July 23, 2014.

Kunz, John (owner of Waterloo Records). Discussion with the author by phone, September 10, 2014.

Leffingwell, Lee (former mayor of Austin). Discussion with the author by phone, April 7, 2014.

Levine, Howard (singer with People's Choice). Discussion with the author by phone, March 11, 2015.

Lozano-Hunter, Olga (regular dancer at the Broken Spoke). Discussion with the author, Whites' ranch, April 13, 2014.

McHenry, Scott (dancer and regular patron of the Broken Spoke). Discussion with the author, Whites' ranch, April 13, 2014.

Minus, Rich (songwriter/singer/former MCA recording artist). Discussion with the author, Broken Spoke, November 10, 2014.

Mitchell, Brenda (director of *Honky-Tonk Heaven*). Discussion with the author at a private residence and Broken Spoke, April 13, 2014.

Montague, Mollee Jo (granddaughter of James and Annetta White). Discussion with the author, Whites' ranch, April 13, 2014.

Moore, Brad (cofounder of Roots Music Series, University of Texas Press). Discussion with the author, Abuelita's Mexican Kitchen, August 28, 2014.

Moser, Margaret (former music writer for the *Austin Chronicle*). Discussion with the author, Broken Spoke, September 2, 2014.

Nachtigal, Birdie (eighty-plus-year-old regular country dancer at the Broken Spoke). Discussion with the author by phone, May 6, 2014.

Nachtigal, Jim (eighty-plus-year-old regular country dancer at the Broken Spoke). Discussion with the author by phone, May 6, 2014.

Needham, John (partner with Riverside Resources). Discussion with the author by phone, November 9, 2014.

Needham, Joshua (son of John Needham). Discussion with the author by phone, November 10, 2014.

Nelson, Willie. E-mailed statement forwarded by his daughter, Lana Nelson, October 3, 2014.

Nunn, Gary P. (singer/songwriter). Discussion with the author, by phone, October 5, 2013.

Parton, Dolly (singer/songwriter/entertainer/actress). Prepared statement forwarded by her personal assistant, Teresa Hughes, March 6, 2014.

Patoski, Joe Nick (professional music reviewer and author). Discussion with the author by phone, April 11, 2014.

Peacock, Gary (brother of Mike Peacock/husband of Ginny White). Discussion with the author, Whites' ranch, April 13, 2014.

Peacock, Marcia (wife of Gary Peacock). Discussion with the author, Whites' ranch, April 13, 2014.

Peacock, Mike (husband of Ginny White, bartender and assistant manager at Broken Spoke). Discussion with the author, Broken Spoke, June 3, 2013.

Peña, Amado (artist). Discussion with the author, Broken Spoke, September 2013.

Penrod, Jake (singer/songwriter/guitar player). Discussion with the author, Broken Spoke, November 11, 2014.

Quisenberry, Janie (semi-retired professional singer/Austin realtor/former singer with Don Walser's band). Discussion with the author by phone, January 21, 2014.

Reese, Pauline (singer/songwriter/entertainer). Discussion with the author by phone, April 9, 2014.

Reyes, Elizabeth (country dancer and regular patron of the Broken Spoke). Discussion with the author, Whites' ranch, April 13, 2014.

Roberts, Jason (singer/songwriter/fiddle player). Discussion with the author, Broken Spoke, August 1, 2014.

Robison, Bruce (country singer/songwriter). Discussion with the author, Broken Spoke, October 5, 2013.

Russell, Paula (singer/acting coach). Discussion with the author, Starbucks at Brodie Oaks, April 15, 2014.

Shelton, Polk (guitar player/singer with Sunset Valley Boys). Discussion with the author, Broken Spoke, March 19, 2014.

Simpson, Ken (former singer/guitar player for Sunset Valley Boys). Discussion with the author, Broken Spoke, March 18, 2015.

Smith, Bobby Earl (former singer/bass player for Freda and the Firedogs). Discussion with the author at a private residence, April 13, 2014.

Smitheal, Jerry (representative with Riverside Resources). Discussion with the author by phone, October 2014.

Spillers, Mike (country dancer and regular patron of the Broken Spoke). Discussion with the author, Whites' ranch, April 13, 2014.

Strait, George. E-mailed statement forwarded by his agent, Ebie McFarland, EB Media, November 7, 2014.

Stuart, Mark (singer/songwriter/frontman for Bastard Sons of Johnny Cash). Discussion with the author, Broken Spoke, September 3, 2014.

Telford, Larry (keyboard player for the Geezinslaws). Discussion with the author, by phone, January 2014.

Wadsworth, Pebbles (retired director, Performing Arts Center, University of Texas at

Austin/creator of the "Broken Spoke Series"). Discussion with the author, Broken Spoke, February 18, 2014.

Walker, Jerry Jeff (singer/songwriter/guitar player). Discussion with the author at a private residence in Austin, February 28, 2014.

Wall, Chris (singer/songwriter/guitar player). Discussion with the author, Jim's Restaurant, April 7, 2014; Broken Spoke, April 10, 2014.

Warden, Monte (singer/songwriter/guitar player). Discussion with the author, Magnolia Cafe Central, April 14, 2014.

Watson, Dale (singer/songwriter/guitar player/entertainer). Discussion with the author, Broken Spoke, February 8, 2014.

Wertheimer, Steve (owner of Continental Club). Discussion with the author, Continental Club, September 9, 2014.

White, Annetta (wife of James White/co-proprietor of Broken Spoke). Discussion with the author, Broken Spoke, August 2014.

White, James (founder and proprietor of Broken Spoke). Discussion with the author, July 2013–June 2015; at a private residence, February 18, 2016; March 28, 2016.

White, Terri (daughter of James and Annetta White). Discussion with the author, Broken Spoke, May 20, 2013.

White-Peacock, Ginny (daughter of James and Annetta White). Discussion with the author, Whites' ranch, April 13, 2014.

Whitmore, John (CEO of American College Testing [ACT]/former dean, College of Fine Arts, University of Texas at Austin). Discussion with the author, Broken Spoke, March 13, 2014.

Wills, Rosetta (biographer and daughter of Bob Wills). Discussion with the author by phone, November 4, 2014.

Wilson, Eddie (owner of Threadgill's). Discussion with the author, Threadgill's North, October 25, 2014.

Woods, Bobby Dan (longtime Broken Spoke patron). Discussion with the author, Whites' ranch, April 13, 2014.

Wynn, Will (former mayor of Austin). Discussion with the author at a private residence, April 2014.

Index

Family relationships shown after names (e.g. granddaughter) are as related to James White. Page numbers in *italic* type denote photos.

Abbott, Greg, 196, 197
Ace in the Hole Band, 82, 83–85, 202
"Act Naturally" (J. Russell, V. Morrison), 125, 204
Acuff, Roy Claxton, 23, 47, 56–57
Adolph Hofner and the Pearl Wranglers, 55–56
"After Closing Time" (B. Sherrill, N. Wilson, D. Walls), 58
Alan, Buddy, 62
alcohol. *See* drinking
"All American Boy" (B. Parsons, O. Lunsford), 57
All My Best (S. Whitman), 58
Allred, Sammy, 49–51, 152. *See also* Geezinslaws/Geezinslaw Brothers
Allsup, Tommy, 92
"Almost Persuaded" (G. Sutton, B. Sherrill), 58
Alvin Crow and the Pleasant Valley Boys, 7, 70, 73, 74–75, 108, 193, 194. *See also* Crow, Alvin
Ameripolitan music, 9, 105
Ameripolitan Music Awards, 9, 124, 198
Anderson, Carl "Crazy Too Cool Carl," 118–19, 120
Anderson, William "Bill," 203
Andretti, Mario, 202
"Angry All the Time" (B. Robison), 146
"Another Somebody Done Somebody Wrong Song" (C. Moman, L. Butler), 91
Anthony, Ray, 45
Antone, Clifford, 69–70, 78, 79, 81, 125
Antone's, 78, 117. *See also* Antone, Clifford

A Perfect Match (Houston and Mandrell), 58
Arhos, Bill, 65
"Arkansas Traveler" (trad.), 29
Armadillo Road (band), 176
Armadillo World Headquarters "the Dillo," 65, 78, 86, 148
Arthur Murray Dance Studio, 17
Ashlock, Jesse, 70, 75, 91, 120
Asleep at the Wheel: "Broken Spoke Series" at UT, 137; career highlights, 87–88; in Country Music Hall of Fame documentary, 202; Girling party 2016, 195; Grammy Awards, 87; hat display, 114; Jason Roberts with, 200; and progressive country movement, 74–75; in *Wild Texas Wind*, 142. *See also* Benson, Ray
"A-Sleepin' at the Foot of the Bed" (H. Wilson, L. Patrick), 54
Ater, Micah, 164
Atlas missiles, 24
Atwell, "Jumbo" Ben, 59
Austin, Texas: cultural identity and mythos, 77, 116, 125; dance halls, evolution of, 23–25; development 1990s, 131; music venues, 23–25, 65–66, 77–79; recession of early 2000s, 159
Austin American-Statesman, 66, 100, 101, 115, 118, 131, 163, 192
Austin Chronicle, 115–16, 192
Austin City Limits (ACL), 49, 65, 71, 92
Austin Film Society, 159
Austin Latino Music Association Award, 49
Austin Monthly, 10, 192
Austin Music Commission, 131
Austin Pizza Garden, 41
Austin State Hospital, 19
Austin Studios, 159
Austin Sun, 116
Autry, Gene, 29

awards and recognition: Ameripolitan Music Awards, 9, 198; Bud Fisher Lifetime Achievement Award (James), 91; international recognition, 205; magazine recognition, 137; mural, Facebook offices, 10; SXSW Audience Choice (documentary film), 11, 204; Texas Treasure Business Award, 9–10, 193

Baland, Joe Sr. (stepfather), 20, 33–34, 36, 42, 68, 73, 100
Baland, Lena (nee Fuchs) (mother), 18–21, 38, 68, 73
Ball, Earl Poole, 164
Ball, Marcia: in Country Music Hall of Fame documentary, 202; with Freda and the Firedogs, 66, 72–73, 74, 75, 76; and Gordon Fowler, 198; HAAM benefit, 200; "If There's a Willie, There's a Way" campaign, 132; on Texas Playboys, 92–93
Ballard, Lee, 38, 42
Baptist Church, 33
Bare, Bobby, 47, 57–58, 202
Bashful Brother Oswald, 47
"Bashful Brother Oswald," 57
Bastard Sons of Johnny Cash (BSOJC), 166
"battle dances," 44
Bauerle family, 18
Baumann, Chris, 101–2
beer: home brew, 19, 21; pull-tab cans, 55; service/sales, 35, 36, 112–14; ten cent nights, 86. See also drinking
Beer, Bait and Ammo" (K. Fowler), 147
Bell, Rusty, 65
bell, traditional ringing of, 102, 121
belly dancers convention, 121
Benson, Ray: Ameripolitan Awards show, 9; career highlights, 87–88, 167; in Country Music Hall of Fame documentary, 202; Girling party 2016, 195, 197; and Harvey Hilderbran, 99; hat display, 114; HEB commercial, 176; height and ceiling issues, 8; and progressive country movement, 74–75. See also Asleep at the Wheel

Bevo's, 66
Big Iron Band, 176
Big Sandy and His Fly-Rite Boys, 9
billboards for fiftieth anniversary, 197
Bill Dorsey and the Melody Drifters, 36
Billy Bob's Texas, 15
"Bing Crosby of Country," 55
Bishop, Virginia (great-grandmother), 67
Bleiburg, Larry, 15
"Blue Eyes Crying in the Rain" (F. Rose), 197
Bob Wills Day, Turkey, Texas, 115
"Bob Wills Show," 30
Born for Trouble (W. Nelson), 132
Bosner, Paul, 65
boxing matches, 120–21
Brazos Valley Boys, 47–49
Brittingham, Mike, 203
Broken Arrow (film), 32–33
"Broken Spoke Day," 193
Broken Spoke Legend (J. White), 163–64
"The Broken Spoke Legend" (J. White), 7, 108–9
Broken Spoke Records (label), 163–64
"Broken Spoke Series" at University of Texas, 131, 137–40
"Broken Spoke Speech," 4, 6–7, 111
"Broken Spoke University," 108
Bromberg, David, 91
Brooks, Leo, 61
Brown, Jim Ed, 47, 54–55
Brown, Junior, 123, 152
Brown, Mack, 149, 151
Brown, Sarah, 82
"brown baggin,'" 35, 112–13
Browns (trio), 55
"The Bruce and Kelly Show," 146
Bryant, James "Bubba," 97–98
Buckdancer's Choice, 75
Bud Fisher Lifetime Achievement Award, 91
Building a Fire (S. King), 200
building/property repairs/improvements, 39–40, 43, 100, 112, 119, 184
"Bunny Hop" (R. Anthony, L. Auletti), 45
Bunny Hop dance, 45
burglary, 163
Burrow, Doris Gerald "D. G.," 35

INDEX

Burrus Mills and Elevator Company, 29
"Bury Me Not on the Lone Prairie" (trad.), 29
Busey, Gary, 142
Bush, George W., 149, 150, 172
Bush, Johnny, 9, 88–89
Business News Daily, 181
Butt family, 176
BYOB. *See* "brown baggin'"

Cabal, Ron, 83
Cactus Theater, 22
Cadillac, James's, 5, 94, 137, 172
Caine, Michael, 169
Calderon, Moises "Blondie," 174
Campbell, Billy, 79
Campbell, Earl, 50, 87
Campbell, James "Doc" (uncle), 38–39
Campbell, John Eaton (great-great-grandfather), 19, 107
Campbell, Lavinia (nee Davidson) (great-great-grandmother), 107
Campbell, Margaret "Maggie" (great-grandmother), 107
Cannon, Dyan, 114
Cantu, Ed, 120
Capitol Theater, 22–23
Carbone, John, 178
Carey, Ashley (granddaughter), 109–10, 120, 191
Cargill, Henson, 47, 61–62
Carpenter, Liz, 81
Casey, Betty, 16
Cash, Johnny, 2, 155
Cash, Roseanne, 118
Cason, Buzz, 144
Castle Creek, 66
"Cattle Call" (T. Owens), 200
C-Boy's Heart & Soul, 204
Chairman's Nights, 99
Chandler, Jon, 164
Chaparral (band), 154
Chaplin, Blondie, 117
Chapman, Dave "Stinky," 97–98
character profiles of James and Annetta White: Ashley (granddaughter), 109–10; author, 4, 5–7, 8–9; Bobby Dan Woods,

101; Chris Wall, 123–24; George Strait, 83; James Hand, 169; Jason Roberts, 200; John Kuntz, 81; Kevin Fowler, 147; Kinky Friedman, 172, 173; Mack Brown, 149; Marcia Ball, 73; Willie Nelson, 134; Will Wynn, 125
Cherokee Cowboys, 174
Chesterfield Supper Club, 49
chicken-fried steak, 38, 84, 89, 91, 114, 123
Clark, Dennis, 163
Clark, Guy, 202
Clark, Roy, 2
Clayjon Gas Company, 51
Clayton, Bill "Billy," 89, 123
Cleaves, Slaid, 199–200
Cleveland, Malcolm, 119–20
clothing. *See* dress/clothing
Cobb, Thomas, 48
"Cocaine Blues" (T. J. Arnall), 2
Coe, David Allan, 50
Cohn, Nudie, 162–63
"Cold Beer, Hot Women and Cool Country Music" (B. Cason, B. Hofeldt), 144
Cole, Bob, 51
Coleman, Keith, 92
college football, 59, 60–62
Colley, Sarah. *See* "Minnie Pearl"
Colter, Jessi, 202
"The Comancheros" (T. Franks), 55
Comin' Right at Ya (Asleep at the Wheel), 87
Commander Cody and His Lost Planet Airmen, 82
Como, Perry, 49
competition/rivalry with other clubs, 73, 78, 80, 86, 100
conjunto music, 91
Contemporary Austin–Jones Center, 22
Continental Club, 9, 77–78, 144
Cooder Graw (band), 166
Cook, Chuck, 43
Cook, David, 73
Cook, Ed, 141
cooking and food service, 36–37, 38, 79–80, 140–41. *See also* chicken-fried steak
Cooper, Dewey, Sarah, 33
Coplin, Nancy, 131

"Cotton-Eyed Joe" (trad.), 44–45, 55
Cotton-Eyed Joe dance, 44–45
"Couldn't Do Nothin' Right" (G. Nunn, K. Brooks), 118
"Country Caruso," 88
Country Music, 76
country music, origins of, 29. *See also* western swing
Country Music Association of Texas, 91
"Country Music Day in Texas," 91
Country Music Hall of Fame: Acuff, Roy, 23; Little Jimmy Dickens, 54; museum documentary, 202–3; Ray Price, 175; Ritter, Tex, 23; Strait, George, 83; Tubb, Ernest, 23, 53; Willie Nelson, 134; Wills, Bob, 23
Country Music Revue, 85–86
cowboy mythos and culture, 22, 29, 105–6, 202. *See also* western culture
cowboys and hippies, 72–73, 74, 75–77, 86, 88
Cowboy's restaurant, 41
Cowjazz, 176
"Cowpoke" (S. Jones), 122
Crabtree, Roger, 70
"Crazy Arms" (C. Seals, R. Mooney), 174
Crazy Heart (film), 48
"Crazy Too Cool Carl," 118–19
Crazy Water Crystals, 30
Creager, Roger, 176
Crider's Rodeo & Dancehall, 15
Crosby, Ronald Clyde. *See* Walker, Jerry Jeff
crossover country. *See* hybrid country sound
Crow, Alvin, 74, 77, 92, 120; Bear Eagle with, 96; "Broken Spoke Series" at UT, 137; Don Walser video, 122; and Doug Sahm, Doug, 91; and fiftieth anniversary celebration, 192, 193; and George Strait, 83; with George W. Bush, 150; hat display, 114; "If There's a Willie, There's a Way" campaign, 132, 136; on James's cd, 164; James's friendship with, 70–71; and Jerry Jeff Walker, 94; Joe Nick Patoski on, 76; profile of, 6–7; and Smith, Bobby Earl, 73; on *Texas Highways* cover, 134, 137. *See also* Alvin Crow and the Pleasant Valley Boys

Crow, Jason, 164
Crow, Josh, 70
Crow, Rick, 70
Crow, Stephanie (nee Geller), 70–71, 108, 120
Crowell, Rodney, 202
Cuban Missile Crisis, 31–32
cultural identity and music/dance, 15–17, 18, 23–25, 29, 105, 126, 145
Cummings, Kris, 76
Cure (the), 154
CWS Partners LLC, 203

Dacus, Smokey, 92
Dailey, Mike, 83
Dallas (TV show), 106, 111
Dallas Times Herald, 61
Damon Meredith and The Western Caravan, 43
The Dance (film), 203
Dance Across Texas, 100
Dance across Texas (Casey), 16
dance halls/dance culture, 15–17, 23–25. *See also* cultural identity and music/dance
dance lessons at Broken Spoke, 8, 41, 125, 168, 184–85
dance/music culture, 105, 126, 145. *See also* cultural identity and music/dance
dance styles and characterizations, 16–17, 44–45, 111
"Dance with Who Brung You" (J. White), 164–65
Dancing with the Stars, 176–78
Daniel, Lee, 10, 203, 204
Dave (film), 203
Dave Perry and the Texas Swing Boys, 43
Davidson, Lavinia (great-great-grandmother), 107
Day, Jimmy, 52, 74, 95
Dayton, Jesse, 9, 147, 192
Dean Martin Presents Music Country, 2
decor/furnishings, 7–8, 39–40, 95–96
"Deep in the Heart of Texas" (J. Hershey, D. Swander), 3
Delk, Josh, 184, 186
Derailers, 9, 96, 123, 143–45, 204, 205
Dessau Dance Hall, 23

Dexter, Al, 16
D. G. Burrow and the Western Melodies, 35
Dickens, James "Little Jimmy," 47, 54
Digby, Amber, 9
Dillo. *See* Armadillo World Headquarters "the Dillo"
Dixie Chicks, 146, 171–72
Dobkin, Gene, 87
documentaries at/of Broken Spoke: *Honky Tonk Heaven: The Legend of the Broken Spoke*, 10–11, 203–4; Mollee Jo's video, 8–9; *Spoke*, 203; *They Called Us Outlaws*, 202–3
Doggett, Lloyd, 72–73
Domino, Floyd, 87, 199
"Don't Squeeze My Sharmon" (C. Belew, V. Givens), 59
"Don't Worry (about Me)" (M. Robbins), 200
Don Walser Band Reunion and Tribute, 198–200
Dorsey, Bill, 36
Douglas, Sam Wainwright, 10–11, 203–4
"Doug Saldana," 91
dress/clothing: bling, 4, 202; dress code, 73, 111; Fiddle Fest, 186; James's personal style, 4, 25, 162, 202; Ray Price, 174; Terri's style, 184; and western culture, 36, 43, 47–48, 53, 126, 162–63, 174, 200, 202
Dressen, Al, 89, 95, 121–22, 181
drinking: Annetta's introduction to, 33; by band members, 36, 53, 55; "brown baggin,'" 35, 112–13; Colorado Bulldogs, 107–8; and dance hall culture, 23; family members, 20, 36, 68, 161; and fights, 40; legal age, 2, 45, 65, 71, 72, 86, 120; Lone Star beer, 124, 126; mixed-beverage liquor license, 34, 112–13; by staff, 36, 141; by underage minors, 72, 114. *See also* beer
Dromgoole, John, 128
Duarte, Brian, 168
Dutton, Stephen, 109
Duvall, Robert, 127, 128, 169
Dylan, Bob, 91

Eagle, Bear, 96
Eddins, Jeff, 195
Edens, Jeremy, 176
Egan, Mary. *See* Hattersley, "Sweet Mary" and Cleve
Eleven Hundred Springs, 178
Ellington, Duke, 45
"El Paso" (M. Robbins), 1
"El Rancho Grande" (S. Ramos, J. Del Morale, B. Costello), 51, 153
Elvis tribute artists, 176
Ely, Joe: Ameripolitan Music Award, 9; at Broken Spoke, 93, 118, 136; "Broken Spoke Series" at UT, 137, 138; Flatlanders, 148, 202–3; Kuntz wedding, 81
Emery, Ralph, 49, 51
Emmons, Buddy, 174
Emmons, Donald "Winker," 127
Endangered Species (film), 70
English, Paul, 52
Entertainment Weekly, 137
Erlewine, Mark, 198
Erlewine Guitars, 198
Ernest Tubb's Texas Troubadours, 70
Erwin, Martie and Emily, 171
Espinoza, Alex (great-grandson), 191
Espinoza, Brenn (great-granddaughter), 191
Esquivel, Jessie, 176
Evans, Dale, 29
expansion (1965), 43

Facebook offices mural (Austin), 10
"Faded Love" (B. Wills, J. Wills), 30, 126
"Fade into You" (D. Roback, H. Sandoval), 154
Fair Alcohol Consumption Act (1973), 65
Faires, Michelle Randolph, 10
Fajardo, Phil, 199
family highlights: early married life, 39–42; "extended" family, 70–71, 127–28, 141, 190–92; history and background, 33, 38–39, 107–8; hobbies, 71, 122; holiday parties, 141; James' birth and childhood, 19–21; small business ethic, 161–62, 190–92
Farm Aid, 134

"Father of Austin Country Music," 79
Fender, Freddie, 151, 195
Fender Telecaster, 82
"Fiddle Fest," 186
fiftieth anniversary celebration, 192–95
fighting: among minors, 72; bouncers, 98; boxing matches, 120–21; and dance hall culture, 23, 40; and dress code, 73; girl fights, 95, 98
Finazio, Phil, 120–21
fire/fire code incident(s), 42, 100
Fisher, Bud, 91
"500 Miles Away From Home" (B. Bare, C. Williams), 58
Flanz, Neil, 164
Flatlanders, 148, 202–3
Flores, Bobby, 9
Flores, Rosie, 9, 123
Folkins, Gail, 15
food. *See* cooking and food service
Foote, Tom, 83–85
Forbes, 181
"For the Good Times" (K. Kristofferson), 174
For the Last Time (Bob Wills and His Texas Playboys), 3
Fortress Steak House, 41, 112
Fort Sam Houston, San Antonio, 32
Fowler, Gordon, 198
Fowler, Kevin, 147–48
Fowler, Wick, 198
Fractured Times (Hobsbawm), 202
Franklin, Jim, 78
Franks, Tillman, 47, 58
"Frank Sinatra of country music," 174
"Fraulein" (L. Williams), 168–69
Frayne, George, 82
Freda and the Firedogs, 66, 72–73, 74, 75, 76
Freeman, George, 112
Freightshakers, 9
Friday Night Lights (film), 70
Friday Night Lights (TV series), 159
Friedman, Richard Samet "Kinky," 50, 172–73
Frizzell, Lefty, 16
Fromholtz, Steven, 72

Fuchs, Lena (mother), 18–21, 38, 68, 73
Full Circle (Roddy), 176
Funston, Frederick, 32

gambling, 33, 53, 97
Gammage, Joel, 127–28
Gammage, Manny, 127
gangsters, 39
Garrett, Pitt, 190
Garrido, Augie, 164
Gary P. Nunn and the Sons of the Bunkhouse, 117. *See also* Nunn, Gary P.
Gary Puckett and the Union Gap, 202
Geadelmann, Eric, 202–3
Geezinslaws/Geezinslaw Brothers, 47, 49–51, 62, 114, 137, 152, 153, 170–71
Geil, Kevin, 168
Geller-Crow, Stephanie, 70–71, 108, 120
"General Burgoyne's March" (unk.), 44
"The Gentle Giant," 54
George Strait and the Ace in the Hole Band, 82, 83–85, 114, 146, 202
Gibbons, Bob, 139
Gilkyson, Eliza, 118
Gilmore, Jimmie Dale, 132, 137, 138, 148, 202–3
Gil's Club, 47
Gimble, Emily, 197
Gimble, Johnny, 77, 137, 197
Girling, Bettie and Robert, 88, 195
Git Gone (band), 176
Glauninger, Frank Otto "Dutch," 97
"Golden Chain Troubadour," 52
Gosfield, Reuben "Lucky Oceans," 87
Grace, Michael, 115
Gracey, Joe, 65, 92
Grammy Awards: Asleep at the Wheel, 87; Charles Townsend, 3; Cindy Cashdollar, 122; Dixie Chicks, 172; Houston, David, 58; Kitty Wells, 153; Rick Trevino, 151; Willie Nelson, 114
Gray, Claude, 197
"The Great Speckled Bird" (trad.), 56
Green, Don (and Cathy), 107, 108, 113, 120, 122, 123
Green, Pat, 166
Greene, Jack Henry, 47, 54

Greezy Wheels (band), 186
Gregg, Red and Marie, 122
Griffin, Patty, 185
Grouchy and the Texas Pioneers, 96–97 89
Gruene Hall, 15
Grumbles, John "Bunky," 97
Guion, David Wendel, 29
Guitar Player, 82
Guns N' Roses, 154

Haggard, Merle, 77, 174
Hagman, Larry, 106
Haile, Lauré, 17
Hale, Terry, 83, 202
Hallmark, Rosemary, 40–41
Hammer of the Honky-Tonk Gods (Kirchen), 82
Hancock, Butch, 148, 202–3
Hancock, Wayne "The Train," 9
Hand, James "Slim," 9, 168–69, 170
Hank Thompson and His Brazos Valley Boys, 47–49
Harmeier, Mike, 178
Harris, Emmylou, 202
Harrison, Tony, 200, 202
hats, western, 73, 114, 127–28, 152
Hattersley, "Sweet Mary" and Cleve, 186
Health Alliance for Austin Musicians (HAAM), 200
health issues, 160–61, 181, 183, 186, 187, 190, 195
HEB grocery, 176, 190
Hedderman, Bobby, 78
Hee Haw, 2, 62
Heinen, Heidi, 193, 195
"Hell Cat" (K. Geil), 168
Heller, Joseph, 172
"Hello Walls" (W. Nelson), 197
Henderson, Nat, 100
Henson, Rick, 82, 114, 143, 163–64
Henson, Weldon, 176–78, 183, 192
"Here We Go Again" (D. Lanier, R. Steagall), 91
Hernández, José María De León "Little Joe," 169–70
"He Stopped Loving Her Today" (B. Braddock, C. Putman), 118
Heybale (band), 9

"Hey Good Lookin'" (H. Williams), 125
Hidalgo, David, 151
"High Noon" (D. Tiomkin, N. Washington), 22
High Riding (A. Crow), 70
Hilboldt, Jamie, 202
Hilderbran, Harvey "H.," 98–99, 193
Hill, Tee-Jay, 176
Hill, Tommy, 85
Hillyer, Matt, 178
hippies and cowboys, 72–73, 74, 75–77, 86, 88
historical markers, 10, 107
Hobsbawm, Eric, 202
Hofeldt, Brian, 144–45, 192, 204, 205
Hofner, Adolph, 55–56
"Hokey Pokey" (La Prise, Macak, Baker), 45
Hokkanen, Eric, 164
holiday performances, 85–87
Holloway, Rick, 119–20
Holly, Buddy, 117, 148
Holly, María Elena, 148
Hollywood Saddlery, 163
Holm, Jenny, 10
"Home on the Range" (trad.), 29
honeymoon, 39
Honeysuckle Rose (film), 114
"honky-tonk," definitions of, 15–16, 23
Honky Tonk Angels (Parton, Lynn, and Wynette), 153
"Honky Tonk Blues" (A. Dexter, J. Paris), 16
Honky Tonk Heaven: The Legend of the Broken Spoke (documentary film), 10–11, 203–4
"Honky-Tonk Man" (J. Horton, T. Franks, H. Hausey), 50
Honky-Tonk: Portraits of Country Music (Horenstein), 203
Honky-Tonk Trail (A. Crow), 164
Horenstein, Henry, 203
Horton, Johnny, 155
Horton, Pappy Hal, 47
Hosek, Denise, 187–88
Hot Club of Cowtown, 9
Hot Texas Country (Bush), 89
The Housewives of Beverly Hills (TV show), 50
Houston, David, 47, 58
How Country Are Ya? (K. Fowler), 147

Hubbard, Ray Wylie, 72
Hub City Movers (band), 148
Huckaby, Ronnie, 85
Hughes, Doug, 86
Hughes, Jeff, 154–55
"Humpty Dumpty Heart" (H. Thompson), 48
Hunter, Craig, 188, 190
Hurd, Cornell, 89, 96, 105, 123, 190, 192
Hutchens, Carl, 200
hybrid country sound, 72–73, 74–76

"Ida Red" (trad.), 30
"I Dreamed of a Hillbilly Heaven" (E. Dean, H. Sothern), 22–23
"If There's a Willie, There's a Way" campaign, 132–34, 135, 136
IL Club, 66
"I Love You, I Love You" (D. Walls, N. Wilson, S. Lyons), 58
immigrants and dance/music culture, 15–17, 18, 29, 105
"I'm So Lonesome I Could Cry" (H. Williams), 91
"Indian Love Call" (O. Harbach, O. Hammerstein, R. Friml), 58
Ingram, Jack, 154, 190, 192, 194
international recognition, 205
Intveld, James, 9
I Play To Win (Steinmark), 61
Irving, Amy, 114
Irwin, Charlie, 198
I Saw the Light (film), 203
"I Saw the Light" (H. Williams), 145
"It Wasn't God Who Made Honky-Tonk Angels" (J. Miller), 153
"It Won't Be Long" (R. Acuff), 56

Jacques, Wayne "Chojo," 200
James, Elana, 9
Jarratt, Josh, 176
Jennings, Waylon, 2, 65, 66, 117
Jiménez, Flaco, 91, 151, 195
"John Deere Tractor" (L. Hammond), 199
Johnny's Place, 23–24
Johnson, Claudia Alta "Lady Bird" and family, 80, 154

Johnson, Jay Lynn Jr. (landlord) and family, 33–34, 160, 182–83
Johnson, Lyndon Baines, 114
Johnson, "Sleepy," 91
John T. Floore's Country Store, 15
Jolly Giants, 54
"The Jolly Rancher," 195
Jones, George, 16, 32
Jones, Louis Marshall "Grandpa," 2, 62
"Just in Time" (A. Green, B. Comden, J. Styne), 188
"Just Like Heaven" (B. Williams, L. Tolhurst, P. Thompson, R. Smith, S. Gallup), 154

Kalish, Howard, 199
"Kansas City" (J. Leiber, M. Stoller), 30
Karow, Ron, 112
Karp, Louis, 81
Keeling, Don "Skinny," 199
keg *vs.* bottled beer, 113
Kelso, John, 100–101
Kimmie Rhodes and the Jackalope Brothers, 73
King, Claude, 24, 47, 55
King, Shelley, 200
"King of Country Music," 56
"King of the Road" (R. Miller), 49
The King of Western Swing: Bob Wills Remembered (R. Wills), 115
Kirby, Beecher Ray, 57
Kirchen, Bill, 81–82
Kirchen, Louise, 82
Kiser, Bob, 92
Knack, Will, 164
Knudsen, Charles, 97
Kristofferson, Kris, 134, 136, 174, 202
Kunz, John, 80–81

La Familia (band), 169–70
"Laredo Rose" (R. Minus), 195
"The Last Letter" (R. Griffin), 54
Last of the Breed (Price), 174–75
"The Last Thing I Needed First Thing This Morning" (D. Farar, G. Nunn), 118
Lavender Hill Express, 117
Layton, David, 10

INDEX

Leavell, Chuck, 117
LeBlanc, L. J., 20
LeBlanc, Lulu "Lou," 20
Leffingwell, Lee, 193
"Legislators' Nights," 59, 99
Lenz, Kim, 9
"Let the World Keep on a Turnin'" (B. Owens), 62
Levine, Howard T., 86–87
Levitan, Ken, 202–3
Lewis, Gibson D. "Gib," 89–90, 98–99, 122–23
Lewis, Jerry Lee, 169
Light Crust Doughboys, 29–30
Lightfoot, Gordon, 155
"Li'l Winker," 127
Lindsay, Sherman, 198
line dancing, ban on, 45, 111
liquor license. *See* mixed-beverage liquor licence
"Little Doug Sahm," 91
Live at Gruene Hall (J. Walker), 123
Live from Deep in the Heart of Texas (Commander Cody and His Lost Planet Airmen), 82
"The Live Music Capital of the World," 105, 125, 131
"Llano Estacado" (Cooder Graw, M. Martindale), 166
local characters and regulars, 96–98, 100–102, 122, 125–28, 187–88, 190. *See also* politicians
Locke, William Wayne "Rusty," 185
Locklin, Hank, 16, 32
"London Homesick Blues" (G. Nunn), 118
"Lonesome, On'ry and Mean" (R. Johnson), 2
Lone Star beer, 124, 126
Longhorn football team, 59
Los Super Seven, 151
Lost Gonzo Band, 118
Loudermilk, Charles Elzer. *See* Louvin, Charlie
Louisiana Hayride, 51, 55, 56, 91
Louvin, Charlie, 47, 59–60
"Love in the Hot Afternoon" (K. Westberry, V. Matthews), 91

"Love Song of the Waterfall" (B. Nolan, B. Barnes, C. Winge), 58
Lowden, Aubrey "Blue," 95
Lozano-Hunter, Olga, 188, 190
Luckenbach, Texas, 93
Luckenbach Dance Hall, 15
Ludicker, Dennis, 195
lunch service, 38
Lynn, Loretta, 153
Lytle, Donald (Johnny Paycheck), 174

Magelsky, Kelly, 202–3
Maggie D's, 98
"Maiden's Prayer" (B. Wills), 83
Maines, Lloyd, 172
Maines, Natalie, 171
Mandrell, Barbara, 58
Marchese, Jake "Sidecar," 168
Marcus, Kathy, 81
"Maria Elena" (L. Barcelata), 55
Martinez, Ramiro, 37
Mary Hattersley and her Blazing Bows, 186
mascots, 7–8, 127, 163
Mathis, Denny, 168
"May the Bird of Paradise Fly up Your Nose" (N. Merritt), 54
McAuliffe, Jack, 101
McAuliffe, Leon, 92
McCall, Darrell, 174
McCanlies, Tim, 169
McCoy, Houston, 37
McDonald, Maria J., 10
McGraw, Tim, 146
McHale's Navy, 153
McHenry, Scott, 188
McKnight, Peyton, 59, 100
McLeese, Donald, 131
McNulty, Brian, 10–11
McRae, Rick, 202
Meech, Sarah Gale, 9
Mellencamp, John "Cougar," 134
Melody Drifters, 36
Meredith, Damon, 43
Meyers, Augie, 195
Midnight Jamboree, 53
Mike and the Moonpies, 178
military careers, 19–20, 31–32, 34, 58

Miller, Roger, 49, 174
Miller, Townsend, 66, 118
Miller Imaging and Digital Solutions, 10
"Minnie Pearl," 2, 193
Minus, Rich, 195
missiles, James's work with, 24, 31–32
Mitchell, Brenda Green and family, 10–11, 203–4
Mitchell, Pete, 70
Mitchell, Scott, 10
mixed-beverage liquor license, 34, 112–13
monkey "Skeeter," 42
Montague, Mollee Jo (granddaughter), 8–9, 127, 128, 141, 181
Montesino Ranch, 204
Moore, Brad, 190
Moose Head Tavern, 19, 23
Moreland, Doug, 178
"More Than Yesterday" (L. Dickens), 58
Morgan, Whitey, 9
Morrison, Van, 87
Moser, Margaret, 115–17
Mother (N. Maines), 171
Moulton, Zach, 178
"Mountain Dew" (S. Wiseman), 95
"Mountain of Love" (V. Del Rio, L. Martin), 58
movie industry in Austin area, 159, 169
movies and western culture, 22–23, 29, 32–33
movies featuring the club, 142–43
"Mr. Bojangles" (J. Walker), 93
"Mr. Jukebox," 70
"Mr. Record Man" (W. Nelson), 51–52
"Mr. Western Show Business," 30
Mueller, Kay, 186
mural, Facebook offices (Austin), 10
Murphey, Michael Martin, 118
museum room and displays, 114–15, 163
Music City Texas Theater, 15
music/dance culture, 15–17, 18, 29, 105, 126, 145
"My Elusive Dreams" (B. Sherrill, C. Putman), 58
"My Maria" (B. Stevenson, D. Moore), 99
"My Old Hometown" (H. Johnson, K. Barrett), 32

Nachtigal, Jim and Birdie, 126–27
Naishtat, Elliott, 9, 193
Nantie Margaret. *See* White-Grunewald, Margaret "Nantie" (aunt)
Nashville Now, 49
National Agricultural Hall of Fame, 134
National Geographic, 137
National Heritage Award (Don Walser), 199
National Register of Historic Places, 9, 15
National Wildflower Research Center, 154
Natural Gardener, 41, 128
Needham, John, 183
Nelson, Ira Doyle "Pop," 119–20
Nelson, Lana, 41, 69, 134
Nelson, Paula, 166
Nelson, Willie: and Asleep at the Wheel, 87, 88; and *Austin City Limits*, 65; and Bobby Bare, 57; at Broken Spoke, 47, 51–52, 53, 90, 120; "Broken Spoke Series" at UT, 137; career highlights, 2, 51–52, 134–35, 197; and Darrell Royal, 90; Gary P. Nunn, covers of, 118; and Ginny White, 67, 69; income tax issues, 132–34, 135, 136; and Johnny Bush, 88; lifetime achievement award, 138; in museum room, 114; with Ray Price, 174–75; on Whites's dedication, 134; and Whites's grandchildren, 184
"Neon Angel," 153
Neon Boots Dancehall and Saloon, 15
Nickel Beer Nights, 113–14
Night Riders, 48–49
Nix, Jody, 114
Nixon, Mojo, 9
Nofziger, Max, 131
Norman, Jack, 141
Norman, Luciana "Lou," 38
"Not Forgotten You" (B. Robison), 146
"Not Ready to Make Nice" (D. Wilson, E. Robison, M. Maguire, N. Maines), 171
Nudie's Rodeo Tailors, 162
Nunn, Gary P.: with Alvin Crow, 74; with Bear Eagle, 96; at Broken Spoke, 126; "Broken Spoke Series" at UT, 137, 138; and B. W. Stevenson, 99; career highlights, 117–18; and fiftieth anniversary celebration, 193; hat display,

114; "If There's a Willie, There's a Way" campaign, 132

Oak Hill, Texas, 18–19, 33, 41, 107, 128
"Ocean Burial" (G. Allen, E. Chapin), 29
O'Connell, Chris, 87
O'Daniel, W. Lee, 29–30
One Knite Saloon, 66
"On the Road Again" (W. Nelson), 114, 197
On the Trail of Negro Folksongs (Scarborough), 44
opening of Broken Spoke, 33–34, 35
"Operation Cyclone," 108
Oppel, Rich, 101
"Orange Blossom Special" (E. Rouse), 44
Orbison, Roy, 117
Osment, Haley Joel, 169
"outlaw" country music, 2, 65–66, 202–3
Owens, Alan Edgar "Buddy," 62
Owens, Alvis Edgar "Buck," 2, 62, 125, 143

"padding" in music, 121–22
painting as hobby, 71
Palmer, Lester, 43
"Panhandle Poor Boy" (K. Fowler), 147
Paramount Theater, 22
Park, Craig, 198
Parnell, Lee Roy, 50, 152
Parsons, John, 203–4
Parton, Dolly, 142–43, 153
"Party Dolls and Wine" (J. Barnhill), 91
"The Party's Over" (W. Nelson), 197
"Pass Me By (If You're Only Passing Through)" (H. Hall), 155
Patoski, Joe Nick, 74, 75–77
Patton, James Andrew (great-grandfather), 19, 41, 107
Patton Elementary School, 165
Patton Rock Store, 41, 107
Patton-White, Rosa (grandmother), 19, 20
"Paul Jones" dance, 44
"The Pavarotti of the Plains," 199
Paycheck, Johnny, 174
payments to performers: 1960s profiles, 34, 36, 43–44; in beer and food, 34; Bob Wills, 46; George Strait, 84; Ray Price,
174; at Sportsman's Inn, 24; Willie Nelson, 47
Peacock, Gary and Marcia, 162, 183
Peacock, Ginny (nee White). *See* White, Virginia "Ginny"
Peacock, Jackson Colt (grandson), 69, 191
Peacock, James Lamar (grandson), 69, 70, 165, 191
Peacock, Mike, 161–62, 165, 184, 191
Pearl, Minnie, 2, 193
Peña, Amado, 169–70, 175
Penrod, Jake, 200
People's Choice (band), 86–87, 98, 111, 113, 121
Performing Arts Center (PAC), UT, 131, 137–40
Perkins, Joseph "Pinetop," 81
Perry, Dave, 43
Perry, Rick, 117
Pershing, John J., 32
Perskin, Spencer, 78
Pettigrew, Craig Allan, 124
Phillips, Lou Diamond, 170
Pickens, Slim, 114
Pickle, J. J., 79
"Pick Me Up on Your Way Down" (H. Howard), 59
Pierce, Webb, 91
Pipkin, Turk, 197
Plant, Robert, 185
Pleasant Valley Boys. *See* Alvin Crow and the Pleasant Valley Boys
Poindexter, Clarence Albert ("Al Dexter"), 16
politicians: Ann Richards, 90, 138, 140, 144, 152–53; Clayton "Claytie" Williams, 51, 152–53; George W. Bush, 149, 150, 172; Greg Abbott, 196, 197; "Legislators' Nights," 59, 99; "Speaker's Nights," 89–90, 98–100, 123, 152–53; Will Wynn (mayor), 125, 159, 163
Ponder, Kyle, 178
"Pop a Top" (N. Stuckey), 54–55
postage stamp, Bob Wills, 115
Preston, Leroy, 87
Price, Ray, 9, 95, 124, 174–75
progressive country movement, 2, 65–66, 74–77

property/land issues, 160, 181–84, 203
Pryor, Kerry, 152
Pryor, Richard S. "Cactus," 22, 152
Pryor, Richard "Skinny," 22
Puckett, Gary, 202
Pure Country (Crow), 7, 109
Pure Texas Band, 199

quarter horses, showing/breeding, 71
Queen Theater, 22
"quick, quick, slow, slow," 184
Quisenberry, Janie, 199

"Raindrops Keep Fallin' on My Head" (B. Bacharach, H. David), 91
ranch, White family, 39, 88
Rapp, Ann, 88
Rausch, Leon, 70, 92
Raw Deal (bar), 78
Ray Benson and Asleep at the Wheel. *See* Asleep at the Wheel; Benson, Ray
Raymond, Richard, 99
"Ray Price Shuffle," 174
Red Dog Saloon, 4141
Red Headed Stranger (W. Nelson), 120
Rednex (band), 44
Reed, John X., 73, 76, 164
Reese, Don, 183
Reese, Pauline, 154, 175–76, 193
Regan Outdoor Advertising, 197
R.E.M., 154
Reyes, Elizabeth, 188
Rhodes, Kimmie, 73, 137
Rhone, Preston, 178
Richards, Ann, 90, 138, 140, 144, 152–53
A Ride with Bob (musical), 88
Righteous Brothers, 202
Ritter, Woodward Maurice "Tex," 22–23, 29, 47
Rivera, Bert, 48–49
Rivers, Eddie, 195
Riverside Resources, 181–82
Roadie (film), 70
Robbins, Marty, 1
Roberts, Alexander "Buck," 107
Roberts, Jason, 200, 201
Robison, Bruce and Charlie, 123, 145–46

rock-and-roll, 154
"(Don't Go Back to) Rockville" (B. Berry, M. Stipe, M. Mills, P. Buck), 154
Roddy, Ted, 176
Rodgers, Jimmie, 29, 70
Rodriguez, Johnny, 155
Rogers, Ben, 187
Rolling Stone, 76, 82, 87
Rolling Stones, 116–17
"Rollin' in My Sweet Baby's Arms" (trad.), 118
Rome Inn, 77–78
Roots Music Series (books), 190
Rosas, Cesar, 151
Rouse, Ervin T. and Gordon, 44
Rowdy, mannequin mascot, 7–8, 163
Roy Acuff and His Smoky Mountain Boys, 56
Royal, Darrell K., 59, 60, 90, 138, 164–65
Royal, Edith, 90
rules: bunny hop, ban on, 45; dress code, 73, 111; hats on dance floor, 73; line dancing, ban on, 45, 111; standing on dance floor, 8, 87
"Running out of Reasons to Run" (G. Teren, B. Regan), 152
Russell, Paula, 198
Rutherford, Catlin, 178
"Rye Whiskey" (T. Ritter), 22

saddle display, 163
Sahm, Doug, 90–91, 132, 136, 195
sales tax issues, 113
Sam and Bob in the Morning, 51
Samples, Alvin "Junior," 2
"Sam's Place" (B. Owens, R. Simpson), 125, 204
Sam the Sham and the Pharaohs, 112
San Antonio Rose: The Life and Music of Bob Wills (Townsend), 3
Sanders, Allan, 127
Sanger, David, 195
Scafe, Bruce, 65
Scarborough, Dorothy, 44
Schatzberg, Jerry, 114
Schroeder Hall, 15
Sczepanik, Ray, 185

INDEX

Seale, Mark, 198
Sears, Dawn, 9
Sears, Kenny, 9
Secondhand Lions (film), 169
The 704 (apartments), 7, 101, 181, 184, 203
Shadow on the Ground (Hand), 169
Shaver, Billy Joe, 9, 65, 173, 202
Shelton, Polk, 198
Sherrod, Blackie, 61
"She's About a Mover" (D. Sahm), 91
Shinn, John Bush. *See* Bush, Johnny
Shoji Tabuchi Theatre, 58
Shore, Katie, 195
Short, Harold, 96
Shrake, Edwin A. "Bud," 138, 140
"Silver Wings" (M. Haggard), 87
Simpson, Ken, 198
Simpson, O. J., 149
Sir Douglas Quintet, 90, 195
"Skeeter" the monkey, 42
"Skip a Rope" (J. Moran, G. Tubb), 61
Skyline Club, 47
Small, Michael, 176
Smith, Bobby Earl, 66, 70, 73–74, 76, 92
Smith, Dewayne "Son," 49, 51. *See also* Geezinslaws/Geezinslaw Brothers
Smith, Preston, 107
Smitheal, Jeremy, 183
Smither, Chris, 176
Smoky Mountain Boys, 56
Soap Creek Saloon, 66
Songwriters Across Texas (TV show), 190
Sons of the Bunkhouse (SOBs), 117
South by Southwest Music Festival (SXSW), 11, 106, 154, 159, 166, 203–4
Southfork Ranch trip, 111
Southwest Texas State University, 68
Sparkles (band), 117
"Speaker's Nights," 89–90, 98–100, 123, 152–53
Spillers, Mike, 187–88
Split Rail, 66
Spoke (documentary film), 203
Sportsman's Inn, 24–25, 33
Stagecoach Ballroom, 15
standing on the dance floor rule, 8, 87
Star, Mazzy, 155

State Theater, 22
Steagall, Red, 91
"Steamboat Whistle Blues" (R. Acuff), 56
Steiner, Herb, 70, 164
Steinmark, Freddie, 61
Stevenson, B. W., 72, 99
Stormclouds in Heaven (Hand), 169
Strait, George, 82, 83–85, 114, 146, 202
Street, James, 61
Strehli, Angela, 148
Stricklin, Al, 70, 75, 92
Stuart, Mark, 166
Stubb's Bar-B-Q, 66
Sumlin, Hubert, 117
Sunnyland Special (band), 148
Sunset Riders, 95
Sunset Valley Boys, 198
Super Swing Sausage Revue, 95
"Sweet Child o' Mine" (A. Rose, D. McKagan, I. Stradlin, Slash, S. Adler), 154
swing. *See* western swing dancing

Tabuchi, Shoji, 47, 58
"Take An Old Cold Tater (and Wait)" (E. Bartlett), 54
Taking the Long Way (Dixie Chicks), 171
Tatsch, William "Grouchy" Egardner, 96–97
television shows of/at Broken Spoke, 190
Telford, Larry, 50–51, 170–71
Ten Cent Beer Nights, 86, 113
"Tender Moment" (L. Parnell, M. Bourke, C. Moore), 152
Tennessee Mountain Boys, 54
"Tennessee Waltz" (R. Stewart, P. King), 56
Texas Alcoholic Beverage Commission (TABC), 113
The Texas Connection (TV show), 49
Texas Crude (publisher), 199
Texas culture and mythos, 22, 106, 111, 190, 202. *See also* western culture
Texas Dance Hall Preservation, Inc., 15
Texas Film Awards, 159
Texas Hatters and Texas Custom Boots, 127–28
Texas Highways, 38, 134, 137, 192
Texas Historical Commission, 9–10, 193

Texas Historical Marker, 10, 107
Texas Jamm Band, 85
Texas Monthly, 38, 59, 76, 81, 192
Texas Moon Palace, 3
Texas Music Awards, 148
Texas Music Hall of Fame, 148
Texas Plainsmen, 199
Texas Playboys, 3, 30, 91–93, 121–22. *See also* Wills, Bob
Texas Rangers, 38–39, 107
Texas State Lunatic Asylum, 19
Texas State Society (TSS), 108
Texas State University (TSU), 68
Texas: The Big Picture (film), 168
Texas Top Hand (D. Walser), 122
Texas Top Hands (band), 168, 185–86
Texas Tornados, 90, 195
Texas Treasure Business Award, 9–10, 193
Texas Troubadours (Ernest Tubb's), 70
Texas Western Swing Hall of Fame, 49, 66, 121–22, 181, 185
"T for Texas" (J. Rodgers), 62
That Old Texas Groove (B. Moore), 190
That's a Man (Ingram), 154
That's My Home (J. Roberts), 200
"There Goes My Everything" (D. Frazier), 54
They Called Us Outlaws: Cosmic Cowboys, Honky-Tonk Heroes and the Rising of Redneck Rock (documentary film), 202–3
They Came to Texas: Patton-White-Campbell Families and Connecting Branches (J. White and A. White), 107
This Old House, 159
Thomas, B. J., 91
Thompson, Hank, 47–49, 91
Threadgill, John Kenneth, 78, 79
Threadgill's, 65, 78–79, 148
"The Three Bells" (J. Gilles, b. Reisfeld), 55
Throckmorton, Sonny, 50
"Til There Was You" (M. Wilson), 51
Tin Pan Alley, 15
"Titan of the Telecaster," 82
Tito's Handmade Vodka, 204
T. Nickel House Band, 148
TNN Live, 90
Tolleson, Mike, 78

Tommy Hill and the Country Music Revue, 85
Tornado Records, 91
"Tourist Trap" museum, 114–15
Townsend, Charles, 3, 115
Transwestern (developer), 184, 186, 203
"Trashy Women" (C. Wall), 123
"Travelin' Soldier" (B. Robison), 146
Travis, Randy, 114
Travis (Crooks) and the Western Gentlemen, 36
Travolta, John, 105, 111
Trevino, Rick, 151–52
A Tribute to the Music of Bob Wills and the Texas Playboys (Asleep at the Wheel), 87
Tried and True Music, 95
Trocino, Jesse, 176
The Truth Will Set You Free (Hand), 169
Tubb, Ernest, 16, 23, 47, 52–54, 67, 93, 99
Turk, Nathan, 162
Turkey, Texas, 115
"Turkey in the Straw" (trad.), 29
Turner, Bob, 61
Twitty, Conway, 155
two-step dancing, 72, 184–85, 202
"Two-Stepping Tuesdays," 176–78
Two Tons of Steel, 166, 168

University of Texas: Annetta's job at, 31, 37; "Broken Spoke Series," 131, 137–40; Longhorn football team, 59, 60–62; Royal, Darrell K., 59, 60, 90, 138, 164–65; tower shooting 1966, 37–38
"Unwound" (D. Dillon, F. Dycus), 84
Urban Cowboy (film), 105, 111
USA Today, 17

van Overbeek, Will, v
Van Zandt, Townes, 88
Van Zanten, Catherine, 186
Vaughan, Jimmie, 77–78
Vaughan, Stevie Ray, 78
Velveeta Room, 22
Victory Grill, 66
videos of/at Broken Spoke, 8–9, 122, 171–72
¡Viva Terlingua! (J. Walker), 93, 118
Vulcan Gas Company, 65, 86, 148
"Wabash Cannonball" (trad.), 56

Wadsworth, Pebbles, 137, 138–1139
Wagoneers, 148, 149
wagon wheel tradition, 4, 6, 118–19, 193, 195
Walk Alone (Bastard Sons of Johnny Cash), 166
Walker, Charlie, 47, 59
Walker, Django, 94
Walker, Jerry Jeff: "Broken Spoke Series" at UT, 137; career highlights, 93–95; and Chris Wall, 123; in Country Music Hall of Fame documentary, 202; and fiftieth anniversary celebration, 193, 194; and Gary P. Nunn, 118; with Jack Ingram, 154; Lee Roy Parnell hat incident, 152; with Mary Egan, 186; and progressive country movement, 72, 75–76; with Ray Benson, 88, 137
Walker, Susan, 123
"Walking the Floor over You" (E. Tubb), 53
Wall, Chris, 151, 164, 173; "Broken Spoke Series" at UT, 137, 138; career highlights, 123–24, 126, 149; and fiftieth anniversary celebration, 193
Walser, Don, 81, 114, 122, 123, 198–200
Walter, David, 100
"Waltz across Texas" (T. Tubb), 53, 93, 199
Ward, Paul, 168
Warden, Monte, 124, 148–49
washboard playing, 96
Washington Post, 184
Waterloo Records, 80–81
Watermelon Records, 81
Watson, Dale: and Ameripolitan Music, 9, 105, 198; career highlights, 123, 124–25, 126–27, 188, 189; at C-Boy's Heart & Soul, 204; and Facebook office mural, 10; and fiftieth anniversary celebration, 192; at James's birthday party, 9, 187; as ordained minister, 188; and Ray Benson, 88; Ted Roddy with, 176
Watson, Gene, 91
"Wave on Wave" (D. Neuhauser, J. Pollard, P. Green), 166
"We Are Never Getting Back Together" (T. Swift, M. Martin, Shellback), 58
wedding/honeymoon, 39
Wells, Annetta. *See* White, Annetta (nee Wells)

Wells, Gene, 41
Wells, Kitty (and family), 153
Wells Fargo Bank mural, 192
Wertheimer, Steve, 9, 77–78, 80
Western, Billy, 46
western culture: cowboy mythos and culture, 22, 29, 105–6, 202; dress/clothing, 36, 43, 47–48, 53, 126, 162–63, 174, 200, 202; hats, western, 73, 114, 127–28, 152; James's loyalty to, 6, 111–12; movies, 22–23, 29, 32–33; music and dance, 15–17, 18, 23–25, 29, 105, 126, 145; Texas culture and mythos, 22, 106, 111, 190, 202
Western Melodies, 35
western swing dancing, 17, 29, 184–85
West Texas Walk of Fame, 117
"What Kind of Fool Do You Think I Am?" (A. Carmichael, G. Griffin), 152
"Whiskey River" (J. Bush, P. Stroud), 2, 89
White, Annetta (nee Wells), 120, 150, 191; family and background, 33; health issues, 161; and James, romance with, 31; roles at Broken Spoke, 38; and UT tower shooting, 37–38; wedding/honeymoon, 39; work ethic, 68, 69, 73, 81. *See also* character profiles of James and Annetta White
White, Bruce Lamar (father), 18–19, 162
White, Bruce Lamar Jr. (brother), 19
White, Dudley (uncle), 21
White, James "Doc" (uncle), 38–39
White, James M.: appearance and personal style, 4, 25, 162, 202; birthday parties, 75th, 187–88; Cadillac, 5, 94, 137, 172; D.C. trip, 108; early family life, 19–21; early jobs, 24; health issues, 160–61; marriage, 39; military career, 31–32; musical performances, 94, 109, 118, 125, 144, 204; songwriting, 108–9; television appearances, 176; videos/movies, 8–9, 114, 122, 143; vision for Broken Spoke, 32–33; western culture, loyalty to, 6, 111–12; work ethic, 68, 69, 73, 181. *See also* character profiles of James and Annetta White
White, John Dudley (grandfather), 39

White, Lena (nee Fuchs) (mother), 18–21, 38, 68, 73
White, Margaret "Maggie" (nee Campbell) (great-grandmother), 107
White, Robert Emmett (grandfather), 107
White, Terri (daughter), 191; childhood at Broken Spoke, 40–41; children/grandchildren, 109–10, 141; dance lessons by, 8, 41, 125, 168, 184–85; Mollee Jo's video, 8
White, Virginia "Ginny" (daughter), 191; childhood and Broken Spoke legacy, 67–70; children of, 184; and Derailers, 144; drinking problems, 161; health issues, 190; and husband, Mike Peacock, 161–62, 165; on James's health issues, 161, 183, 187; on leaky roof, 119; on "Li'l Winker," 127; work at the club, 140–41
White family ranch. See ranch, White family
White-Grunewald, Margaret "Nantie" (aunt), 19, 67
White-McCool, Cynthia Ann (half-sister), 20
Whitey, Whiddon, 98
Whitman, Charles Joseph, 37–38
Whitman, Otis Dewey Jr. "Slim," 58
Whitmore, Jon and Jennifer, 139–40
Wick Fowler's Two-Alarm Chili, 198
Wide Open Spaces (Dixie Chicks), 171
Wier, Rusty, 72, 75, 117
Wild Blue Yonder Films, 10–11, 203–4
Wild Texas Wind, 142–43
Williams, Clayton "Claytie," 51, 152–53
Williams, Hank, 16
Williams, Lawton, 168
Willie Nelson and the Record Men, 51–52, 53. *See also* Nelson, Willie
Willis, Kelly, 145, 146
Wills, Bob: at Broken Spoke, 45–46; career highlights, 29–30, 46–47; and Charles Townsend, 3; Country Music Hall of Fame, 23; death of, 91–92; museum room displays, 114, 115; tributes to, 87–88. *See also* Texas Playboys
Wills, Renee, 116
Wills, Rosetta, 30, 115, 116
Wilson, Brent, 124
Wilson, Charlie, 108
Wilson, Eddie, 78–80
"Window Up Above" (G. Jones), 32
Winger, Debra, 105
"Winker Withaneye," 127
"Wolverton Mountain" (M. Kilgore, C. King), 24, 55
Wonderland, Carolyn, 200
Woods, Bobby Dan, 101, 102
"Wooly Bully" (S. Samudio), 112
"Wrapped" (B. Robison), 146
Wunsche Bros. Cafe & Saloon, 204
Wynette, Tammy, 58, 153
Wynn, Will, 125, 159, 163

Yoakum, Dwight, 50
Youman, Dudley, 161
"You Never Even Called Me by My Name" (S. Goodman), 50
Young, Donny. *See* Paycheck, Johnny
Young, Faron, 91, 200
Young, Neil, 134